# 1 MONTH OF
# FREE
# READING

## at

## www.ForgottenBooks.com

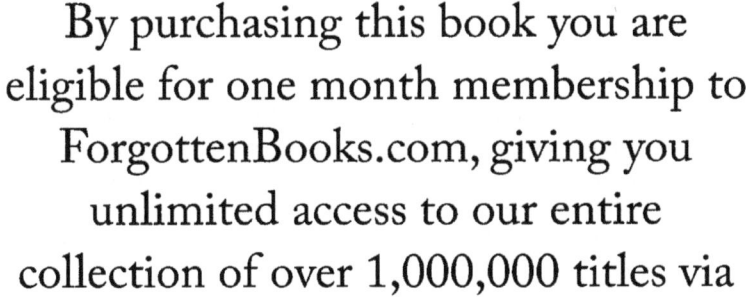

By purchasing this book you are eligible for one month membership to ForgottenBooks.com, giving you unlimited access to our entire collection of over 1,000,000 titles via our web site and mobile apps.

To claim your free month visit:

www.forgottenbooks.com/free151898

ISBN 978-1-5283-8591-6
PIBN 10151898

This book is a reproduction of an important historical work. Forgotten Books uses state-of-the-art technology to digitally reconstruct the work, preserving the original format whilst repairing imperfections present in the aged copy. In rare cases, an imperfection in the original, such as a blemish or missing page, may be replicated in our edition. We do, however, repair the vast majority of imperfections successfully; any imperfections that remain are intentionally left to preserve the state of such historical works.

# OHIO
# SCHOOL
# LAWS

## IN FORCE APRIL 25, 1904

COMPLIMENTS OF
## LEWIS D. BONEBRAKE
### COMMISSIONER

*VK FORMS AND DIRECTIONS TO SERVE*
*4 GUIDE FOR SCHOOL OFFICERS*

# OHIO

# SCHOOL LAWS

## IN FORCE APRIL 25, 1904,

---

## BLANK FORMS AND DIRECTIONS TO SERVE AS A GUIDE FOR SCHOOL OFFICERS.

Springfield, Ohio:
The Springfield Publishing Company,
State Printers.
1904.

# CONSTITUTION OF OHIO

RELATING TO

## PUBLIC SCHOOLS.

### ARTICLE I.

**Sec. 7.** [Of the rights of conscience; necessity of religion and knowledge.] * * * Religion, morality and knowledge, however, being essential to good government, it shall be the duty of the general assembly to pass suitable laws to protect every religious denomination in the peaceable enjoyment of its own mode of public worship, and to encourage schools and the means of instruction.

"The system of public education in Ohio is the creature of the Constitution and statutory laws of the state. It is left to the discretion of the general assembly, in the exercise of the general legislative power conferred upon it (Art II, § 1), to determine what laws are 'suitable' to secure the organization and management of the contemplated system of common schools, without express restriction, except that 'no religious or other sect or sects shall ever have any exclusive right to, or control of, any part of the school funds of this state.' " 21 O. S., 198-205, Day, J.

The compulsory education law comes within this section. 5 C. C., 645.

### ARTICLE II.

**Sec. 26.** [What laws to have uniform operation.] All laws of a general nature, shall have a uniform operation throughout the state; nor, shall any act, except such as relates to public schools, be passed, to take effect upon the approval of any other authority than the general assembly, except, as otherwise provided in this Constitution.

### ARTICLE VI.

**Sec. 1.** [Funds for educational and religious purposes.] The principal of all funds, arising from the sale, or other disposition of lands, or other property, granted or intrusted to this state for educational and religious purposes, shall forever be preserved inviolate, and undiminished; and, the income arising therefrom, shall be faithfully applied to the specific objects of the original grant, or appropriations.

**Sec. 2.** [School funds.] The general assembly shall make such provisions, by taxation, or otherwise, as, with the income arising from the school trust fund, will secure a thorough and efficient system of common schools throughout the state; but no religious or other sect, or sects, shall ever have any exclusive right to, or control of, any part of the school funds of this state.

Religious instruction. or the reading of the Bible in the public schools, is not required by the Constitution. The board of education have the sole management of the schools, and the courts cannot direct what instruction shall be given or what books read. 23 O. S , 211.

A requirement of a board of education that the Bible be read in the schools as an opening exercise cannot be interfered with by the courts, and is not in violation of any constitutional rights. 1 N. P., 140.

It is an unlawful diversion of the school funds of the state of Ohio for a board of education to authorize the teaching of religion as a regular branch of study. Attorney General.

## ARTICLE XII.

**Sec. 2.** [Taxation by uniform rule.] Laws shall be passed, by taxing by a uniform rule, all moneys, credits, investments in bonds, stocks, joint stock companies, or otherwise; and also all real and personal property, according to its true value in money; but burying grounds, public school houses, houses used exclusively for public worship, institutions of purely public charity, public property used exclusively for any public purpose, and personal property, to an amount not exceeding in value two hundred dollars, for each individual, may, by general laws, be exempted from taxation; but all such laws shall be subject to alteration or repeal; and the value of all property, so exempted, shall, from time to time, be ascertained and published, as may be directed by law.

School property is not liable to assessment for street improvement; nor can a judgment be rendered against the board of education for the payment of the assessment out of its contingent fund. 48 O. S., 83.

Sidewalk—School property not assessable for. 48 O. S., 87.

# INTERPRETATION OF STATUTES.

---

**Sec. 23. R. S.** [Interpretation of certain words.] In the interpretation of Parts First and Second, unless the context shows that another sense was intended, the word "bond" includes an "undertaking," and the word "undertaking" includes a "bond"; "and" may be read "or," and "or" read "and," if the sense requires it; words of the present include a future tense, in the masculine, include the feminine and neuter genders, and in the plural include the singular and in the singular include the plural number; but this enumeration shall not be construed to require a strict construction of other words in said Parts, or in this Code.

A construction which gives effect to every section and clause must be favored. 1 O., 381, 385; 2 O., 395, 398; 17 O. S., 52, 68; 3 O., 187, 193; 5 O., 48, 51; 2 O. S., 147, 151.

Each part must harmonize with each other, and a construction of one clause which will neutralize another cannot be correct. 3 O., 187, 193; 2 O., 395, 398; 5 O., 48, 51.

What is plainly implied in a statute is as much a part of it as what is expressed. 50 O. S., 330.

The ordinary and natural import of words consistent with the common sense of the community is to be adopted in arriving at legislative intent. 5 O., 65, 71; 25 O. S., 26, 28.

In considering questions arising under the school legislation of the state, such construction should be placed upon its various enactments, and the several provisions thereof, as will give harmony to our educational system, and secure, as far as practicable, its equal benefits, and the reasonable facilities for their enjoyment to every locality. 21 O. S., 339.

Penal statutes must be construed strictly, and cannot be extended by implication to cases not strictly within their terms. 20 O., 7; 18 O., 11; 38 O. S., 659; 44 O. S., 347.

While the opinion of the state commissioner of common schools cannot have the force of a judicial interpretation, it is of great force as the opinion of an eminent educator, who was at the head of the school system of the state, and presumably familiar with the necessities of the schools. 2 C. C., 366; Stewart, J.

# REVISED STATUTES of OHIO

## PART FIRST—TITLE III

### CHAPTER XIII.

#### STATE COMMISSIONER OF COMMON SCHOOLS.

Sec. 354. [State commissioner of common schools; election and term of; proviso.] There shall be elected triennially, at the general election for state officers, a state commissioner of common schools, who shall hold his office for the term of three years from the second Monday of July succeeding his election; and in case of a vacancy occurring by death, resignation, or otherwise, the governor shall fill the same by appointment. Provided, that the state commissioner of common schools now in office shall continue to hold his office until three years from the second Monday of July succeeding his election. (1884, March 27; 81 v. 89; Rev. Stat. 1880; 70 v. 195, § 102; S. & C., 1362.)

Sec. 355. [His official bond, and oath.] Before entering upon the discharge of his official duties, the commissioner shall give bond in the sum of five thousand dollars to the state, with two or more sureties, to the acceptance of the secretary of state, conditioned that he will truly account for and apply all moneys or other property which may come into his hands in his official capacity, and that he will faithfully perform the duties enjoined upon him according to law; which bond, with his oath of office indorsed thereon, shall be filed with the treasurer of state. (70 v. 195, § 103; S. & C. 1362.)

Sec. 356. [Office; books and papers; prohibitions.] The books and papers of his department shall be kept at the seat of government where a suitable office shall be furnished by the state, at which he shall give attendance not less than ten months in each year, except when absent on public duty; and he shall not, while holding the office of state commissioner of common schools, perform the duties of teacher or superintendent of any public or private school, or be employed as teacher in any college, or hold any other office or position of emolument.    (90 v. 13; 70 v. 195, § 104; S. & C., 1362.)

Sec. 357.  [His duties in visiting the several judicial districts.] The commissioner shall visit annually, each judicial district of the state, superintending and encouraging teachers' institutes, conferring with boards of education or other school officers, counseling teachers, visiting schools and delivering lectures on topics calculated to subserve the interests of popular education.  (70 v. 195, § 105; S. & C., 1362.)

Sec. 358.  [His supervision over school funds; may require reports from certain officers.]   He shall also exercise such supervision over the educational funds of the state as is necessary to secure their safety and right application and distribution according to law. He has power to require of county auditors, boards of education, clerks and treasurers of boards of education, or other local school officers, and county treasurers, copies of all reports by them required to be made, and all such other information in relation to the funds and condition of schools and the management thereof as he deems important.  (70 v. 195, § 106; S. & C., 1362.)

Sec. 359.  [Shall prepare forms, etc.]   He shall prescribe suitable forms and regulations for making all reports and conducting all necessary proceedings under the school laws, and cause the same, with such instructions as he deems necessary and proper for the organization and government of schools, to be transmitted to the local school officers, who shall be governed in accordance therewith.  (70 v. 195, § 107; S. & C., 1363.)

Sec. 360.  [Duties as to distribution of school laws, etc.]   He shall cause as many copies of the laws as are necessary, relating to schools and teachers' institutes, with an appendix of appropriate forms and instructions for carrying into execution all such laws, to be printed in a separate volume, and distributed to each county with the laws, journals, and other documents, for the use of the school officers therein, as often as any change in the laws is made of sufficient importance, in the opinion of the commissioner, to require a republication and distribution thereof.  (70 v. 195, § 108; S. & C., 1363.)

Sec. 361.  [Annual report of commissioner of schools.]   He shall make an annual report, on or before the fifteenth day of November, to the general assembly, when that body is in session, and when not in session the report shall be made to the governor, who shall cause the same to be published, and shall also communicate a copy thereof to the general assembly at the beginning of the next session. (1888, Apr. 11 : 85 v. 192; Rev. Stat. 1880; 70 v. 195, § 109; S. & C., 1363.)

**Sec. 362.** [What it shall present.] In his annual report he shall present a statement of the condition and amount of all funds and property appropriated to purposes of education; a statement of the number of common schools in the state, the number of scholars attending such schools, their sex, and the branches taught; a statement of the number of private or select schools in the state, so far as the same can be ascertained, and the number of scholars attending such schools, their sex, and the branches taught; a statement of the number of teachers' institutes, and the number of teachers attending them, and the number of instructors and lecturers, and the amount paid to each; a statement of the estimates and accounts of the expenditures of the public school funds of every description; a statement of plans for the management and improvement of common schools, and such other information relative to the educational interests of the state as he deems of importance. (70 v. 195, § 110; S. & C., 1363.)

**Sec. 363.** [Shall require reports from private schools, etc. He shall, annually, require of the president, manager, or principal of every seminary, academy, and private school, a report of such facts, arranged in such form as he prescribes, and shall furnish blanks for such reports; and it is made the duty of every such president, manager, or principal, to fill up and return such blanks within the time the commissioner directs. (73 v. 225, § 1.)

**Sec. 364.** [Duties of commissioner on complaint of fraudulent use of money, etc.; appointment of accountant to investigate charges.] When a complaint is made to the state commissioner of common schools, in writing, verified by the affidavits of at least three freeholders and taypayers, resident of any school district in the state, and bearing the certificate of the auditor or auditors of the respective county, or counties, in which said district is located, that said affiants are freeholders and taxpayers, alleging that they have good reason to and do believe that any portion of the school fund of such district has been expended, or is being expended, contrary to law, or has been fraudulently, unlawfully, or corruptly used, or misapplied, by any of the officers of such district, or that there have been fraudulent entries in the books, accounts, vouchers, or settlement sheets thereof, by any such officers, or that any of such officers have not made settlements of their account as required by law, or whenever from information filed in his office, or from other cause, the state commissioner of common schools may deem it necessary for the safety and security of the public funds of any school district, situated in the state of Ohio, he is authorized and required to appoint some trustworthy and competent accountant, for the purpose of investigating such complaint, or allegations, who after being duly commissioned by said state commissioner of common schools and sworn by any person authorized by law to administer oaths, shall forthwith visit such school district and take possession of all the books, papers, vouchers and accounts of such district and investigate the truth of the allegations of such complaint, and the condition of the school fund of such district; and the several officers of such school district, on the application of such examiner, shall immediately place in his possession all their books, accounts, contracts, vouchers, and other papers having reference to the receipts and disbursements of the school funds; and the county auditor and treasurer shall give such examiner free access to all the records, books, papers, vouchers, and accounts of their respective offices having reference to the object of such investigation, and said examiner is authprized, by and with the written consent of the prosecuting attorney, or the judge of the court of common pleas of the county in which such district is located, to require the assistance of the official stenographer of said county, in making such examination; and said stenographer shall receive only such compensation and in the manner provided in section 478, Revised Statutes, upon the certificate of the prosecuting attorney of said county. (94 v. 312; 72 v. 82, § 1.).

Sec. 365. [Powers and duties of examiner; his compensation; payment thereof.] Such examiner shall have authority to call before him forthwith, upon written notice, and examine witnesses, under oath, to be administered by him; and he shall immediately after completing such investigation, report in writing, in duplicate, setting forth the condition of the books, vouchers, and accounts of such district, the amount of school funds received for any and all purposes, and from whatever source, the amount expended, and for what, and the amount actually in the treasury, one copy of which report he shall file in the office of the clerk of the court of common pleas of the county in which such district is situate, and the other copy he shall transmit to the state commissioner of common schools at Columbus; and the examiner so appointed and performing the duties herein required, shall receive as compensation a per diem of five dollars for each day necessarily engaged in the performance of his duties, and shall also receive five cents for each mile by him necessarily traveled in that behalf; but no mileage shall be allowed for a greater distance than from Columbus to such district; and such compensation and mileage shall be paid out of the county treasury upon the warrant of the county auditor, and if the investigation establish the truth of any material allegation in such complaint, then such amount so paid shall be assessed by the county auditor upon the taxable property of the district, to be collected as other taxes are for the use of such county treasurer.   (94 v. 313; 72 v. 82, § 2.)

Sec. 366. . [Adverse report of examiner to be given in charge to the grand jury; duty of prosecuting attorney.]   The judge of the court of common pleas of the proper county shall examine the report so filed in the clerk's office, as provided in section three hundred and sixty-five, and if it appear therefrom that any part of the common school fund has been fraudulently, unlawfully, or corruptly used or misapplied, or that there has been fraud in any of the entries, accounts, vouchers, contracts, or settlements, or that the settlements have not been made as required by law, or that there appears any defalcation or embezzlement on the part of any of the officers of such school district, he shall give the report specially in charge to the grand jury at the term of the court of common pleas next after the filing of the same; and the prosecuting attorney of such county shall forthwith institute and carry forward such proceedings, civil or criminal, or both, against the delinquent officer or officers of such district as is authorized by law. (72 v. 82, § 3.)

# PART SECOND—TITLE III.

## SCHOOLS.

---

# CHAPTER I.

## CLASSIFICATION AND CHANGE OF DISTRICTS.

**Sec. 3885.** [Classification of school districts.] The state is hereby divided into school districts to be styled respectively, city school districts; village school districts; township school districts; and special school districts. (Passed and Approved April 25, 1904.)

Sec. 3886. [City school districts.] Each incorporated city, now existing or hereafter created, together with the territory attached to it for school purposes, and excluding the territory within its corporate limits detached for school purposes, shall constitute a city school district. (Passed and approved April 25, 1904.)

Sec. 3887. Repealed April 25, 1904.

Sec. 3888. [Village school districts.] Each incorporated village now existing or hereafter created, together with the territory attached to it for school purposes, and excluding the territory within its corporate limits detached for school purposes, shall constitute a village school district. (Passed and approved April 25, 1904.)

Sec. 3889. [Change of classification in certain cases; terms of members of boards of education when classification is changed; village districts abolished by surrender of corporate power of municipality.] When a village is advanced to a city, the village school district shall thereby become a city school district; when a city is reduced to a village the city school district shall thereby become a village school district. The members of the board of education in village school districts that are advanced to city school districts, and in city school districts that are reduced to village school districts, shall continue in office until succeeded by the members of the board of education of the new district, who shall be elected at the next succeeding annual election for school board members. Upon the creation and incorporation of a village, the same shall thereby become a village school district, and if said village was, previous to its creation and incorporation, included within the boundaries of a special school district but said special district included more territory than is included within the village limits, said territory shall be, and thereby is, attached to said village school district for school purposes; when a village surrenders its corporate powers the village school district shall be thereby abolished and the territory formerly constituting said village district shall become a part of the township school district or districts of the civil township or townships in which it is situated, and all school property shall pass to and become vested in the township board of education of the civil township in which it is situated; the provisions of section 1536-4 of the Revised Statutes of Ohio in regard to the settlement of the affairs of a village that has surrendered its corporate powers shall also apply to the village school district and the board of education of the same, and in case the village school district is situated in two or more townships any distribution of funds shall be made in proportion to the total tax valuation of the property situated in the several townships. (Passed and approved April 25, 1904.)

**Sec. 3890.** [Township school districts.] Each civil township together with the territory attached to it for school purposes, and excluding the territory within its established limits detached for school purposes, shall constitute a township school district. (Passed and approved April 25, 1904.)

**Sec. 3891.** [Special school districts.] Any school district, now existing, other than a city, village or township school district, and any school district organized under the provisions of chapter 5 of this title, shall constitute a special school district. (Passed and approved April 25, 1904.)

**Sec. 3892.** [Territory must be contiguous.] The territory included within the boundaries of any city, village or special school district shall be contiguous. (Passed and approved April 25, 1904.)

**Sec. 3893.** [Annexation of territory to cities and villages.] Whenever territory is annexed to a city or village, such territory thereby becomes a part of the city or village school district and the legal title to all school property in said territory shall be thereby vested in the board of education of such city or village school district. (Passed and approved April 25, 1904.)

**Sec. 3894.** [Transfer of territory by agreement between boards of education.] A part or the whole of any school district may be transferred to an adjoining school district by the mutual consent of the boards of education having control of such district; to secure such consent it shall be necessary for each of said boards to pass a resolution indicating the action taken and definitely describing the territory to be transferred, and the passage of said resolution shall require a majority vote of the full membership of each board, to be taken by a yea and nay vote and the vote of each member to be entered on the records of such boards; but such transfer shall not take effect until a map showing the boundaries of the territory transferred is placed upon the records of such boards, and copies of the resolution certified to the president and clerk of each board, together with a copy of said map, is filed with the auditor or auditors of the county or counties in which such transferred territory is situated. (Passed and approved April 25, 1904.)

**Sec. 3895.** [Transfer of territory by proceedings in probate court.] Territory can also be transferred from one school district to another in the following manner: A petition signed by not less than one-half of the qualified male citizens who are electors residing in the territory sought to be transferred and accompanied by a correct map of said territory, shall be filed with the clerks of the boards of education interested and if such boards of education fail or refuse to transfer such territory by mutual consent, as provided for in section thirty-eight hundred and ninety-four of the Revised Statutes of Ohio, within sixty days after the filing of said petition and map, the petitioner shall file a copy of said petition and map in the probate court of the county in which such territory is situated, or if the territory be in two or more counties, in the probate court of the county containing the largest proportionate share of the territory to be transferred; the petitions [petitioners] shall be required to give satisfactory security for the costs in the sum of one hundred dollars, conditioned that the sureties shall pay all the costs in case the transfer is not granted; the probate judge shall thereupon fix a day for the hearing of said petition and shall cause to be published for four consecutive weeks, in two newspapers of opposite politics, printed and of general circulation in the county, a notice of the filing of such petition and of the time of the hearing, and he shall also notify the clerks of the boards of education interested of the filing of the petition and the time of hearing; the probate judge is authorized and empowered to hear and determine the case and give judgment for or against such transfer and his judgment shall be final. In case the finding is against the transfer, judgment shall be rendered against the petitioners for the costs of the proceedings, and if the finding is for the transfer, judgment shall be rendered against each of the boards of education interested for one-half of the costs, or if more than two boards are interested judgment shall be rendered against each for its equal proportionate share of the costs. A certified copy of the findings of the court, together with a copy of the map of the territory transferred, shall be filed in the office of the county auditor by the probate judge. (Passed and approved April 25, 1904.)

**Sec. 3896.** [Division of funds and indebtedness when territory is transferred or annexed.] When territory is transferred from one school district to another under the provisions of section 3894 of the Revised Statutes of Ohio, the equitable division of funds or indebtedness shall be determined upon at the time of the transfer. When territory is transferred from one school district to another by proceedings in the probate court, or by the annexation of territory to a city or village, the proper division of funds in the treasury, or in the process of collection, of the board of education of the school district from which the territory is detached, shall, upon application to the probate court of the county in which such territory is situated by either board of education interested, be determined and ordered by said court; in case said board of education is indebted, such indebtedness together with the proper amount of money to be paid to said

2—S. L.

board of education by the board of education of the school district to which the territory is transferred, annexed, or the district created, shall be, in a like manner, determined and ordered by said court. If the territory is situated in two or more counties the application and proceedings shall be had in the probate court of the county containing the largest proportionate share of said transferred territory. The findings of the probate court shall be final. (Passed and approved April 25, 1904.)

# CHAPTER II.

## CITY SCHOOL DISTRICTS.

**Sec. 3897.** [Boards of education in city districts; number of members.] In city school districts the board of education shall consist of not less than two members nor more than seven members elected at large, by the qualified electors of the school district, and of not less than two members nor more than thirty members elected from sub-districts by the qualified electors of their respective sub-districts; provided that in city school districts which at the last preceding federal census contained a population of not less than fifty thousand persons, the board of education shall consist of not less than three members nor more than seven members elected at large, by the qualified electors of such city school districts.

[Existing boards to fix number of members and divide city into sub-districts.] Not later than the first day of July next, after the passage of this act, the present city school board, board of education, school council or other city school legislative body, shall pass a resolution fixing, within the limits prescribed by this act, the number of members of said board of education to be elected at large, and in city school districts where there are members of the board of education to be elected from sub-districts, they shall also, at the same time, fix the number of members of the board of education to be elected by such city sub-districts. The said city school board, board of education, school council or other city school legislative body, in city school districts where there are members of the board of education to be elected

from sub-districts, shall, at the same time, to-wit: Before the first day
of July next, after the passage of this act, subdivide said city school
district into sub-districts equal in number to the number of members
of the board of education in said city school district who are to be
elected from sub-districts therein .established. Said sub-districts
shall be bounded as far as practicable by corporation lines, streets,
alleys, avenues, public grounds, canals, water courses,ward boundaries,
voting precinct boundaries or present school district boundaries, and
shall be as nearly equal in population as possible, and shall be composed of adjacent and as compact territory as possible. The lines of
sub-districts so fixed shall not be changed until after each succeeding
federal census.

[Redistricting.]   Within three months after the official announcement of the result of each succeeding federal census the board of education of each city school district shall redistrict the said city school
district into sub-districts in accordance with the provisions of this act.

[When board fails to divide into districts.]   If the city school
board of education, school council, or other city school legislative body
shall fail to district or redistrict said city school district as herein required, at the time or times herein specified, then and in that event, upon the application of the president of the board of education the state
commissioner of common·schools shall, subject to the requirements
of this act, forthwith district, or re-district said city school districts.

[First election; how conducted.]   Provided also, that school sub-
districts shall be numbered from one up, consecutively, and that a'
the first election for members of the board of education held after
the passage of this act, the members to be elected to the board of education from sub-districts of odd numbers beginning with one, shall
be elected for two years, and those elected from sub-districts of even
numbers shall be elected for four years, and at the expiration of their
respective terms their successors shall be elected for a term of four
years; and provided further, that at the said first election the members
of the board of education at large in all city school districts shall be
elected for terms as follows:   If there be but two members of the
board of education elected at large, one shall be elected for two years
and one for four years, and if there be more than two, and the number
thereof divisible by two, the one-half of such board shall be elected for
two years and one-half for four years but if the whole number of
members elected at large be not divisible by two, then the number to
be elected for two years shall be the quotient obtained by dividing the
whole number to be elected at large, less one, by two, and the remaining members shall be elected for four years.

[Elections held thereafter; change in membership of board.] At the expiration of their respective terms their successors shall be elected for four years. Members elected at large must be electors of the city school district, and members elected from sub-districts must be electors of the city sub-districts from which they are chosen, or of the territory attached to the sub-district for school purposes; a removal from said sub-districts, territory or city school district shall vacate said office. The number of members of the board of education shall not be changed, except at the time of the redistricting herein provided for, within three months after the official announcement of the result of the federal census. All members of boards of education of city school districts, herein provided for shall be elected at the same time and in the same manner as municipal officers are elected. (Passed and approved April 25, 1904.)

Sec. 3897a. [Organization; meetings; president; clerk; nomination by petition.] Boards of education in city school districts shall organize on the first Monday in January after the election held for members of the board of education by the election of one of their members as president and the election of a clerk, who may or may not be a member of the board, the president to be elected for one year and the clerk to be elected for a term not to exceed two years; they shall fix the time of holding regular meetings. Upon the organization of the first boards of education elected under this act, the previously existing boards of education are thereby abolished and said newly elected boards shall be their successors in all respects. Not less than fifteen days before the election of members of boards of education, nominations of candidates therefor may be made by nomination papers, signed in the aggregate for each candidate by not less than twenty-five qualified electors of either sex of the school district, except that in city school districts such nomination papers shall be signed by petitioners not less in number than one for every one hundred persons who voted at the next preceding general election in such city; and whenever each of such candidates shall be so nominated and his or their names shall be presented to the county board of deputy state supervisors of elections of the county in which such district is situated not less than fifteen days prior to the ensuing election, the said board of deputy state supervisors of elections shall publish on two different days prior to such election the names of such candidates in two newspapers of opposite politics in the school district, if there be such printed and published therein, or, if no newspaper is printed therein, by posting such list of names in at least five public places in the school district. (Passed and approved April 25, 1904.)

**Sec. 3897b.** [Trustees of school-teachers' pension fund; number, election and term.] Whenever the board of education of any school district shall declare by resolution, adopted by a majority vote of the members of said board, that it is advisable to create a school-teachers' pension fund for such school district, said school-teachers' pension fund shall be under the charge, management and control of a board to be known as the board of trustees of the school-teachers' [pension fund for such school] district, which board shall be composed of not less than three, nor more than seven, members, as said board of education shall by resolution declare; if composed of less than five members, one of the members of said board of trustees of the school-teachers' pension fund of such school district shall be elected by the board of education of such school district, and the remaining members by the teachers of the public schools, including the teachers of any high schools, of such district, who have accepted the provisions of this act, as hereinafter provided; if such board is to be composed of five or more members, two of the members of said board of trustees of said school district shall be elected by the board of education of such school district, and the remaining members by the teachers of the public schools, including the teachers of any high schools of such school district, who have accepted the provisions of this act, as herein provided; such election of the members of said board by the teachers to be at a meeting called by the superintendent of schools of such school district, the first election to be at a meeting to be called by such superintendent when one-third of the teachers of the public schools of such school district shall have accepted the provisions this act; the members of said board of trustees of the school-teachers' pension fund shall be elected for such length of time as the board of education of such school district shall by resolution declare, to serve not less than one, nor more than three, years, and shall serve until their successors are elected and qualified, such service to be without compensation. (92 v. 149; 94 v. 306; 95 v. 610.)

**Sec. 3897c.** [How fund created.] Whenever the board of education of any school district shall have declared the advisability of creating a school-teachers' pension fund, as herein provided, the clerk of said board of education shall notify each and every teacher in the public schools and high schools, if any, of said school district, by notice in writing of the passage of such resolution, and require said teachers to notify said board of education in writing within thirty days from the date of said notice whether they consent or decline to accept the provisions of this act; and from and after the election of the board of trustees herein provided for, the sum of two dollars ($2) shall be deducted by the proper officers from the monthly salary of each teacher who may have accepted the provisions of this act, and from the salary of such new teachers as may here-after accept the same, as herein provided, said sum to be paid into and applied to the credit of said school-teachers' pension fund, and shall continue to so deduct said sum during the remainder of the term of service of said teacher. All teachers hereafter appointed in said public schools, or high schools, if any, in said school district, shall be notified within thirty days after their appointment by the clerk of such board of education of the election of said board of trustees of said school-teachers' pension fund, and they shall be required to notify said board of education within six months there-after whether they consent or decline to accept the provisions of this act. All moneys received from donations, legacies, gifts, be-quests or from any other source shall also be paid into said fund, or into a permanent fund, and if paid into a permanent fund, the interest only of said fund shall be applied to the payment of pensions. Said board of trustees shall have power to invest said pension fund in the name of said board in bonds of the United States, or the state of Ohio, or of any county in this state, or of any municipal corporation in this state, or of any school district in this state; and said board shall have power to make payments from said pension fund for pensions granted in pursuance of this act. Said board of trustees shall also have power from time to time to make and estab-lish such rules and regulations for the administration of said pen-sion fund as they shall deem best. (92 v. 152; 95 v. 610.)

**Sec. 3897d.** [Retirement and pension of teachers; meaning of term "teacher"; amount of pension; who not entitled to pension; how, when fund insufficient to pay pensions.] Said board of education of said school district, and any union board, or other separate board, if any, having the control and management of the high schools of said school district, shall each of them have power by a majority vote of all the members composing said board to retire on account of physical or mental disability, any male or female teacher under such board who shall have taught for a period aggregating twenty (20) years, whether before or after, or partly before or after, the passage of this act; provided, however, that three-fifths of said period of service shall have been rendered by said beneficiary in the public schools or high schools of said school district, or in the public schools or high schools of the county in which said school district is located, and the re-maining two-fifths of said period of service in the public schools of this state or elsewhere. "The term 'teacher' under this act, shall include all teachers regularly employed by either of said boards in the day schools, including the superintendents of schools, all superintendents of instructon, principals, and special teachers, and in the estimation of years of service, only service in public day schools or day high schools, supported in whole or in part by public taxation, shall be considered. Any teacher shall have the right to retire and become a beneficiary under this act who shall have taught for a period aggregating thirty (30) years, whether before or after, or partly before or after, the passage of this act; provided that three-fifths of said term of service shall have been rendered in the public schools or in the high schools of said school district, or in the public schools or high schools of the county in which said district is located, and the remaining two-fifths of said term of service in the public schools of this state· or elsewhere. Each teacher so retired or retiring shall be entitled during the remainder of his or her natural life to receive as pension, annually, the sum of ten dollars ($10) for each and every year of service rendered as teacher, but in no event shall such pension paid to any teacher exceed the sum of five hundred dollars ($500) in any one year, and said pensions shall be paid monthly during the school year; but in no event shall such pension be paid to any teacher until such teacher shall contribute, or shall have contributed, to said fund a sum equal to twenty dollars ($20) a year for each and every year of service rendered as teacher, but in no event shall this sum exceed six hundred dollars ($600); but should any teacher retiring be unable to pay the full amount of this sum before receiving a pension, the board of trustees shall, in paying the annual pension to such retiring teacher withhold on each month's payment twenty per cent. thereof, until the full amount as above provided shall have been thus contributed to the fund; provided further, that if said pension fund shall at any time be insufficient to meet the pensions so provided for, that during the period that such fund is insufficient to make such payment, the amount in said fund during said period shall be pro-rated between the parties entitled thereto. (92 v. 153; 94 v. 307; 95 v. 611.)

**Sec. 3897e.** [Use of **principal and income.**] Said board of trustees shall have the power to use both the principal and income of said fund for the payment of the premiums herein provided for, and the expense thereof. No portion of said pension fund shall, befo·e its distribution and payment by said board of trustees to the beneficiaries, be liable to be taken or subjected by any writ or legal process against the beneficiary. (92 v. 154; 95 v. 612.)

**Sec. 3897f.** [Monthly certifications of deductions from salaries.] The clerk of the board of education of said school district, and the clerk of the union board of high schools, or other separate board having the control and management of the high schools of said school dis-

trict, if any, shall each of them certify monthly to said board of trustees all amounts deducted from the salaries of the teachers as aforesaid, which amounts, as well as all other moneys contributed to
said fund, shall be set apart as a special fund for the purposes herein
specified, subject to the order of said board of trustees.   All moneys
belonging to said fund shall be paid only on the order of said board
of trustees, entered upon its minutes on warrants signed by the president and secretary of said board.   (92 v. 154; 95 v. 612.)

Sec. 3897g.   [Who custodian of fund; duties.]   The treasurer of
said school district shall be the custodian of said pension fund, and shall
keep the same subject to the order, control and direction of said board
of trustees.   He shall keep books of accounts concerning said fund
in such manner as may be prescribed by said board, which books
of account shall always be subject to the inspection of said board
of trustees or of any member thereof.   Said treasurer shall execute a
bond to said board of trustees with good and sufficient sureties in such
sum as said board of trustees shall require, which bond shall be subject to the approval of said board and be conditioned for the faithful performance of his duties as custodian of said board and treasurer
of said board.   He shall always keep and truly account for all moneys and profits coming into his hands as such treasurer belonging
to such fund, and at the expiration of his term of office shall pay
over, surrender and deliver to his successor all securities, moneys and
other property of whatsoever kind, nature and description which may
be in his hands or under his control as treasurer aforesaid.   Said
treasurer shall be paid for his services under this act as compensation
not to exceed one per cent. annually of the amount paid into said
fund during the year.   (92 v. 154; 95 v. 612.)

Sec. 3897h.   [Rebate in case of resignation or removal; heirs, legatees or assigns of deceased teacher entitled to half amount paid.]   Any
teacher who shall resign or be removed for cause, as aforesaid, shall,
·upon application within three (3) months after such resignation
or removal takes effect, be entitled to receive one-half of the total
amount paid by such teacher into such fund.   In case of the death
of any teacher, the heirs, legatees or assigns of the deceased teacher
shall be entitled to receive one-half of the total amount paid by such
teacher into such fund upon application therefor, with proof of claim
to the satisfaction of the board of trustees.   (92 v. 154; 94 v. 308; 95
v. 613.)

Sec. 3897i.   [Rules and regulations.]   The board of trustee shall
make such rules and regulations as it may deem expedient or necessary for its government; which rules and regulations must be

adopted, and when adopted, may be amended, by a vote of not less than two-thirds of all the members of said board of trustees.   (94 v. 308; 95 v. 613.)

**Sec. 3897j.**  [Transfer of fund now existing to trustees herein created.]   Upon the election and organization of a board of pension trustees under this act in any school district of this state, any school-teachers' pension fund heretofore created for said district under any former act, shall be transferred to the board of trustees created under this act by the board or persons having control thereof; and all beneficiaries now receiving pensions from the fund transferred as aforesaid, shall continue to receive pensions under this act.   (95 v. 613.)

**Sec. 3897k.**  [Deductions, fines, penalties and assessments, disposition of.]   The board of education in any school district which has created, or shall hereafter create, a teachers' pension fund, shall pay monthly into said teachers' pension fund all deductions, fines, penalties and assessments made against any of the teachers or other employes of said board for violation of any of the rules or orders of the said board.   (Passed and approved April 25, 1904.)

**Sec. 3897l.**   [Board of education may contribute to pension fund.]   The board of education in any school district which has created or shall hereafter create, a teachers' pension fund, may pay semi-annually, out of the contingent fund of such school district, into said teachers' pension fund, not to exceed two per cent. of the gross receipts of said board of education raised by taxation to be applied to the payment of teachers' pensions as hereinbefore provided. (Passed and approved April 25, 1904.)

**Sec. 3898.**  [Attached territory, assignment of and voting in.] When territory is attached to a city school district for school purposes, it shall be the duty of the board of education to assign such territory to the sub-district or sub-districts adjoining the same, and a map showing such assignment shall be made a part of the record of the board; the electors residing in said attached territory shall be entitled to vote for school officers and on all school questions in the sub-district to which they are assigned, and in the election pre cinct nearest their residence; and in case the board fails to perform this duty, the electors residing in said attached territory shall be entitled to vote in the sub-district and precinct nearest their residence An elector residing in the city, but not in the city school district, shall not be entitled to vote in said city school district.   (Passed and approved April 25, 1904.)

**Sec. 3899.**  Repealed 89 v. 79.

**Sec. 3900.**  [Redistricting of city districts.]   The redistricting of a city school district shall not affect the membership of the then existing board of education in said city school district; all the members thereof shall continue to serve for the full term for which they were elected, but after the expiration of said terms the election of members of the board of education from sub-districts shall be by the sub-districts as redistricted. (Passed and approved April 25, 1904.)

**Sec. 3901.** [**Schools for deaf children.**] Boards of education of city school districts are authorized and empowered to establish and maintain, under their management and control one or more day schools for the education of the deaf youth of school age of the district, the expense of conducting the same to be paid from the school funds of the district in the same manner and from the same funds as other school expenses are paid. (Passed and approved April 25, 1904.)

**Sec. 3902.** Repealed April 25, 1904.

**Sec. 3903.** Repealed April 25, 1904

## CHAPTER III.

### VILLAGE SCHOOL DISTRICTS.

**Sec. 3904.**   Repealed April 25, 1904.

**Sec. 3905.**   Repealed April 25, 1904.

**Sec. 3906.**   Repealed April 25, 1904.

**Sec. 3907.**   Repealed April 25, 1904.

**Sec. 3908.**   [**Board of education in village** districts; membership; **election and term.**] The board of education of village school districts shall consist of five members elected at large at the same time and in the same manner as municipal officers are elected, for the term of four years from the first Monday in January after their election or until their successors are elected and qualified. At the first municipal election held after the passage of this act there shall be a board of education elected in all village districts as provided for herein, two to serve for two years, and three to serve for four years, and at the municipal election held every second year thereafter, their successors shall be elected for the term of four years. Upon the organization of said boards, upon the succeeding first Monday in January after their election, the previously existing village boards of education shall be thereby abolished and the newly elected and organized board shall be their successors in all respects. (Passed and approved April 25, 1904.)

**Sec. 3909.**   [**Newly created village districts; election in.**] In all incorporated villages not now organized as school districts and in all villages hereafter created, there shall be a board of education elected as provided for in section 3908 of the Revised Statutes of Ohio; provided, however, that if said election be a special election held in a newly created village, the members elected shall serve for the terms as indicated in said section 3908, from the first Monday in January after the last preceding election for members of boards of education, and the board shall organize on the second Monday after the special election. (Passed and approved April 25, 1904.)

**Sec. 3910.**   [**Voting in attached territory.**] Electors residing in territory attached to a village school district for school purposes, shall be entitled to vote for school officers and on all school questions, at the regular voting place in the village to which such territory is attached, and should said village be divided into voting precincts, it shall be the duty of the board of education of such village school district to assign such territory to the adjoining precinct or precincts and to have a map prepared showing such assignment, said map to be made a part of the records of the board, and the electors residing in such attached territory shall be entitled to vote in the precinct to which they are assigned, but in case no assignment of territory is made, the elector shall vote in the precinct nearest his residence. An elector residing in a village, but not in a village school district, shall not be entitled to vote in said village school district. (Passed and approved April 25, 1904.)

**Sec. 3911.** [Organization; president; clerk; regular meetings.] Boards of education of village school districts shall organize on the first Monday in January after the election of the board, by the election of one of their members president, and the election of a clerk who may or may not be a member of the board, the president to be elected for one year and the clerk to be elected for a term not to exceed two years; and they shall fix the time of holding regular meetings. (Passed and approved April 25, 1904.)

**Sec. 3912** Repealed April 25, 1904.

**Sec. 3913.** Repealed April 25, 1904.

**Sec. 3914.** Repealed April 25, 1904.

# CHAPTER IV.

## TOWNSHIP SCHOOL DISTRICTS.

**Sec. 3915.** [Boards of education in township districts; member-ship; election and term.] The board of education of township school districts shall consist of five members elected at large at the same time and in the same manner as the township officers are elected, for the term of four years from the first Monday in January after their election [or] until their successors are elected and qualified. At the first town-ship election held after the passage of this act, there shall be a board of education elected in all township districts as provided for herein, two to serve for two years, and three to serve for four years, and at the township election held every second year thereafter, their success-ors shall be elected for the term of four years. Upon the organization of said boards, upon the succeeding first Monday in January after their election, the previously existing township boards of education shall be thereby abolished and the newly elected and organized boards shall be their successors in all respects. (Passed and approved April 25, 1904.)

**Sec. 3916.** [Attached territory; voting in.] Electors residing in territory attached to a township school district for school purposes, shall be entitled to vote for school officers and on all school questions, at the regular voting place in the township to which such territory is attached, and should such township be divided into different voting precincts, it shall be the duty of the board of education of the town-ship district, to assign such attached territory to the adjoining pre-cinct or precincts; if territory is attached to more than one precinct, a map shall be prepared showing such assignment and said map shall be made a part of the records of the board of education, and electors shall be entitled to vote according to such assignment, but in case no assignment of territory is made, the electors shall vote in the precinct nearest to their residence. An elector residing in the township, but not in the township school district, shall not be entitled to vote in said township school district. (Passed and approved April 25, 1904.)

**Sec. 3917.** Repealed April 25, 1904.

**Sec. 3918.** Repealed April 25, 1904.

**Sec. 3919.** Repealed 90 v. 76.

**Sec. 3920.** [Organization; president; clerk; regular meetings.] Boards of education of township school districts shall organize on the first Monday in January after the election of the board, by the election of one of their members president and the election of a clerk who may or may not be a member of the board, the president to be elected for one year and the clerk to be elected for a term not to exceed two years; and they shall fix the time of holding regular meetings. (Passed and approved April 25, 1904.)

**Sec. 3921.** [Sub-districts recognized.] The division of township school districts into sub-districts as they exist at the time of the passage of this act, shall continue and be recognized for the purpose of school attendance, but the board of education is authorized to increase or diminish the number or change the boundaries of the sub-districts at any regular meeting, a map designating such changes to be entered upon its records. (Passed and approved April 25, 1904.)

**Sec. 3921a.** [Director of sub-districts; election; term; duties.] In all township districts the schools of which are not centralized or consolidated there shall be elected by ballot on the second Monday of April, 1905, and annually thereafter in each sub-district, by the qualified electors thereof, one competent person, having the qualifications of an elector therein to be styled director. In all cases of tie votes at an election for director the judges of election shall decide the election by lot; and in other cases of failure to elect directors or in case of a refusal to serve, or in case where vacancies exist from any cause, the township board of education shall appoint a director for such sub-district. The director of each sub-district shall post written or printed notices in three or more conspicuous places in his sub-district at least six days prior to the election, designating the day and hour of opening, and the hour of closing the election. The election shall be held at the school house in the sub-district. The meeting shall be organized by appointing a chairman and secretary, who shall act as judges of the election under oath or affirmation, which oath or affirmation may be administered by the director of the sub-district, or any other person competent to administer such an oath or affirmation, and the secretary shall keep a poll-book and tally-sheet, which shall be signed by the judges, and delivered within eight days to the clerk of the township board of education. .The qualified electors of the sub-district may hold other meetings at any time upon the call of the director or of any five electors. Five days' notice shall be given of such meetings by posting notices in five public places in the vicinity. The director of each sub-district shall preside at the school meetings of the district, record their proceedings, and shall act as the organ ·of communication between the inhabitants and the township board of education. He shall take charge of the school house and property belonging thereto under the general order and direction of the township board of education and preserve the same and when so ordered by the board shall make all temporary repairs of the school house, furniture and fixtures, and provide the necessary fuel for the school, reporting the cost thereof to the board of education for payment. The director of each sub-district shall take the enumeration of his sub-district and return the same to the clerk of the township board of education in the manner prescribed by law. (Passed and approved April 25, 1904.)

Sec. 3922. [Centralization by suspension of one or more sub-district schools.] The board of education of any township school district is authorized to suspend the schools in any or all sub-districts in the township district, but upon such suspension the board must provide for the conveyance of the pupils residing in such sub-district or sub-districts to a public school in said township district, or to a public school in another district, the cost of such conveyance to be paid out of the funds of the township school district; or the board may abolish all the sub-districts providing conveyance is furnished to one or more central schools, the expense of such conveyance to be paid out of the funds of the district. When transportation of pupils is provided for, the conveyance must pass within at least the distance of one-half of a mile from the respective residence of all pupils, except when such residences are situated more than one-half of a mile from the public road; but boards of education shall not be required to provide transportation for pupils living less than one-half of a mile from the school house. (Passed and approved April 25, 1904.)

Sec. 3923. [Joint sub-districts abolished.] Joint sub-districts are hereby abolished and the territory of such districts, situated in the township in which the school house of the joint sub-district is not located, shall be attached for school purposes to the township school district in which said school house is located, and shall constitute a part of said township school district, and the title of all school property located in said joint sub-district, is hereby vested in the board of education of the township to which the territory is attached. A map of such attached territory shall be prepared under the direction of the board of education of the township district to which such territory is attached and shall be made a part of the records of said board and a copy of the same shall be filed with the auditor of the county in which said territory is situated, or if the territory be in two or more counties, said map shall be filed with the auditor of each county. (Passed and approved April 25, 1904.)

**Sec. 3924.** Repealed April 25, 1904.

**Sec. 3925.** Repealed April 25, 1904.

**Sec. 3926.** Repealed April 25, 1904.

**Sec. 3927.** Repealed April 25, 1904

**Sec. 3927-1.** Repealed April 25, 1904.

**Sec. 3927-2.** [Centralization, submission of question to vote.] A township board of education may submit the question of centralization, and upon the petition of not less than one-fourth of the qualified electors of such township district, must submit such question to a vote of the qualified electors of such township district, and if more votes are cast in favor of centralization than against it, at such election, it shall then become the duty of the board of education, and such board of education is required to proceed at once to the centralization of [the] schools of the township, and if necessary purchase a site or sites and erect a suitable building or buildings thereon; provided, that if, at the said election, more votes are cast against the proposition for centralization than for it, the question shall not again be submitted to the electors of said township district for a period of two years. When the schools of a township have been centralized, such centralization shall not be discontinued within three years thereafter, and then only by petition and election as required herein and if at such election more votes are cast against centralization than for it, the division into sub-districts as they existed prior to centralization, shall be thereby re-established at the next regular election and sub-district directors shall be elected as provided in section 3921a of this act. (Passed and approved April 25, 1904.)

## AN ACT.

To provide aid for the support of normal schools.

*Be it enacted by the General Assembly of the State of Ohio:*

**Sec. 1.** That the trustees of any township in the state of Ohio, in which a normal school is organized and conducted or may be established hereafter, are authorized to levy annually a tax, not exceeding two mills on the dollar upon all the taxable property of the township for the purpose of aiding in the support of such normal school.

**Sec. 2.** Before the tax may be levied, the question of making a levy for the purpose named in section 1, herein, shall be submitted to the qualified electors of the township, at a special or general election to be held in such township, due notice of which shall be given at least twenty days prior to the election, by publication in some newspaper of general circulation in the township; and provided a majority of the votes cast at such election upon said question of tax levy is in favor of levying the tax, then the trustees of the township thereafter shall make the levy annually and report the same to the county auditor for collection as other taxes, and when collected, to be paid over to the duly qualified and acting treasurer of the board of trustees of such normal school.

**Sec. 3.** At any time after four years from the date of an election held in accordance with the provisions of section 2 of this act, another election may be petitioned for and shall be ordered by the trustees of the township, provided the petition shall be signed by at least forty per cent. of the qualified electors of the township. (Passed and approved April 25, 1904.)

# CHAPTER V.

## SPECIAL SCHOOL DISTRICTS.

**Sec. 3928.** [Formation of special school district, proceedings for.] A special school district may be formed of any contiguous territory, not included within the limits of an incorporated city or village, which has a total tax valuation of not less than one hundred thousand dollars. To establish a special school district, a petition signed by not less than ten male citizens who are electors of the proposed special district shall be filed in the office of the probate judge of the county in which such special district is situated or if said district is situated in two or more counties, then with the probate judge of the county having the greatest total tax valuation in said proposed district; said petition shall set forth the desires of the petitioners, shall contain a description of the territory to be included in the proposed special district, and shall be accompanied by a statement giving the total tax valuation of said territory certified to by the county auditor or auditors and also an accurate map of the territory to be included in said district, the same to be prepared to the satisfaction of the probate judge; said petition shall also be accompanied by an undertaking of one or more of the petitioners, with security to the satisfaction of the judge, in the sum of one hundred dollars, conditioned that the parties entering into the undertaking shall pay all the costs of the proceedings if a special school district is not created, and in such case the probate judge shall render judgment against the parties to the undertaking for all the costs of the proceedings. In case the petition is granted the costs shall be taxed against the special school district thereby authorized and shall be paid by the board of education of said special school district, thereafter elected, from any funds that may come into its possession. A remonstrance signed by one or more of the male citizens who are electors of the proposed district may be filed with the probate judge and shall be considered on the hearing of the petition. Nothing herein contained shall be so construed as to abolish any special school district now existing, but all such districts whether created under the provisions of a general or special act, including the territory now constituting such special district, shall, unless changed under the provisions of. this chapter, continue to be and remain and be recognized and regarded as legal special school districts, excepting, however, such special school districts which do now or may hereafter include within their boundaries an incorporated city or village, and in such cases such special district shall become a city or village school district with or without territory attached or detached, as the case may be. And all officers and members of boards of education of existing special school districts heretofore created, whether by special or general act, shall continue to hold and exercise their respective offices and the powers thereof, until their successors are elected and qualified as provided herein; provided that all such officers of such districts created by special act shall hold such offices only until the first Monday of January following the first election for school officers to be held after the passage of this act, at which election their successors shall be elected. (Passed and approved April 25, 1904.)

**Sec. 3929.** [Further proceedings in probate court.] Upon the filing of a petition in the probate court for the establishment of a special school district, the judge thereof shall fix a time for the hearing of the same, which shall be within sixty days of the filing thereof; he shall thereupon cause to be published for four consecutive weeks, in two newspapers of opposite politics, printed and of general circulation in the county .where the petition is filed, notice of the filing of such petition and the time of the hearing thereon; such notices shall also be mailed to the clerk or clerks of the board or boards of education having territory in the proposed special school district. The probate judge is authorized to hear and determine the question of the establishment of such special school district, may subpoena and examine witnesses under oath, may change the boundaries of the proposed special school district, shall fix and determine the amount of money due and payable to said special district from the surplus money in the treasury or in process of collection in the district or districts from which it was formed, or in case of the indebtness of such district or districts, he shall determine the amount of money due and payable by the special school district to the district or districts from which it was formed, and in either case the amount so found due shall be [a] valid and binding obligation upon the board of education of such district or districts. The fees in cases involving the establishment of special school districts shall be the same as in civil cases, and the jurisdiction of the probate court in such cases shall be exclusive. (Passed and approved April 25, 1904.)

Sec. 3930. [Boards of education in special districts; membership; election and term.] The board of education of special school districts shall consist of five members elected at large at the same time and in the same manner as the township officers are elected, for the term of four years from the first Monday in January after their election or until their successors are elected and qualified. At the first township election held after the passage of this act, there shall be a board of education elected in all special districts as provided for herein, two to serve for two years, and three to serve for four years, and at the township election held every second year thereafter, their successors shall be elected for the term of four years. Upon the organization of said boards, upon the succeeding first Monday in January after their election the previously existing boards of education of special school districts shall be thereby abolished and the newly elected and organized boards shall be their successors in all respects. (Passed and approved April 25, 1904.)

Sec. 3931. [Elections, how conducted.] Elections in special school districts shall be held by the regular election officers of the township in which such special districts are situated and if a special district is situated in two or more townships, the election shall be held by the election officers of the different townships for the electors residing in each township respectively. At least twenty days prior to the first election held under this act, it shall be the duty of the clerk of the board of education of each special school district to notify the deputy supervisors of elections of the county in which the district is situated, or if said district be in two or more counties, he shall notify the deputy supervisors of each county, of the names of the voting precincts having territory in such special school district, and the probable number of electors in each precinct, in order that said deputy supervisors shall be enabled to prepare ballots and election supplies and distribute the same to the proper precincts, and in each precinct there shall be separate ballots, ballot boxes, poll books and tally sheets for each school district having voters therein. (Passed and approved April 25, 1904.)

Sec. 3932. [Election in newly created special district.] When a special school district is created, a mass meeting of the electors in such district shall be called by the posting of notices in five public places in the district setting forth the time and place of said meeting and signed by at least three electors of the district. The electors assembled at said meeting shall elect a chairman and secretary and fix the time for holding the first election for members of the board of education, the time so fixed shall not be within twenty-five days of the time of holding said mass meeting. The chairman and secretary of said meeting shall immediately post notices in five public places within the district, giving the date of the election and shall notify the deputy state supervisors of elections as provided in section 3931 of the Revised Statutes of Ohio. The board thus elected, shall organize on the second Monday after the election and the term of the members shall be as indicated in section 3930 of the Revised Statutes of Ohio, from the first Monday in January after the last preceding annual election for members of boards of education, or until their successors are elected and qualified. (Passed and approved April 25, 1904.)

Sec. 3933. [Organization of board of education; president; clerk; regular meetings.] Boards of education of special school districts, shall organize on the first Monday in January after the election of the board, by the election of one of their members president and the election of a clerk who may or may not be a member of the board, the president to be elected for one year and the clerk to be elected for a term not to exceed two years; and they shall fix the time of holding regular meetings. (Passed and approved April 25, 1904.)

Sec. 3934. [Transportation of pupils in special districts.] Boards of education of special school districts are authorized to provide for the conveyance of pupils of said districts to the school or schools of the districts, the expense of said conveyance to be paid from the school funds of the special school districts; provided, however, that boards of education of such districts as provide transportation for the pupils thereof, shall not be required to transport pupils living less than one-half of a mile from the school house, transportation of such pupils being optional with the board of education. Provided, further, that when any pupils of said district reside at a greater distance than one and one-half miles from the school house the board of education shall be required to provide for the conveyance of such pupils and the expense thereof to be paid from the school funds of said special school district. (Passed and approved April 25, 1904.)

Sec. 3935. [Abandonment or continuance of special district, election for.] When a petition is signed by not less than one-third of the electors residing within the territory constituting a special school district, whether created under the provisions of a general or special act, praying for the abandonment or continuance of such district, shall be presented to the board of education of said district, or when said board shall, by a majority vote of the full membership of the board, decide to submit the question of abandoning or continuing the special school district, it shall be the duty of the board to fix the time of holding said election at either a special or general election and the clerk of the board shall notify the deputy state supervisors of elections, as provided in section 3931 of the Revised Statutes of Ohio, of the date of such election and the nature of the same and said supervisors of elections shall provide for the same. The clerk of the board of education shall also post notices of said election in five public places within the district. If said election be submitted at a special election in a district situated in two or more election precincts, the election shall be held at the precinct nearest the school house in said special district, by the election officers of the precinct, and all the electors of said district shall vote at said precinct. If the district is situated in two or more counties, the deputy state supervisors of the county in which said nearest election precinct is situated, shall have charge of the election. If said question is submitted at a regular election, it shall be conducted in the same manner as the election of members of the board of education. The ballot shall be in the regular form, but without the circle at the top, and shall have printed thereon "Abandonment of Special School District, Yes;" "Abandonment of Special School District, No;" or "Continuance of Special School District, Yes;" "Continuance of Special School District, No," as the case may be. The expense of said election shall be paid in the same manner as are other school election expenses, and returns of said elections shall be made to the board of education of the special school district and if more votes are cast for abandonment than against it, or against continuance than for it, said boards shall certify the result to the board or boards of education of the township or townships having territory in said special district and the territory of said special district shall thereby revert to the township school district or districts from which it was originally taken, except as hereinafter provided for in the case of indebtedness of the special district. Otherwise said district shall continue to be and remain and be recognized and regarded as a legal special school district as theretofore constituted. The legal title of the property of the special school district shall in the event of abandonment or failure to continue become vested in the board or boards of education of the township or townships in which such property is situated. And the school funds of said special district shall be paid into the treasury of the township district and. if said special district be in two or more townships, it shall be divided between them in proportion to the total tax valuation of property in the several districts, but the abandonment of a special school district shall not be deemed complete until the board of education of said district shall have provided for the payment of any indebtedness that may exist. (Passed and approved April 25, 1904.)

Sec. 3936.     Repealed April 25, 1904.

Sec. 3937.     Repealed April 25, 1904.

Sec. 3938.     Repealed April 25, 1904.

Sec. 3939.     Repealed April 25, 1904.

Sec. 3940.     Repealed April 25, 1904.

Sec. 3941.     Repealed April 25, 1904.

Sec. 3941a.     Repealed 89 v. 96.

Sec. 3942.     Repealed April 25, 1904.

Sec. 3943.     Repealed April 25, 1904.

Sec. 3944.     Repealed April 25, 1904.

Sec. 3945.     Repealed April 25,1904.

Sec. 3946.     Repealed April 25, 1904.

Sec. 3946a.     Repealed 94 v. 64.

Sec. 3947.     Repealed April 25, 1904

Sec. 3948.     Repealed April 25, 1904.

Sec. 3949.     Repealed 90 v. 76.

Sec. 3950.     Repealed April 25, 1904.

# CHAPTER VI.

## SCHOOL FUNDS.

**Sec. 3951.** ["The state common school fund" and "The Ohio State University fund."]   For the purpose of affording the advantages of a free education to all the youth of the state, there shall be levied annually a tax on the grand list of the taxable property of the state, which shall be collected in the same manner as other state taxes and the proceeds ·of which shall constitute "the state common school fund," and for the purpose of higher, agricultural and industrial education, including manual training, there shall be levied and collected in the same manner a tax on the grand list of taxable property of the state, which shall constitute "the Ohio state university fund." The rate for such levy in each case shall be designated by the general assembly at least once in two years; and if the general assembly shall fail to designate the rate for any year the same shall be for "the state common school fund" ninety-five one-hundredths of one mill, each year for the years 1902 and 1903, and one mill each year thereafter; for the "Ohio state university fund," fifteen one-hundredths of one mill upon each dollar of valuation of such taxable property, each year for the years 1902 and 1903, and ten-hundredths of one mill each year thereafter. (95 v. 439; 94 v. 81; 92 v. 59; 88 v. 159; 70 v. 195, § 126.)

**Sec. 3951a.** [Ohio and Miami university fund; admission of pupils.] For the purpose of affording adequate support to the Ohio university and to the Miami university there shall be levied annually a tax on the grand list of taxable property of the state of Ohio, which shall be collected in the same manner as other state taxes and the proceeds of which shall constitute the "Ohio and Miami university fund." The rate of such levy shall be designated by the general assembly at least once in two years, and if the general assembly shall fail to designate the rate for any year, the same shall be for the said "the Ohio and Miami university fund" three one-hundredths (.03) of one mill upon each dollar of valuation of such taxable property. Said Ohio university and Miami university shall admit free of tuition all residents of this state who shall conform to the standards of admission. (92 v. 41.)

**Sec. 3951b.** [Distribution of fund.] The said "Ohio and Miami university fund" shall be distributed and paid annually, seven-twelfths (7-12) thereof to the treasurer of the Ohio university upon the order of the president of the board of trustees of said Ohio university, and five-twelfths (5-12) thereof to the treasurer of the Miami university upon the order of the president of the board of trustees of the said Miami university. (92 v. 41.)

**Sec. 3952.** [Interest upon proceeds of salt and swamp lands.] The state shall pay interest annually, at the rate of six per cent per annum, upon all money which has been paid into the state treasury on account of sales of lands commonly called "salt lands," and upon all money heretofore paid, or which may hereafter be paid into the state treasury on account of sales of swamp lands granted to the state of Ohio by act of congress; the money received from such sales shall constitute an irreducible debt of the state; and the interest shall be apportioned annually on the same basis as the state common school fund is apportioned, and distributed to the several counties as provided in section *thirty-nine hundred and fifty-six*. (70 v. 195, § 132; 49 v. 40, § 1; S. & C. 1338.)

**Sec. 3952-1.** [Proceeds of sale of swamp lands to go to common school funds; how funded, and interest distributed.] The net proceeds that may hereafter be paid into the state treasury, from the sales of swamp lands granted to the state of Ohio by act of Congress passed September 28, 1850, be and the same is hereby appropriated to the general fund for the support of common schools; and the state of

Ohio is hereby pledged to pay the interest, annually, on any and all sums of money which may be paid into the state treasury, from the sales of said lands, from the receipt of such money into the treasury aforesaid; and the interest arising as aforesaid shall be funded, annually, until the first day of January, in the year eighteen hundred and fifty-five; after which time the interest shall be annually distributed to the several counties in this state, in proportion to the number of male inhabitants above the age of twenty-one, as the law shall be ascertained for the apportionment of representatives; and the proportion of interest due to each and every such county shall be distributed for the support of common schools, in the respective counties, in the manner prescribed in the "act to provide for the support and better regulation of common schools". (1883, March 5; 80 v. 39; R. S. 1880; 49 v. 40; S. & C. 1338.)

Sec. 3953. [The "common school fund."] The money which has been and may hereafter be paid into the state treasury on account of sales of lands granted by congress for the support of public schools in any original surveyed township, or other district of country, shall constitute the "common school fund,"of which the auditor of state shall be superintendent, and the income of which shall be applied exclusively to the support of common schools, in the manner designated in this chapter. (70 v. 195, §§ 127, 128; S. & C. 1335.)

Sec. 3954. [Accounts of common school fund; how kept, etc.] The common school fund shall constitute an irreducible debt of the state, on which the state shall pay interest annually, at the rate of six per cent. per annum, to be computed for the calendar year, and the first computation on any payment of principal hereafter made to be from the time of payment to and including the thirty-first day of December next succeeding; and the auditor of state shall keep an account of the fund, and of the interest which accrues thereon, in a book or books to be provided for the purpose, with each original surveyed township and other district of country to which any part of the fund belongs, crediting each with its share of the fund, and showing the amount of interest thereon which accrues and the amount which is disbursed annually to each. (70 v. 195, §§ 128, 129; S. & C. 1335.)

Sec. 3955. [Bequests, etc., in trust for common school fund.] When any grant or devise of land, or any donation or bequest of money or other personal property, is made to the state of Ohio, or to any person, or otherwise, in trust for the common school fund, the same shall become vested in said fund; and when the money arising therefrom is paid into the state treasury, proper accounts thereof shall be kept by the auditor of state, and the interest accruing therefrom shall be applied according to the intent of the grantor, donor, or devisor. (70 v. 195, § 131; S. & C. 1336.)

**Sec. 3956.** [Apportionment of school funds by auditor of state.] The auditor of state shall apportion the state common school fund to the several counties of the state semi-annually, upon the basis of the enumeration of youth therein, as shown by the latest abstract of enumeration transmitted to him by the state commissioner of common schools; before making his February settlement with county treasurers he shall apportion such amount thereof as he shall estimate to have been collected up to that time, and, in the settlement sheet which he transmits to the auditor of each county, shall certify the amount payable to the treasurer of his county; before making his final settlement with county treasurers each year, he shall apportion the remainder of the whole fund collected, as nearly as the same can be ascertained, and in the August settlement sheet which he transmits to the auditor of each county shall certify the amount payable to the treasurer of his county; in each February settlement sheet he shall also enter the amount of money payable to the county treasurer on the apportionment of interest specified in section *thirty-nine hundred and fifty-two;* he shall also enter in each February settlement sheet the amount of money payable to the county treasurer on account of interest for the preceding year on the common school fund, and designate the source or sources from which the interest accrued; he shall transmit with each February settlement sheet a certified statement, showing the amount of interest derived from the common school fund payable to each original surveyed township or other district of country within the county; and the treasurer of each county shall, at each semi-annual settlement with the auditor of state, retain in the county treasury, from the state taxes collected by him, the amount of the funds be-cin mentioned shown by the settlement sheet of the auditor of state to be payable to him at that time; but if such amount for any county exceeds the amount of state taxes collected therein, the auditor of state shall draw an order on the treasurer of state, in favor of the treasurer of such county, for the balance of school funds due his county, and transmit the same to such county treasurer, and the treasurer of state shall pay such order upon its presentation to him. (70 v. 195, §§ 120, 130; S. & C. 1359.)

**Sec. 3957.** [To what county common school fund paid when county line divides original surveyed township.] If parts of an original surveyed township or fractional township are situate in two or more counties, the amount of interest on common school fund due to such township shall be paid in the manner provided in the last section, to the treasurer of the county wherein the greatest relative portion of such township is situate; but if it be uncertain in which county such portion is situate, the amount of interest due to such township shall be paid to the treasurer of the oldest county in which any part of the township is situate. (70 v. 195, § 130.) ·

Sec. 3958. [Boards of education to make local tax levy.] Each board of education shall, annually, at a regular or special meeting held between the third Monday in April and the first Monday in June, fix the rate of taxation necessary to be levied for all school purposes, after the state funds are exhausted; said levy shall be divided by the board of education into four funds, namely, first, Tuition Fund; second, Building Fund; third, Contingent Fund; fourth, Bonds, Interest and Sinking Fund, and a separate levy shall be made for each fund; provided, that in every city school district, said levies shall be submitted to the board of review of the city, which shall consider the same, and approve or reduce said levies, or any part thereof, and return the same to the board of education, and said levies shall then become valid and effective as so approved or reduced; but if said board of review fail or neglect to act upon said levies within ten days after the receipt of the same from the board of education, then said levies shall become valid and effective without the action of said board of review. (Passed and approved April 25, 1904.)

Sec. 3958a. Repealed April 25, 1904.

Sec. 3958-1. Repealed April 25, 1904.

Sec. 3958-2. Repealed April 25, 1904.

Sec. 3959. [Maximum tax levy for school purposes; when greater tax may be levied.] The local tax levy for all school purposes shall not exceed twelve mills on the dollar of valuation of taxable property in any school district, but said levy shall not include any special levy for a specified purpose, provided for by a vote of the people. A greater tax than is authorized herein may be levied for any or all school purposes if the proposition to make such levy shall have been first submitted, by the board of education, to a vote of the electors of the school district, under a resolution prescribing the time, place and nature of the proposition to be submitted, and approved by a majority of those voting on the proposition; notice of said election must be given by publication of the resolution for three consecutive weeks prior thereto in some newspaper published and of general circulation in the district, or by posting copies thereof in five of the most conspicuous places in the district for a like period, if no such paper is published therein. (Passed and approved April 25, 1904.).

**Sec. 3960.** [Rate of levy to be certified to county auditor.] The amount of the levy fixed by the board of education under sections *thirty-nine hundred and fifty-eight* and *thirty-nine hundred and fifty-nine* shall be certified to the county auditor in writing, on or before the first Monday in June of each year, who shall assess the entire amount upon all the taxable property of the district, and enter it upon the tax duplicate of the county, and the county treasurer shall collect the same, at the same time and in the same manner as state and county taxes are collected, and pay it to the treasurer of the district upon the warrant of the county auditor; and unless the county treasurer is paid a fixed salary he shall receive one per centum on all money so collected, and no more. (Passed and approved April 25, 1904.)

**Sec. 3961.**    Repealed April 25, 1904.

**Sec. 3961a**    Repealed April 25, 1904.

**Sec. 3962.**    Repealed April 25, 1904.

**Sec. 3963.** [Tax levy and funds of district in two or more counties.] When a school district is composed of territory in two or more counties the rate of taxation shall be ascertained by the board of education of such district and shall be certified to the auditors of the several counties and such county auditors shall place the same on the tax duplicate and the same shall be collected as provided in section *thirty-nine hundred and sixty* of the Revised Statutes of Ohio. The funds belonging to a district composed of territory in more than one county shall be paid by the treasurers of the other counties to the treasurer of the county having the greatest tax valuation in said district; the auditors of the other counties shall make settlement on account of such funds with the auditor of the county having said greatest tax valuation; and the treasurer of the district shall make the settlement required by section *thirty-nine hundred and sixty-six* of the Revised Statutes of Ohio, with such auditor. (Passed and approved April 25, 1904.)

**Sec. 3964.** [Apportionment of school fund by county auditor.] Each county auditor shall, immediately after each annual settlement with the county treasurer, apportion the school funds for his county; the state common school fund shall be apportioned in proportion to the enumeration of youth in each of the several school districts within the county, but if an enumeration of the youth of any district has not been taken and returned for any year, such district shall not be entitled to receive any portion of said fund; the local school tax collected from the several districts shall be paid to the districts from which it was collected; money received from the state on account of interest on the common school fund shall be apportioned to the school districts and parts of school districts within the territory designated by the auditor of state as entitled thereto, in proportion to the enumeration of youth therein, and all other money in the county treasury for the support of the common schools, and not otherwise appropriated by law, shall be apportioned annually in the same manner as the state common school fund. (Passed and approved April 25, 1904.)

Sec: 3965. [Distribution of money after apportionment.] The auditor shall immediately after such apportionment is made, enter the same in a book to be kept for that purpose, and furnish a certified copy of the apportionment to each school treasurer and clerk of his county; and he shall give to each of such treasurers an order on the county treasurer for the amount of money payable to him, and take his receipt therefor. (70 v. 195, § 120.)

Sec. 3966. [Apportionment of common school fund by county auditor when county line divides original surveyed township.] When an original surveyed township or fractional township is situate in two or more counties, and the land granted thereto by congress for the support of public schools has been sold, the auditor of the county, to whose treasurer the interest on the proceeds of such sale is paid, shall apportion such interest to the counties in which such township is situate, in proportion to the youth of the township enumerated in each; such auditor shall certify to the auditor of each of the other counties the amount so ascertained to belong to the part of the township situate in his county, and transmit to the treasurer of each of such counties an order on the treasurer of his own county for such amount; and the auditor of each county shall apportion the amount of such interest belonging to the part of the township in his county, to the districts or parts of districts entitled thereto, in proportion to the enumeration of youth therein, and certify and pay the same to the proper school officers, as provided in the preceding section. (70 v. 195, §§ 121, 122; 72 v. 63, § 36.)

Sec. 3967. [Certificate of apportionment by county auditor.] The certificate of apportionment furnished by the county auditor to the treasurer and clerk of each school district shall exhibit the amount of money received by each district from the state, the amount received from any special tax levy made for a particular purpose as well as the amount received from local taxation of a general nature; the amount received from the state common school fund and the common school fund shall be designated the "tuition fund" and shall be appropriated only for the payment of superintendents and teachers; the funds received from special levies shall be designated in accordance with the purpose for which the special levy was made and shall be paid out only for such purpose, but when a balance remains on [in] such fund after all expenses incident to the purpose for which it was raised shall have been paid, such balance shall become a part of the contingent fund and it shall be the duty of the board of education to make such transfer by resolution; the funds received from the local levy for general purposes shall be designated as indicated in section *thirty-nine hundred and fifty-eight*, so as to correspond to the particular purpose for which the levy was made; all moneys coming from sources not enumerated herein shall be placed in the contingent fund. (Passed and approved April 25, 1904.)

**Sec. 3968.** [Depositories for school funds, boards of education may provide.] The board of education of any school district shall have authority to provide by resolution for the deposit of any or all moneys coming into the hands of the treasurer of the board. Provided, however, that no bank shall receive a larger deposit than the amount of its paid-in capital stock, and in no event to exceed three hundred thousand dollars ($300,000.00). In school districts containing two or more banks such deposit shall be made in the bank or banks, situated in the district, that shall offer at competitive bidding the highest rate of interest which in no case shall be less than two per cent. for the full time the funds or any part thereof are on deposit, and such bank or banks shall give a good and sufficient bond of some approved guaranty company in a sum at least equal to the amount deposited, and it shall be the duty of the treasurer of the school district to see that a greater sum than that contained in the bond is not deposited in such bank or banks and said treasurer and his bondsmen shall be liable for any loss occasioned by deposits in excess of such bond; the board shall determine in such resolution the method by which such bids shall be received, the authority which shall receive them, the time for which such deposits shall be made and all details for carrying into effect the authority herein given, but all such proceedings in connection with such competitive bidding and deposit of such moneys shall be conducted in such a manner as to insure full publicity and shall be open at all times to public inspection; if in the opinion of a board of education there has been any collusion between the bidders, said board may reject any or all bids and may provide for the deposit of funds in a bank or banks without the district as hereinafter provided for in districts not having two or more banks located therein. In all school districts containing less than two banks the board of education may, after the adoption of a resolution providing for the deposit of its funds, enter into a contract with one or more banks that are conveniently located and offer the highest rate of interest, which shall in no case be less than two per cent. for the full time the funds or any part thereof are on deposit, and said bank or banks shall give good and sufficient bond of some approved guaranty company in a sum at least equal to the amount deposited and it shall be the duty of the treasurer of the school district to see that a greater sum than that contained in the bond is not deposited in such bank or banks, and said treasurer and his bondsmen shall be liable for any loss occasioned by deposits in excess of such bond; said resolution and contract shall set forth fully all details necessary to carry into effect the authority herein given and all proceedings connected with the adoption of said resolution and the making of said contract shall be conducted in such a manner as to insure full publicity and shall be open at all times to public inspection. When a depository is provided as authorized herein and the funds are deposited therein, the treasurer of the school district and his bondsmen shall be relieved of any liability occasioned by the failure of the bank or banks of deposit or by the failure of the guaranty company acting as surety for such bank or banks or by the failure of either of them, except as herein provided in cases of excessive deposits. (Passed and approved April 25, 1904.)

Sec. 3969. [When a board of education fails to provide proper school facilities the county commissioners shall act.] If the board of education in any district fail in any year to estimate and certify the levy for a contingent fund as required by this chapter, or if the amount so certified is deemed insufficient for school purposes, or if it fail to provide sufficient school privileges for all the youth of school age in the district or to provide for the continuance of any school in the district for at least seven months in the year, or to provide for each school an equitable share of school advantages as required by this title, or to provide suitable school houses for all the schools under its control, or to elect a superintendent or teachers, the commissioners of the county to which such district belongs, upon being advised and satisfied thereof, shall do and perform any or all of said duties and acts, in as full a manner as the board of education is by this title authorized to do and perform the same; and the members of a board who cause such failure shall be each severally liable, in a penalty not to exceed fifty nor less than twenty-five dollars, to be recovered in a civil action in the name of the state upon complaint of any elector of the district, which sum shall be collected by the prosecuting attorney of the county, and when collected shall be paid into the treasury of the county, for the benefit of the school or schools of the district. (Passed and approved April 25, 1904.)

4—S. L.

**Sec. 3970.** [County auditor to collect fines, etc., and inspect section sixteen accounts.] The auditor of each county shall collect, or cause to be collected, all fines and other money, for the support of common schools in his county, and pay the same to the county treasurer; he shall inspect all accounts of interest accruing on account of section sixteen or other school lands, whether the same is payable by the state or by the debtors; and he shall take all proper measures to secure to each school district in his county the full amount of school funds to which it is entitled. (70 v. 195, § 120.)

**Sec. 3970-1.** [Sinking fund; board of commissioners of.] In any school district having a bonded indebtedness, for the payment of which together with interest, no provision has been made by a special tax levy for that particular purpose, it shall be the duty of the board of education of such district and such board shall annually, on or before the 31st day of August, set aside from its revenue a sum equal to not less than one-fortieth of said indebtedness together with a sum sufficient to pay the annual interest thereon. The board of education of every district shall provide a sinking fund for the extinguishment of all its' bonded indebtedness, which sinking fund shall be managed and controlled by a board of commissioners designated as the "Board of Commissioners of the Sinking Fund of —————" (inserting the name of the district), which shall be composed of five electors thereof, and who shall be appointed by the court of common pleas of the county in which such district is chiefly located, provided, that in city or village districts the board of commissioners of the sinking fund of the city or village may be the board of commissioners of the sinking fund of the school district; the commissioners of the sinking fund shall serve without compensation and shall give such bond as the board of education may require and approve, provided that any surety company authorized to sign such bonds may be accepted by such board of education as surety, and the cost thereof, together with all necessary expenses of the commissioners of the sinking fund shall be paid by said commissioners out of the funds under their control. (Passed and approved April 25, 1904.)

**Sec. 3970-2.** [How sinking fund invested.] The board of commissioners of the sinking fund shall invest the sinking fund in bonds of the United States, of the State of Ohio, of any municipal corporation, county, township or school district within the state of Ohio or in bonds of its own issue. All interest received from such investments shall be deposited in the treasury to the credit of said sinking fund, and reinvested in a like manner; at no time shall there be over one thousand dollars kept on deposit if investment can be made without jeopardizing the prompt redemption of bonds falling due. For the extinguishment of any bonded indebtedness included in said sinking fund, the board of commissioners of the sinking fund is authorized to sell or use any of the securities or money in said fund. (Passed and approved April 25, 1904.)

Sec. 3970-3. [Refunding, renewing or extending bonded debt.] The board of commissioners of the sinking fund may refund, extend or renew the bonded debt of the school district or any part thereof, existing at the time of the taking effect of this act, by issuing the bonds of said school district for such periods, not exceeding twenty years, in such denomination, payable at such place and at a rate of interest not to exceed the rate previous to such refunding, extension or renewal; provided that the aggregate amount of the refunding, extending or renewing bonds so issued shall not exceed that of the bonds so refunded, extended or renewed. (Passed and approved April 25, 1904.)

Sec. 3970-4. [Reports of sinking fund; how orders are drawn.] The clerk of the board of commissioners of the sinking fund shall make an annual report to the board of commissioners of the sinking fund, giving a detailed statement of the sinking fund, such report shall be filed at such time as the board shall designate and other reports may be required by the board when the same shall be deemed necessary. Orders on the sinking fund shall be drawn by the same authority and in the same manner as other orders for the payment of money from the school funds. (Passed and approved April 25, 1904.)

## CHAPTER VII.

### PROVISIONS APPLYING TO ALL BOARDS.

**Sec. 3970-10.** [School elections; separate ballots and ballot-boxes; returns and canvass of vote.] The election of members of boards of education shall be governed and controlled by the general election laws of the state. There shall be separate poll-books and tally-sheets used for all elections for school purposes, and the ballots of the electors at said elections shall be deposited in a separate ballot-box. In city school districts the ballots for each sub-district shall contain the names of the candidates for member of the board of education from such sub-district and also the names of the candidates to be elected at large. Returns of all school elections shall be made to the clerk of the board of education not less than five days after the election, and it shall be the duty of the board of education to canvass said returns at a meeting to be held on the second Monday after the election, and the result thereof shall be entered upon the records of the board; in case of a tie vote, the same shall be decided by said board of education, by lot. (Passed and approved April 25, 1904.)

**Sec. 3970-11.** [Notice of elections.] The clerk of each board of education shall publish a notice of all school elections in a newspaper of general circulation in the district, or post written or printed notices of said elections in five public places in the district, at least ten days before the holding of the same, which notices shall specify

the time and place of such election and the number of members of
the board of education to be elected and the term for which they
are to be elected, or the nature of the question to be voted upon.
(Passed and approved April 25, 1904.)

Sec. 3970-12. [Women may vote and be voted for, for school
officers.] Every woman born in the United States, or who is a wife
or daughter of a citizen of the United States, who is over twenty-one
years of age and possesses the necessary qualifications in regard to
residence, as is provided for men, shall be entitled to vote, and to
be voted .for, for member of the board of education and upon no
other question. The law relating to registration shall apply to women
upon whom the right to vote is conferred, but the names of such
women may be placed on a separate list. (Passed and approved
April 25, 1904.)

Sec. 3971. [Corporate powers of board of education; sales of
property exceeding three hundred dollars in value; exchange of real
estate with municipal corporation.] The boards of education of all
school districts now organized and established, and of all school districts organized under the provisions of this title, shall be and they
are hereby declared to be bodies politic and corporate, and, as such,
capable of suing and being sued, contracting and being contracted
with, acquiring, holding, possessing, and disposing of property, both
real and personal, and taking and holding in trust, for the use and
benefit of such districts, any grant or devise of land, and any donation or bequest of money or other personal property, and of exercising such other powers, and having such other privileges as are
conferred by this title; but when a board of education decides to
dispose of any property, real or personal, held by it in its corporate capacity, exceeding in value three hundred dollars, it shall sell
the same at public auction, after giving at least thirty days' notice
thereof, by publication in some newspaper of general circulation, or
by posting notices in five of the most public places in the district in
which such property is situate. Provided, that when such board
has twice offered a tract of real estate for sale at public auction, as
hereinbefore provided, and the same is not sold, the board may
sell said real estate at private sale, either as an entire tract, or in
parcels thereof, as the board may deem best, and the president and
secretary of the board shall execute and deliver the deed or deeds
necessary to complete such sale or sales. Provided, that upon a
vote of a majority of the members of any board of education, and
a concurring vote of the council of any municipal corporation, that
an exchange of any real estate held by such board of education for
school purposes, for real estate held by such municipal corporation

for municipal purposes, will be mutually beneficial to such school district, and to such municipal corporation, such exchange may be made by conveyances, to be executed by the mayor and clerk of the municipal corporation, and by the president and clerk of such board of education. (1888, March 30; 85 v. 133; 80 v. 36; Rev. Stat. 1880; 70 v. 195, § 37; S. & C. 1350.)

Sec. 3972. [Title to property vested in boards of education; resolutions and orders to remain valid until changed; contracts, bonds and tax levies protected.] All property, real or personal, which has heretofore vested in and is now held by any board of education for the use of public or common schools in any district, is hereby vested in the board of education provided for in this title, having under this title jurisdiction and control of the schools in such district; and all resolutions and orders passed by any board of education shall remain in full force and effect until duly altered or repealed, and nothing in this act contained shall be construed to in any way affect the validity of any contract made nor bonds or certificates of indebtedness issued, by any board of education of any school district, whether created under the provisions of a general or a special act; and all school funds, whether arising from taxation, sale of bonds, or otherwise, in the hands of or belonging to any board of education of any school district, whether created under the provisions of a general or a special act, and all taxes levied by any such board not collected, shall be transferred to the credit of the board of education elected, under the provisions of this act, to succeed the board having such funds to its credit or which made the levy for the uncollected taxes. (Passed and approved April 25, 1904.)

Sec. 3973. [School property exempt from taxation.] All property, real or personal, vested in any board of education, shall be exempt from tax, and from sale on execution, or other writ or order in the nature of an execution. (70 v. 195 § 72.)

Sec. 3974. [Conveyances and contracts.] All conveyances made by a board of education shall be executed by the president and clerk thereof; no member of a board shall have any pecuniary interest, either direct or indirect, in any contract of the board, or be employed in any manner for compensation by the board of which he is a member, except as clerk or treasurer; and no contract shall be binding upon any board unless it be made or authorized to be made at a regular or special meeting of the board. (70 v. 195, §§ 21, 38.)

Sec. 3975. [Boards of education may accept bequests, gifts or endowments; limitation on same.] Any board of education may, by the adoption of a resolution, accept any bequest made to them by will or may accept any gift or endowment from any person or corporation, upon the conditions and stipulations contained in the will or connected with the gift or endowment; and for the purpose of enabling such boards to carry out the conditions and limitations upon which the bequest, gift or endowment is made, they are authorized to make all rules and regulations that may be required to fully carry into effect the provisions of said bequest, gift or endowment; but no such bequest, gift or endowment shall be accepted by any board of education when the conditions of the same shall remove any portion of the public schools from under the control of said board. (Passed and approved April 25, 1904.)

Sec. 3976. [Process against boards and how served.] The process in all suits against a board of education shall be by summons, and shall be served by leaving a copy thereof with the clerk or president of the board. (70 v. 195, § 68.)

Sec. 3977. [Prosecuting attorney and city solicitor to act as legal adviser of boards of education.] The prosecuting attorney shall be the legal adviser of all boards of education in the county in which he is serving, except in city school districts, he shall prosecute all actions against a member or officer of a board of education for malfeasance or misfeasance in office, he shall be the legal counsel of said boards or the officers thereof in all civil actions brought by or against them and shall conduct the same in his official capacity; provided, that when said civil action is between two or more boards of education in the same county said prosecuting attorney shall not be required to act for either of them. In city school districts the city solicitor shall be the legal adviser and attorney for the board of education and shall perform the same services for said board of education as is herein required of prosecuting attorneys for other boards of education. The duties herein prescribed shall devolve upon any official serving in a capacity similar to that of prosecuting attorney or city solicitor for the territory wherein a school district is situated, regardless of his official designation. No prosecuting attorney, city solicitor or other official acting in a similar capacity shall be a member of the board of education. No compensation in addition to such officers' regular salary shall be allowed for such services. (Passed and approved April 25, 1904.)

Sec. 3978. [Special meetings, how called.] A special meeting of a board of education can be called by the president or clerk of the board or by any two members thereof, by serving a written notice of the time and place of such meeting upon each member of the board, either personally or at his residence or usual place of business, said notice to be signed by the official or member calling the meeting. (Passed and approved April 25, 1904.)

**Sec. 3979.** [Oath of members and other officers.] Each person elected or appointed a member of a board of education, or elected or appointed to any other office under this title, shall, before entering upon the duties of his office, take an oath or affirmation to support the constitution of the United States and the constitution of the state of Ohio, and that he will perform faithfully the duties of his office; which oath or affirmation may be administered by the clerk or any member of the board. (71 v. 15, § 42.) .

**Sec. 3980.** Repealed April 25, 1904.

**Sec. 3981.** [Vacancies in board of education, how filled.] Vacancies in any board of education arising from death, non-residence, resignation, removal from office, failure of person elected or appointed to qualify within ten days after the organization of the board or of his appointment, removal from the district, or from other cause, shall be filled by the board of education at its next regular or special meeting or as soon thereafter as possible for the unexpired term. A majority vote of all the remaining members of the board can fill any vacancy or vacancies that may exist in said board. (Passed and approved April 25, 1904.)

**Sec. 3982.** [Quorum; majority of all members required in certain cases; roll call; pay roll.] A majority of the board of education shall constitute a quorum for transaction of business; upon a motion to adopt a resolution authorizing the purchase or sale of property, either real or personal, or to employ a superintendent, teacher, janitor, or other employe, or to elect or appoint an officer, or to pay any debt or claim, or to adopt any text book, the clerk of the board shall call, publicly, the roll of all the members composing the board, and enter on the record required to be kept the names of those voting "aye" and the names of those voting "no"; if a majority of all the members of the board vote "aye," the president shall declare the motion carried; and upon any motion or resolution any member of the board may demand the yeas and nays, and thereupon the clerk shall call the roll and record the names of those voting "aye" and those voting "no," provided, that boards of education may provide for the payment of superintendents, teachers and other employes by payroll if deemed advisable, but in all cases the roll call and record, provided for herein shall be complied with. (Passed and approved April 25, 1904.)

**Sec. 3983.** [Absence of president or clerk.] If, at any meeting of the board, either the president or the clerk is absent, the members present shall choose one of their number to serve in his, place pro tempore; and if both are absent, both places shall be so filled; but on the appearance of either at the meeting, after his place has been so filled, he shall immediately assume the duties of his office. (70 v. 195; § 31.)

**Sec. 3984.** [Record of proceedings and attestation thereof.] The clerk of the board shall record the proceedings of each meeting, in a book to be provided by the board for that purpose, which shall be a public record; the record of proceedings at each meeting of the board shall be read at its next meeting, corrected if necessary, and approved, and the approval shall be noted in the proceedings; and after such approval the president shall sign the record, and the clerk shall attest the same. (70 v, 195, § 29; 71 v. 15, § 42.)

**Sec. 3985.** [Boards to make rules; illegal meetings.] The board of education of each district shall make such rules and regulations as it may deem necessary for its government and the government of its appointees and the pupils of the schools; and no meeting of a board of education not provided for by its rules or by law shall be legal unless all the members thereof have been notified as provided for in section *thirty-nine hundred and seventy-eight.* (Passed and approved April 25, 1904.)

**Sec. 3986.** [Board may make and enforce rules for vaccination.] The board of each district may make and enforce such rules and regulations to secure the vaccination of, and to prevent the spread of smallpox among the pupils attending or eligible to attend the schools of the district, as in its own opinion the safety and interest of the public require; and the boards of health and councils of municipal corporations, and the trustees of townships, shall, on application of the board of education of the district, provide at the public expense, without delay, the means of vaccination to such pupils as are not provided therewith by their parents or guardians. (69 v. 22, § 1.)

**Sec. 3986-1.** [Display of U. S. flag.] All boards of education be authorized and required to display the U. S. national flag upon all school houses under their control, during all day school sessions in fair weather, and to be displayed on the inside of the school house on all other days, and said boards of education shall make all rules and necessary regulations for the care and keeping of such flags, the expense of the same to be paid out of the contingent funds of such boards. (92 v. 86.)

**Sec. 3.** [Terms of office of existing officers of boards of education, 1904.] All existing officers of boards of education and school councils shall hold their respective offices until boards of education are elected and organized under the provisions of this act; but no officer elected or appointed to fill a vacancy occurring in any such office shall be appointed to serve for a longer period than that ending on the 31st day of August, 1905. (Passed and approved April 25, 1904.)

# CHAPTER VIII.

## SCHOOL HOUSES AND LIBRARIES.

**Sec. 3987.** [School houses.] The board of education of any district is empowered to build, enlarge, repair and furnish the necessary school houses, purchase or lease sites therefor, or rights of way thereto, or rent suitable school-rooms, provide all the necessary apparatus and make all other necessary provisions for the schools under its control; also, the boards shall provide fuel for schools, build and keep in good repair all fences inclosing such school houses, plant when deemed desirable shade and ornamental trees on the school grounds, and make all other provisions necessary for the convenience and prosperity of the schools within the sub-districts. (89 v. 95; 83 v. 84; 82 v. 86; Rev. Stat. 1880; 70 v. 195, § 55.)

**Sec. 3987-1.** [Regulating use of school houses.] That when, in the judgment of any board of education, it will be for the advantage of the children residing in any school district to hold literary societies, school exhibitions, singing schools, religious exercises, select or normal schools, the board of education shall authorize the opening of such school houses for the purposes aforesaid. And the board of education of any school district shall have discretionary power to authorize the opening of such school houses for any other lawful purposes; provided, however, that nothing herein contained shall be construed to authorize any board of education to rent or lease any school house when such rental or lease shall in any wise interfere with the public schools in such district, or for any purpose other than such as is authorized by this act. (91 v. 44; 89 v. 147; 87 v. 240; 86 v. 11.)

**Sec. 3988.** [Directions for bidding, and for letting contracts.] When a board of education determines to build, repair, enlarge or furnish a school house or school houses, or make any improvement or repair provided for in this chapter, the cost of which will exceed in city districts, fifteen hundred dollars, and in other districts five hundred dollars, except in cases of urgent necessity, or for the security and protection of school property, it shall proceed as follows:

(1) The board shall advertise for bids, for the period of four weeks, in some newspaper of general circulation in the district, and two such newspapers, if there are so many; and if no newspaper has a general circulation therein, then by posting such advertisement in three public places therein, which advertisement shall be entered in full by the clerk, on the record of the proceedings of the board.

(2) The bids, duly sealed, shall be filed with the clerk by twelve o'clock, noon, of the last day stated in the advertisement.

(3) The bids shall be opened at the next meeting of the board, be publicly read by the clerk, and entered in full on the records of the board.

(4) Each bid shall contain the name of every person interested in the same, and shall be accompanied by a sufficient guarantee of some disinterested person, that if the bid be accepted, a contract will be entered into, and the performance of it properly secured.

(5) When both labor and materials are embraced in the work bid for, each must be separately stated in the bid, with the price thereof.

(6) None but the lowest responsible bid shall be accepted; but the board may, in its discretion, reject all the bids, or accept any bid for both labor and material which is the lowest in the aggregate for such improvement or repair.

(7) Any part of a bid which is lower than the same part of any other bid, shall be accepted, whether the residue of the bid is higher or not; and if it is higher, such residue shall be rejected.

(8) The contract shall be between the board of education and the bidders, and the board shall pay the contract price for the work, when it is completed, in cash, and may pay monthly estimates as the work progresses.

(9) When two or more bids are equal, in the whole, or in any part thereof, and are lower than any others, either may be accepted, but in no case shall the work be divided between the makers thereof.

(10) When there is reason to believe that there is any collusion or combination among the bidders, or any number of them, the

bids of those concerned therein shall be rejected. (Passed and approved April 25, 1904.)

**Sec 3989.** Repealed April 25, 1904.           •

**Sec. 3990.** [When boards may appropriate property.] When it is necessary to procure or enlarge a school house site, and the board of education and the owner of the proposed site or addition are unable from any cause to agree upon the sale and purchase thereof, the board shall make an accurate plat and description of the parcel of land which it desires for such purpose, and file the same with the probate judge of the proper county; and thereupon the same proceedings of appropriation shall be had which are provided for the appropriation of private property by municipal corporations. (70 v. 195, § 65.)

**Sec. 3991.** [Bond issue, vote on.] When the board of education of any school district determines that it is necessary for the proper accommodation of the schools of such district to purchase a site or sites to erect a school house or houses, to complete a partially built school house, to enlarge, repair or furnish a school house, or to do any or all of said things, and that the funds at the disposal of said board or that can be raised under the provisions of section 3994 of the Revised Statutes of Ohio, are not sufficient to accomplish said purpose and that a bond issue is necessary, the board shall make an estimate of the probable amount of money required for such purpose or purposes and at a general election or a special election called for that purpose, shall submit to the electors of the district the question of the issuing of bonds for the amount so estimated; notices of the election required herein shall be given in the manner as provided in section *thirty-nine hundred and seventy dash eleven.* (Passed and approved April 25, 1904.)

**Sec. 3992.** [Bond issue, when election favorable.] If a majority of the electors, voting on the proposition to issue bonds, shall vote in favor of said issue, the board shall be thereby authorized to issue bonds for the amount indicated by the vote provided for in section *thirty-nine hundred and ninety-one,* the issue and sale of said bonds to be provided for by a resolution fixing the amount of each bond, the length of time they shall run, the rate of interest they shall bear, and the time of sale which may be by competitive bidding at the discretion of the board; the bonds shall bear a rate of interest not to exceed six per cent. per annum payable semi-annually, shall be made payable within at least forty years from the date thereof, be numbered consecutively, made payable to the bearer, bear date of the day of sale and be signed by the president and clerk of the board of education; the clerk of the board shall keep a record of the number, date, amount, and the rate of interest of each bond sold, the amount received for the same, the name of the person to whom sold, and the time when payable, which record shall be open to the inspection of the public at all reasonable times; and the bonds so issued shall in no case be sold for a less sum than their par value. nor bear interest until the purchase money for the same shall have been paid by the purchaser. (Passed and approved April 25, 1904.)

Sec. 3993. [Tax levy for bonds to be certified to county auditor.] When an issue of bonds has been provided for under sections *thirty-nine hundred and ninety-one* and *thirty-nine hundred and ninety-two* the board of education shall certify annually, to the county auditor or auditors as the case may require, a tax levy sufficient to pay said bonded indebtedness as the same shall fall due together with accrued interest thereon; the county auditor or auditors shall place said levy on the tax duplicate and it shall be collected and paid to the board of education in the same manner as other taxes are collected and paid. The tax levy provided for herein shall be in addition to the tax levy provided for under section *thirty-nine hundred and fifty-nine* and shall be kept in a separate fund by the board of education and applied only to the payment of the bonds and interest for which it was levied. (Passed and approved April 25, 1904.)

Sec. 3994. [Bond issue without vote; limitations.] The board of education of any school district may issue bonds to obtain or improve public school property, and in anticipation of income from taxes, for such purposes, levied or to be levied, may, from time to time, as occasion requires, issue and sell bonds, under the restrictions and bearing a rate of interest specified in section *thirty-nine hundred and ninety-two* and shall pay such bonds and the interest thereon when due, but shall provide that no greater amount of such bonds shall be issued in any year than would equal the aggregate of a tax at the rate of two mills, for the year next preceding such issue, but the order to issue bonds shall be made only at a regular meeting of the board and by a vote of two-thirds of the full membership of the board, taken by yeas and nays and entered upon the journal of the board; but in no case shall a board of education issue bonds under the provisions of this section in a greater amount than can be provided for and paid with the tax levy provided for under section *thirty-nine hundred and fifty-nine* of the Revised Statutes of Ohio, and paid within forty years after the bond issue on the basis of the tax valuation at the time of the bond issue. (Passed and approved April 25, 1904.)

Sec. 3995. Repealed April 25, 1904.

**Sec. 3996.** Repealed April 25, 1904.

**Sec. 3997.** Repealed April 25, 1904.

**Sec. 3998.** * Repealed April 25, 1904.

**(3998-1) Sec. 1.** [Boards of education authorized to provide for establishment, etc., of public library; taxation.] That the board of education of any city, village or special school district may by resolution, provide for the establishment, control and maintenance, in such school district, of a public library, free to all the inhabitants of such district, and for that purpose may acquire by purchase the necessary real property, and erect thereon a library building; it may acquire from any library association, by purchase or otherwise, its library and property; may receive donations and bequests of money 'or property for such library purposes and may maintain and support libraries now in existence and controlled by the board of education; and such board of education may annually make a levy upon the taxable property of such school district, in addition to all other taxes allowed by law, of not to exceed one mill for a library fund to be expended by such board of education, for the establishment, support and maintenance of such public library. (96 v. 8.)

**(3998-2) Sec. 2.** [Board of library trustees; how constituted; qualifications; terms; vacancies; compensation; powers.] The board of education may provide for the management and control of such library by a board of trustees to be elected by said board of education as herein provided. Such board of library trustees shall consist of seven members, who shall be residents of the school district, and no one shall be eligible to membership on said library board who is or has been for a year previous to his election, a member or officer of the board of education. The term of office shall be seven years, except that at the first election the terms shall be such that one member shall retire each year. Should a vacancy occur in said board, it shall be filled by the board of education for the unexpired term. The members of said library board shall serve without compensation and until their successors are elected and qualified. Such library board in its own name shall hold the title to and have the custody, management and control of all libraries, branches, stations, reading rooms, and of all library property, real and personal, of such school district, and the expenditure of all moneys collected or received from any source for library purposes for such district. It shall have power to employ a librarian and assistants, but previous to such employment the compensation of such librarian and assistants shall be fixed. Such library board shall have the power, by a two-thirds vote of its members, to purchase or lease grounds and buildings, and erect buildings for library purposes. It may accept any gift, devise or bequest for the benefit of such library. No member of the library board shall be interested, directly or indirectly, in any contract made by the board. The library board shall report annually in writing to the board of education. (96 v. 8.)

(3998-3) **Sec. 3.** [When library to be under control of such board.] Whenever in any city, village or special school district a library established or controlled by a board of education shall contain twenty-five thousand or more volumes, it shall be managed, governed and controlled by a board of trustees elected by the board of education as provided in section 2 of this act. (96 v. 9.)

(3998-4) **Sec. 4.** [Library fund; how provided and maintained; payments from.] Said board of library trustees shall annually, during the month of May, certify to the board of education the amount of money that will be needed for increasing, maintaining and operating said library during the ensuing year in addition to the funds available therefor from other sources; and such board of education shall annually levy on each dollar of taxable property within said school district, in addition to other levies authorized by law, such assessment not exceeding one mill, as shall be necessary to realize the sum so certified, the same to be placed on the tax duplicate and collected as other taxes. The proceeds of the said tax shall constitute a fund to be known and designated as the library fund: Payments therefrom shall only be made upon the warrant of the board of trustees of the library, signed by the president and secretary thereof. (96 v. 9.)

(3998-5) **Sec. 5.** [Board of education may contract with library association for use of library.) The board of education in any city, village or special school district shall have power to contract annually with any library corporation or other organization owning and maintaining a library, for the use of such library by the residents of such district, and it shall have power to levy annually a tax not exceeding one mill on the taxable property of such district to pay for the same; and such board of education shall require an annual report in writing from such library corporation or other organization. (96 v. 9.)

(3998-6) **Sec. 6.** [School library.] The board of education of any school district of the state, in which there is not a public library operated under public authority and free to all the residents of such district, may appropriate annually not to exceed two hundred and fifty dollars annually from its contingent fund for the purchase of books, other than school books, for the use and improvement of the teachers and pupils of such school district. The books so purchased shall constitute a school library, the control and management of which shall be vested in the board of education, which board shall have power to receive donations and bequests of money or property for such library. (96 v. 9.)

(3998-7) **Sec. 7.** [Museum.] The board of education of any school district, or any board of trustees managing and controlling a library in any school district, may found and maintain a museum in connection with and as an adjunct to such library, and for such purposes may receive bequests and donations of money or other property. (96 v. 9.)

(3998-8 ) **Sec. 8.** [Taking effect; existing laws.] This act shall take effect and be in force on and after November 15, 1902, and all acts or parts of acts not inconsistent herewith under which existing libraries are maintained, governed and controlled, shall be and remain in full force and effect. (96 v. 10.)

(3998-9) **Sec. 1.** [City board of education may acquire private library; shall be made a public library; board of managers; vacancies in board.] That whenever in any city organized under chapter 4, division 2, of title 12, of the Revised Statutes of Ohio, there is a library owned by a private incorporated or unincorporated association which the owners, or managers thereof, are willing to dispose of and to transfer to the board of education of such city or school district within which said city is situate, the said board of education is hereby authorized to acquire from said association by purchase, or otherwise, said library and the property used by said association for library purposes. Upon acquiring title to said library and property, the said board of education shall declare the same to be a public library and shall elect a board of managers therefor, consisting of six persons, two of whom, at the first election shall be elected for a period of three years, two for a period of two years, and two for a period of one year, and thereafter, upon the expiration of said terms, and all succeeding terms, said managers shall be elected for three years. And said board of education shall fill vacancies in said board of managers for unexpired terms in like manner, and said board of managers shall at all times be amenable to and under the control of said board of education as to tenure of office and authority and shall serve without compensation. The president of said board of education shall be ex-officio a member of said board of managers, but otherwise, no member of said board of education shall be a member of said library board. (95 v. 74.)

(3998-10.) **Sec. 2.** [Powers and duties of managers.] Said board of managers shall have the care, custody, control and management of said library and property, under such rules and regulations as they shall prescribe and shall have the power to receive donations of land, money and other things of value, and to hold, dispose of, or use the same for the benefit of such library. The use of said library shall be free to all residents of said city and territory thereto attached for school purposes. Said board shall have the power to lease or rent suitable place for the use of said library and establish a reading room or rooms in connection therewith. (95 v. 74.)

(3998-11.) Sec. 3. [Organization of board; librarian and assistants.] Said board of managers shall elect from their number a president, vice-president, and secretary, and shall appoint a librarian and such assistants and employes as may be necessary for the proper conduct of said library. The term of office of said appointees shall be at the pleasure of the board, but shall not exceed three years. (95 v. 74.)

(3998-12.) Sec. 4. [Tax levy; expenditure of funds.] For the purpose of paying for such library purchased and of maintaining and increasing said library and reading rooms, the said board of education may levy upon the general tax duplicate of the school district within which such city is situate, a tax not to exceed six-tenths of one mill on each dollar of valuation of the taxable property of said school district which shall be levied, assessed and collected as other taxes levied by said board and shall be in addition thereto. The proceeds of said tax when collected, shall constitute and be called the library fund, and shall be paid to the treasurer of the school district, who shall disburse same only upon warrant of said board of managers, signed by the president and secretary thereof. Said board of managers shall expend said fund in the purchase of books, pamphlets, papers, magazines, periodicals, journals, furniture, and such other property as may be necessary for such library and reading rooms and in the payment of all proper charges for maintenance including the compensation of the librarian and other employes of said board. No part of said fund shall be transferred or used for any other purpose than as provided in this section. All money heretofore appropriated, received, or collected by tax levied for public library purposes in said city, or school district, and remaining unexpended shall be transferred to said library fund, and be expended by said board of managers in accordance with the provisions of this act. (95 v. 74.)

Sec. 3999. [In certain cities board may appoint managers of library.] In cities not having less than twenty thousand inhabitants, the board of education having custody of any public library therein, may, at any regular meeting, adopt a resolution providing for a board of managers of such library, and shall thereupon elect by ballot, two persons to serve as members of such board for a term of three years, two persons to serve for a term of two years, and two persons to serve for a term of one year; and annually thereafter two persons shall be elected to serve for a term of three years; all vacancies in such board shall be filled by the board of education by ballot, and a person so elected shall serve during the unexpired term of his predecessor; the president of the board of education shall be a member of the board of managers, ex-officio; and the board of managers shall at all times be amenable to and under the control of the board of education, as to tenure of office and authority, and shall serve without compensation.

[**Board of trustees in Cincinnati; how** appointed; terms.] Provided, that in cities of the first grade of the first class upon the expiration of the terms of office of the trustees of the public library therein, heretofore appointed under this section, as amended April 3c, 1891, there shall be appointed as successors to said board, a board of trustees of said library consisting of seven persons, as follows: Two by the board of education of the school district within which such city is situated, two by the board having charge of the high schools of such city, two by the directors of the university in such city, one of each of said appointees shall hold his office for two years, and one for three years; and one by the judges of the court of common pleas of the county within which such city is situated, who shall hold his office for a period of three years; and thereafter said boards and said judges shall, upon the expiration of the terms of office of said appointees, and each three years thereafter, appoint successors to said trustees. The appointee aforesaid of the judges of the court of common pleas shall succeed in said board of trustees the president of the board of education, who theretofore was, by virtue of his said office, a member of said board of trustees, and thereafter the right of such president of said board of education aforesaid of membership in said board of, trustees of said library shall cease.

[**Vacancies.**] All vacancies in said board of trustees of said library shall be filled by the respective bodies having the power of appointment. Provided, however, that nothing herein shall be construed in any wise to abridge the term of office or curtail the powers or duties of the trustees of the public library in cities of the first grade of the first class, appointed under this section as amended April 30, 1891, during the terms of office for which they were appointed. (93 v. 192; 88 v. 446; 64 v. 100, § 1; S. & S. 722.)

Sec. 3999*a*. [Residents of Hamilton county entitled to use of city library.] Each and every resident of the county within which is situated any city of the first grade of the first class, having therein established a public library, shall be entitled to the free use of such library, reading rooms and any branch or department of the same, and all the privileges thereof, upon such terms and conditions not inconsistent herewith, as the board of trustees of such library may prescribe. (94 v. 204; 93 v. 193.)

Sec. 3999*b*. [Powers of trustees in Cincinnati.] The board of trustees of the public library in cities of the first grade of the first class shall have sole and exclusive charge, custody and control of the public library in such city, including all property, both real and personal, used and occupied by such library, whether acquired heretofore or hereafter, and shall have full power to make all rules and regulations necessary for the proper government, maintenance, care and management thereof, and to provide therefor. Said board of trustees shall have power over, and exclusive control of, the library fund hereinafter provided for, and of the expenditure of all moneys collected to the credit thereof. They shall have power and it shall be their duty to establish in said city and throughout the county within which is situated said library, reading rooms, branch libraries and library stations in connection with said library, and to lease and furnish said rooms, buildings or parts thereof as are required for such purposes, and to pay all necessary expenses connected therewith. They shall have power, and it shall be their duty to purchase and pay for all books, periodicals, magazines and other literature and supplies necessary, in their judgment, for said public library, reading rooms, branch libraries and library stations, and to incur the necessary expenditures for the encouragement and advancement of the best use of such library, reading rooms, branch libraries and library stations by the public; all such purchases, payments and expenditures to be made out of said library fund hereinafter provided for.

[Employment of librarian and assistants.] They shall have power, and it shall be their duty, to employ a librarian, assistant librarians, and other necessary assistants for such public library, reading rooms, branches and stations, to fix the compensation of persons so employed, and to pay the same out of said library fund. Said library board may fix the term of any such person employed by them for any period not to exceed one year. (93 v. 193.)

Sec. 3999*c*. [Tax for library purposes in Cincinnati.] For the purpose of increasing, maintaining and managing the public library in cities of the first grade of the first class, for which a board of trustees shall have been appointed, as provided in section 3999, the said board of trustees may levy annually a tax of not exceeding five-tenths of a mill on each dollar of valuation of the taxable property of the county wherein is situated such city, to be assessed, collected and paid in the same manner as are other taxes levied throughout the county. Said levy shall be certified by said board of trustees to the auditor of the county in which said city is situated, and shall be placed by said auditor on the tax duplicate and collected as other taxes. The money realized from said levy, and all moneys received or collected by said trustees for the library, shall be placed in the treasury of said county, subject to the order of said board of trustees of said library. Said fund shall be known as the library fund of said county, of which the county treasurer shall be the custodian, and no money shall be drawn therefrom, except upon the requisition of the board of trustees of said library, certified by the president and secretary of said board, directed to the county auditor, who shall draw his warrant on the county treasurer therefor. Any part of said funds unexpended during any year shall remain to the credit of said library fund. (94 v. 204; 93 v. 194.)

Sec. 3999c-1. [Provisions relating to tax and expenditures for library purposes in Cincinnati.] The provisions, requirements, limitations and inhibitions of sections 1005, 1006, 1007, 1008 and 1009 of the Revised Statutes of Ohio, shall apply to and govern the levying of taxes and the making of appropriations and expenditures for library purposes in and for any city of the first grade of the first class situate in any county having a board of control, in all respects and as fully as said sections apply to and govern any such county in the levying of its taxes and in providing for its yearly expenditures; and it shall be unlawful in any such county to levy any tax for library purposes or to make any expenditure from any library fund, created under section 3999c of the Revised Statutes, without the action thereon of the county auditor and of the board of county commissioners and of the board of control, in the manner prescribed in and by said several sections 1005, 1006, 1007, 1008 and 1009: Provided, however, that in the year 1902 the report required by said section 1008 shall be made by the board of trustees of any public library of any such city on or before the first Monday of May of said year, and that the statements required by said section 1005 shall be made by the county auditor, as to the tax for library purposes in such cities, on or before the first Monday of June of said year, and the first appropriation of funds provided for by this act shall be made for the six months ending December 31st, 1902, in accordance with said section 1007. The secretary of the board last named shall, on demand, furnish to the county auditor, board of county commissioners, and board of control any information relating to the finances of said board, which either may deem necessary in the proper discharge of the duties imposed by this act. The provisions of section 2834b of the Revised Statutes shall apply to all contracts, agreements, obligations and orders involving the expenditure of money, entered into or made by the board of trustees of the public library of any such city, and any action of any such board, contrary to the provisions of said section, shall be void, except that the certificate of the county auditor required by said section shall not be necessary in case of current expenditures, or in case of any other expenditures not exceeding five hundred dollars, or in case of contracts for the employment of officers, assistants or other employes of such board. (95 v. 361.)

**Sec. 3999d.** [Disposition of unexpended fund heretofore raised for library purposes in Cincinnati.] The amount of any fund heretofore raised by a levy or tax by the board of education in such city for school library purposes, and all library funds remaining unexpended, shall be transferred from the respective funds to the library fund herein created, to be expended and paid out as herein provided for funds produced by a levy made by said board of trustees, and any and all funds, bonds, stocks or other species of property held by the board of education of such city, or by any of the departments of such city for the benefit of the public library thereof, shall be transferred to the board of trustees of such public library, to be held and controlled by them subject to the terms of the respective donations. (93 v. 194.)

**Sec. 3999e.** [Who ineligible as members of the library board.] No member of any of the boards exercising the power of appointment of the trustees of the public library, as provided in section 3999, shall be appointed or elected a member of said library board. (94 v. 204.)

**(3999f) Sec. 1.** [Carnegie donation, library trustees may accept.] That the board of trustees of the public library of the school district of Cincinnati be and it is hereby authorized to receive and accept the said donation of Andrew Carnegie npon the terms and conditions therein expressed, the branch libraries constructed under the provisions of said donation to be by said library trustees and their successors equipped, furnished and maintained, and forever kept open for the free use of the public. (95 v. 902.)

**(3999g) Sec. 2.** [Bonds for sites, equipment, etc., of libraries.] That for the purpose of providing the sites and furnishing the equipment necessary for said branch libraries the said board of trustees is hereby authorized and empowered to borrow as a fund therefor such sum as be necessary, not exceeding one hundred and eighty thousand dollars, and to issue registered or coupon bonds therefor, which shall be known and designated as "The Public Library bonds of the school district of Cincinnati," and shall be issued in such sums and be made payable at such times and places as shall be deemed best by said board.  Said bonds shall be signed by the president and secretary of said board and a record kept thereof.  They shall bear a rate of interest not exceeding three and one-half per centum per annum, and shall not be sold for less than par, nor until after four successive weekly advertisements in two newspapers published and of general circulation in said city.  For the purpose of paying the interest and providing a sinking fund for the final redemption of said bonds, the said board of trustees shall levy annually a tax upon the taxable property of said school district sufficient in amount to pay the said interest upon said bonds, and to provide a sinking fund for their final redemption.  The said tax shall be certified annually by said trustees to the auditor of the county in which said school district is situate, and shall be by him placed upon the tax duplicate of said district in addition to all other taxes allowed by law, and said tax shall be levied, assessed and collected as other taxes.  The proceeds of said tax, when collected, shall be credited to the said library trustees as trustees of the sinking fund for the payment of the said bonds and interest.  Said trustees shall pay therefrom the said annual interest upon said bonds, and the portion assessed and collected for the sinking fund shall be invested by them in bonds of the United States, state of Ohio, or the city of Cincinnati, and from the proceeds of said investment they shall pay the said bonds at maturity.  (95 v. 902.)

(3999*h*) **Sec. 3.**  [Power of trustees to lease or purchase sites, etc.; contracts for branch libraries; title to property.]  Said library trustees shall have power to purchase or lease and to hold land necessary for suitable sites on which to erect said branch libraries, and shall use said fund in the payment therefor, and in suitably equipping said libraries for use.  It shall require the affirmative vote of not less than two-thirds of the members of said board to purchase or lease any such land or to make any contracts concerning the erection of such branch libraries.  Purchases made may be for cash or on time, and if on time, said board may issue its obligations for the deferred payments and secure the same by mortgage upon the land purchased.  Said trustees shall have power and they are hereby authorized to make all necessary contracts for the construction, furnishing and equipping of such branch libraries. The title to the land acquired under this act shall be taken in the name of "The trustees of the Public Library of the school district of Cincinnati," and shall be held by them in trust for public library purposes, and said trustees shall have the care, custody, management, and control of all property provided for public library purposes under this act. (95 v. 903.)

(3999*i*) Sec. 4. [Exemptions from taxes, execution, etc.] All property, real and personal, vested in such library board or used for library purposes, shall be exempt from taxation, and from sale on execution, or any writ or order in the nature of an execution. (95 v. 903.)

(3999*j*) Sec. 5. [Donations, taxes, etc.] Said trustees shall have the right to receive and accept donations of land, money, or other thing of value, and to invest, use, or dispose of the same in the interest of the library. (95 v. 903.)

(3999*k*) Sec. 6. [Power of trustees to control funds; contracts for buildings, etc.] The said library trustees, and their successors shall be the trustees of said fund so as aforesaid raised and provided, and shall have the control and disbursement of the same. They may maintain and defend suits, appoint, employ, and pay officers and agents. No contract shall be made for any part of the construction of said library building, or for any work to be done in connection therewith, which shall involve the expenditure of more than five hundred dollars, save upon public advertisement for not less than thirty days in two newspapers, printed and of general circulation in said city, inviting proposals therefor. Said trustees shall have power to take such security from any officer, agent, or contractor chosen, appointed, or employed by them as they shall deem advisable. They shall not become surety for any officer, agent or contractor, or be interested directly or indirectly in any contract concerning said library. (95 v. 903.)

(3999*l*) Sec. 7. [Officers of trustees; depositories of funds, etc.] The said trustees shall choose from their number a president, vice-president, secretary and treasurer, and may select a depository within said city which shall be a national bank or trust company organized under the laws of this state in which to deposit any funds coming into the hands of said treasurer, and they may make contracts for the safe keeping of said funds and the payment of interest thereon. (95 v. 904.)

Sec. 4000. [Cleveland public library.] The public library board of the city of Cleveland shall consist of seven suitable persons, residents of said city, no one being a member or officer of the board of education. The members of the library board shall serve without compensation and hold their offices for three years and until their successors shall have been elected and qualified, except that at the first election two of the board shall be elected for one year, two for two years, and three for three years. After said first election so many shall be elected each year as equals the number whose term expires that year. They shall be elected by roll-call as in other cases by the board of education of the city of Cleveland, at its first regular meeting after the third Monday in April, 1886, and annually thereafter as hereinbefore provided. The board of education shall have power at any time to fill vacancies in the library board for unexpired terms by election as aforesaid. (1886, April 28; 83 v. 104; 80 v. 172; Rev. Stat. 1880; 75 v. 101, § 1.)

**Sec. 4001.** [**Powers and duties of** library board.] Such library board shall report in writing to the board of education once each year, and oftener if required by the latter, shall have exclusive charge and control of the public library of the city, and shall have full power to make all rules and regulations for the government and management thereof; to employ a librarian and such assistants and help as may be needed for the care and protection of the library, and to attend to the drawing and return of books; but prior to such employment the compensation of such librarian, assistants and help, shall be fixed by the library board, by a majority of the members thereof voting in favor of such compensation, on roll-call by the secretary, and such librarian, assistants and help shall be employed by a vote in the same manner. (1883, April 18; 80 v. 172; 78 v. 132; Rev. Stat. 1880; 76 v. 50, § 2.)

**Sec. 4002.** [**Library tax, and how expended.**] For the purpose of increasing and maintaining the public library in said city, and the territory thereto attached for school purposes, such library board may levy annually a tax of eight-tenths of one mill on each dollar valuation of the taxable property of the city, and the territory thereto attached for school purposes, to be levied, collected and paid in the same manner as are school taxes of the city; all money appropriated, received or collected by tax for the library, shall be expended under the direction of the library board in purchasing such books, pamphlets, papers, magazines, periodicals, journals and other property as may be deemed suitable for the public library and in payment of all other charges and expenses, including compensation of the librarian, assistants and help that may be incurred in increasing and maintaining the library, and all claims against said fund shall be approved by the president and secretary of said library board and paid upon the warrant of the auditor of the board of education in the manner now provided by law for the payment of claims against said city. (94 v. 26; 91 v. 268, 123; 90 v. 96; 80 v. 172, 173; Rev. Stat. 1880; 76 v. 50, § 3; 95 v. 438.)

(4002-1.) Sec. 1. [Cleveland library board to hold title and control property.] Said library board, in its own name shall hold the title to and have the custody, management and control of all property of said library board, both real and personal, whether acquired heretofore, or hereafter, and shall have power over, and the executive control of the expenditures of moneys collected for the purpose of purchasing lands, and erecting buildings and also have complete custody, management and control of all public libraries and branches and stations thereof, and the reading rooms connected therewith. (92 v. 590.)

(4002-2) Sec. 2. [Can purchase, lease or condemn.] Said library board shall have power, by a two-third vote of its members entered upon its journal, to purchase grounds and erect suitable library buildings, and to lease grounds and suitable library buildings, and in case suitable grounds cannot be purchased, to condemn the grounds desired, by virtue of the power of eminent domain, and erect thereon suitable and appropriate buildings for library use. The title to such grounds so purchased or condemned and buildings erected shall be taken to and vest in the said library board. (92 v. 590.)

(4002-3.) Sec. 3. [Proceedings to condemn.] When it is deemed necessary by said library [board] to condemn or appropriate private property, whereon to erect library buildings, said library board in making such appropriation shall proceed in accordance with the provisions of section 2235 and subsequent sections found in chapter 3, division 7, title 12 of the Revised Statutes of Ohio and acts amendatory thereof and supplementary thereto. (92 v. 590.)

(4002-4.) Sec. 4. [Donations.] Said board may by resolution accept any gift, devise or bequest of property, real and personal, for the benefit of the library. (92 v. 590.)

(4002-5) Sec. 5. [Exempt from tax and execution.] All property, real or personal, vested in any public library board shall be exempt from taxation and from sale on execution or other writ or order in the nature of an execution. All conveyances made by such library board shall be executed by the president and secretary thereof. (92 v. 590.)

(4002-6) Sec. 6. [Oath.] Each person appointed a member of such board shall, upon entering upon the duties of his office, take an oath or affirmation, to obey the constitution of the United States and the constitution of the state of Ohio, and that he will faithfully perform the duties of his office. (92 v. 590.)

**(4002-7) Sec. 7.** [Organization.] Said library board at its first meeting in June after the passage of this bill, and annually thereafter in June, shall organize by choosing a president, a vice president and a secretary, and in the absence of the president or his inability to act, the vice president shall perform the duties of the president. (92 v. 590.)

**(4002-8) Sec. 8.** [Annual report.] Said library board shall make an annual report to the board of education stating the condition of their trust, the various sums of money received from the library fund and from other sources and how much moneys have been expended, and for what purposes; the number of books and periodicals on hand; the number added by purchase, gifts or otherwise during the year; the number lost or missing, the number of books loaned out and the general character of the books, with other statistics, information and suggestions as they may deem of general interest. (92 v. 590.)

**(4002-9) Sec. 9.** [No member of board to be interested in contract, except; validity of contract.] No member of such library board shall have any pecuniary interest, either directly or indirectly, in any contract made with the board or be employed in any manner or have any compensation from the board of which he is a member, except as secretary, and no contract shall be binding upon such board unless it be made or authorized to be made at a regular or special meeting of the board. (92 v. 590.)

**(4002-10) Sec. 10.** [Use of library and reading room.] Every library and reading-room established under this act shall be free to the use of the inhabitants of such city and those who reside in the territory thereto attached for school purposes, subject, however, to such rules and regulations as the library board may deem necessary to adopt and publish, to protect and preserve property therein in order to render the use of said library and reading-room of the greatest benefit to the greatest number; and said library board may exclude and cut off from the use of said library and reading-room any and all persons who shall wilfully violate any of such rules and regulations. (92 v. 590.)

**(4002-11) Sec. 11.** [Bonds to pay for land and building.] Said library board may issue bonds with interest coupons attached, to obtain land and building for a public library and to furnish the same and to pay the cost and expense thereof, and in anticipation of income from taxes for such purposes levied or to be levied, may from time to time, as occasion requires, or at any time after the passage of this bill, issue and sell bonds, bearing interest, payable semi-annually, at a rate specified therein, not exceeding five per cent. (5%) per annum, and in such sums and at such times as the library board may determine, which bonds shall be numbered consecutively, made payable to the bearer and be signed by the president and secretary of the board and denominated "public library bonds of the city of Cleveland, Ohio," and the secretary of said board shall keep a record of the number, date, amount and rate of interest on each bond sold, the sum for which and the name of the person to whom sold, and the time when payable, which record shall be open to the inspection of the public at all reasonable times, and the bonds so issued shall in no case be sold for a less sum than the par value nor bear interest until the purchase money for the same shall have been paid by the purchaser and such library board shall pay such bonds and the interest thereon when due, provided that the total issue of bonds shall not exceed two hundred and fifty thousand dollars ($250,000). (92 v. 590.)

(4002-12) Sec. 12. [Resolution to issue; sale of.] The order to issue such bonds shall be made only at a regular meeting of such board and by a vote of five-sevenths of all the members thereof, taken by yeas and nays and entered on the journal of the board, and such bonds shall be sold to the highest bidder after being advertised once a week for four (4) consecutive weeks in a newspaper having a general circulation in the county where such bonds are issued, and if there shall be more than one newspaper in such city having a general circulation in the county where such bonds are issued, then the sale of such bonds shall be advertised in at least one additional newspaper of such general circulation in such county, the advertisement shall state the total number of bonds to be sold, the amount of each, how long they are to run, the rate of interest to be paid thereon, whether annually or semi-annually, the law or section of law authorizing their issue, day, hour and place in the county where they are to be sold, and the privilege shall be reserved by such board to reject all or any bids, and if said bids are rejected said bonds shall be advertised and the moneys arising on premiums of the sale of said bonds as well as the principal shall be credited to said fund on account of which the bonds are issued and sold and shall be used for the purpose provided in this section. (92 v. 590.)

(4002-13) Sec. 13. [Sinking fund.] For the purpose of creating a sinking fund for the extinguishment of the bonds provided for in the preceding section, said library board may annually until the payments of the bonds are fully provided for, levy and collect a tax in addition to other taxes now authorized to be levied by it, which shall not exceed two-tenths of one mill upon the taxable property of the city of Cleveland and the territory thereto attached for school purposes, which tax shall be paid into the treasury of said city and on order of the director of accounts of said city paid over to the sinking fund commission hereafter provided for and by them applied by order of the library board to the extinguishment of the bonds in the preceding section provided and to no other purpose whatever, and the taxes so levied shall be certified and placed on the tax list and collected in the same manner as school taxes of said city and such tax shall be a lien upon the property whereon they are assessed and the same as state and county taxes and subject to the same penalties if delinquent. (92 v. 590.)

(4002-14) **Sec. 14.** [Trustees of sinking fund.] In such city there shall be a board designated as "the trustees of the library sinking fund of the city of Cleveland" composed of three (3) citizens thereof, to be appointed by the court of common pleas in the county in which such city is situated. The first appointment shall be one for the term of one year, one for the term of two years, and one for the term of three years and all trustees appointed thereafter shall serve for three years, except in case of vacancy, which shall be filled by said court for the unexpired term, and before any person appointed as a member of such board shall assume the duties of his office he shall give bond to the state of Ohio in the sum of five thousand dollars ($5,000) with not less than two sureties to faithfully discharge his said duties. (92 v. 590.)

(4002-15) **Sec. 15.** [Their organization.] Such trustees immediately after appointment and qualification shall organize by appointing one of their number as president and the director of accounts of such city shall act as secretary of said board of trustees and the library board shall provide such trustees with a place of meeting, and regular meetings of such trustees shall be held on the second Monday of January and July of each year, but other meetings may be called by the president or any member of the board. Their proceedings shall be recorded in a journal kept for that purpose which shall at all times be open to the inspection of the library board or any member thereof and all questions relating to the purchase or sale of securities, payment of bonds or interest shall be decided by a viva voce vote with the name of each member voting recorded on the journal and no question shall be decided unless approved by a majority of the whole board. (92 v. 590.)

**(4002-16) Sec. 16.** [Their duty to certify tax.] The trustees of such sinking fund shall in the month of May in each year and oftener, if required, certify to the library board the rate of tax, not exceeding the limit herein provided, necessary to provide a sinking fund for the payment of the bonds issued by authority of this bill together with the amount necessary to be levied to provide for the payment of the interest thereon, and the library board shall levy the amount so certified as under this act provided and for the full amount so certified, but said library board may increase the amount so reported, provided the total amount so levied does not exceed the limitation provided in this bill. (92 v. 590.)

**(4002-17) Sec. 17.** [Investments by.] The trustees of such sinking fund shall invest all moneys received by them in bonds of the United States, state of Ohio, city of Cleveland, city of Cincinnati, city of Columbus, and the city of Toledo, and they shall give preference to the bonds of the city of Cleveland, where they can be purchased at a price equal to, or, less than the bonds of the United States, or of the state of Ohio, taking into consideration the rate of interest paid on each, and the interest received shall be reinvested in like manner and at no time shall there be more than $5,000 kept on deposit if investment can be made, and said trustees shall provide for the payment of all interest on, said bonds herein authorized to be issued, together with the principal thereof at maturity of said bonds, from said funds so invested by them. (92 v. 590.)

**(4002-18) Sec. 1.** [Cleveland may appropriate from school fund for library.] In all cities, which, by the last federal census, had, and all those which hereafter, on the first day of March, in any year, as ascertained by any federal census, may have, a population exceeding ninety thousand and less than two hundred thousand inhabitants, it shall be lawful to appropriate from the school fund, an amount equal to the proceeds of one-tenth of one mill of the tax levy, to maintain or assist in maintaining the public library and pay in part the cost and expense of supporting and running any public library in said cities in addition to the one-tenth of one mill now authorized by law to be raised by taxation for that purpose; provided, that this act shall not be construed to authorize any increase in levies for school purposes, including libraries in said cities, over that made in 1877. (75 v. 11.)

### IN TOLEDO.

**(4002-19) Sec. 1.** [Toledo public library; tax for library.] In any city of the third grade of the first class, the city council may, by a resolution passed by a majority of the members elected thereto, declare it to be essential to the interests of such city, to establish and maintain therein a public library and reading room. That thereafter the said city council shall, annually, levy a tax of thirty-five one-hundreths (35-100) of one mill on the dollar on the taxable property of such city for that purpose, to be called the library fund; and which levy shall be certified to the county auditor of the county, and by him placed on the tax duplicate of the county and collected as other taxes. (94 v. 166; 1888, April 12; 85 v. 209; Rev. Stat. 1880; 70 v. 142.)

(4002-20) Sec. 1a. Repealed April 14, 1900. (94 v. 166.)

(4002-21) Sec. 2. [Board of trustees.] The custody and management of such public library and reading-room, as well as its entire administration, shall be committed to a board of trustees, nine in number, of whom the mayor of such city for the time being shall be one, and the others shall be appointed by the common council, four of whom shall be appointed from such names as shall be nominated to the common council by the board of education of said city, and shall be citizens of approved learning, discretion, and fitness for such office. They shall hold their office for the term of four years, and until their successors are duly elected and qualified; provided, that the trustees first appointed, other than the mayor, shall be elected respectively for terms of one, two, three, and four years, from the first day of January next following their election, two for each term. Any vacancy caused by the death, resignation, or removal of a trustee, or otherwise, shall be filled for his unexpired term by appointment of the common council. No trustees shall have compensation as such. (1888, April 12; 85 v. 209, 210; Rev. Stat. 1880; 70 v. 142.)

(4002-22) Sec. 3. [Transfer of libraries to such board by the board of education.] As soon as said board of trustees shall be elected and organized, it shall be the duty of the board of education in such city to transfer to the custody and control of such board of trustees whatever public library or libraries may be in its possession or control, except such books of reference, maps or charts as the board of education may think proper to retain for use in school buildings; and thereafter no tax shall be levied by such board of education for a library fund. (1888, April 12; 85 v. 209, 210; Rev. Stat. 1880; 70 v. 142.)

(4002-23) Sec. 4. [Organization of trustees; regulations; powers; deposit of library funds; warrants; power to purchase or condemn grounds; issue and sale of public library building bonds; payment of said bonds and interest; title to grounds purchased; librarians and assistants.] Said trustees shall immediately after their appointment, meet and organize by the election of one of their number as president, and by the election of such other officers as they may deem necessary. They shall make and adopt such by-laws, rules and regulations for their own government and guidance of the library, reading-room and employes as may be expedient and not inconsistent with this act. They shall have power over and the exclusive control of the expenditure of all moneys collected to credit of the library fund, and of the supervision, care, custody and control of the grounds and buildings constructed for such purpose, or rooms leased or set apart for such purpose; provided, that all moneys collected for such library, including proceeds of the bonds herein authorized, and all others, shall be deposited in the treasury of said city to the credit of the library fund, and shall be kept separate and apart from other funds, and the city auditor shall issue his warrant when drawn upon by said board of trustees, or by its proper officers duly authorized. Said board shall have the power, by a two-third vote of said trustees entered upon its journal, to purchase grounds, and in case suitable grounds cannot be purchased, to condemn the grounds desired, and erect thereon suitable and appropriate building or buildings for the use of said library; the cost of such ground and buildings not to exceed in the aggregate the sum of $45,000; and for such purpose said board is authorized and empowered to borrow money upon bonds as hereinafter provided to pay for the same, not to exceed in the aggregate, the sum of $45,000; and the said boards of trustees is authorized to issue and sell its bonds, for the above named amount, with coupons for interest, divided into and payable in fifteen consecutive annual payments; the first of which shall become due three years after their issue. Said bonds shall be denominated "The Public Library Building Bonds" of said city, and shall be for the sum of $500 each, payable to bearer, and bear interest at the rate not exceeding four and one-half per cent. per annum, payable semi-annually. Said bonds and coupons shall be signed by the president of said board and attested by its secretary; and in making sale of said bonds the said board of trustees shall be governed by the provisions of an act of the general assembly passed March 22, 1883 (O. L., vol. 80, p. 68), entitled "an act providing for the sale of public bonds." To meet the payment of said bonds and interest, the said board of trustees shall appropriate and set apart annually from said library fund, a sum sufficient for such purpose, not to exceed one-half of the tax revenues collected for such year. The title to such grounds so purchased shall be taken to and vest in the trustees of the public library of such city; said trustees shall be held and considered to be special trustees thereof for such city. Said board shall have power to appoint suitable librarians and necessary assistants, fix salaries of same, and shall, in general, carry out the spirit and intent of this act in establishing and maintaining the best public library and reading-room with the means at their disposal. (1888, April 12; 85 v. 209, 210; Rev. Stat. 1880; 70 v. 142.)

(4002-24) Sec. 4a. [Additional bonds authorized to be issued for certain purposes.] For the purpose of enabling said board of trustees to construct said building or buildings so as to make it or them fire-proof, and thereby insure protection to the large and valuable library to be kept therein, and to pay the increased cost of such construction, and complete said building or buildings, and provide necessary furniture for same, and to pay for grading the library grounds and constructing walks, said board of trustees is hereby authorized to issue and sell additional bonds to an amount not in excess of thirty-five thousand dollars ($35,000); said additional bonds shall bear interest, be issued, sold, the proceeds deposited, drawn, used, and the interest and principal paid, as provided, and subject in all respects to all the conditions named in said original section 4, for the bonds therein authorized, except as follows: the bonds hereby authorized, shall mature, three thousand dollars ($3,000.00) July 1, 1890; five thousand dollars ($5,000.00) July 1, 1906; and five thousand dollars ($5,000.00) July 1, of each succeeding year until July 1, 1911, when seven thousand dol'ars ($7,000.00) shall mature, but if it be found unnecessary to issue all of said bonds, those not issued shall be those last to mature as aforesaid; and the rate of interest shall not exceed four per cent. on those bonds to mature July 1, 1906 and thereafter; and said board shall annually appropriate and set apart such additional sum as may be necessary to pay said bonds and the interest thereon as the same mature. (1889, March 12; 86 v. 79.)

(4002-25) Sec. 4b. [Purchase of a site for library.] That on the request of said board by a two-thirds vote of all of the trustees, entered on its journal, any such city of the third grade of the first class, may purchase, appropriate, enter upon and hold, any real estate within its limits, by it deemed necessary for the purpose of providing said public library with suitable library grounds and extensions or additions thereto. The cost and expense of acquiring such grounds, extensions or additions shall be paid for by the trustees of such public library, out of any moneys in its hands or due and owing to it from the public library fund. (88 v. 92.)

(4002-26) **Sec. 4c.** [Appropriation of private property.] That when it is deemed necessary by any such city of the third grade of the first class to appropriate private property as heretofore provided in said supplementary section 4b, any such city shall proceed in making such appropriation under and in accordance with the provisions of section 2235 and the subsequent sections thereto as found in chapter 3, division 7, title 12 of the Revised Statutes of this state, in so far as the same are applicable. (88 v. 335.)

(4002-27) **Sec. 4d.** [Additional building bonds.] For the purposes specified in said original section four (4) and the first section supplemental thereto, section 4a, and to complete the carrying out of such purposes, and paying therefore, said board of trustees is hereby authorized to issue and sell additional bonds to an amount not in excess of five thousand dollars ($5,000.00) ; and such additional bonds shall be issued and sold and their proceeds disposed of and their payment including interest provided for, in all respects in the same manner and subject to the same conditions, as provided in said supplemental section 4a for the bonds to mature July 1, 1906, and thereafter, except that those hereby authorized shall mature July 1, 1912. (89 v. 419.)

(4002-28) **Sec. 5.** [Library to be free, subject to reasonable rules.] Every library and reading room established under this act, shall be and remain forever free to the use of the inhabitants of such city, subject, however, to such reasonable rules and regulations as the library board may find and deem necessary to adopt and publish, to protect and preserve the property therein, in order to render the use of said library and reading room of the greatest benefit to the greatest number; and said board may exclude and cut off from the use of said library and reading room, any and all persons who shall wilfully violate any of such rules and regulations. (1888, April 12; 85 v. 209, 211; Rev. Stat. 1880; 70 v. 142.)

(4002-29) **Sec. 6.** [Annual report to city council.] The said board of trustees shall make an annual report to the city council, stating the condition of their trust, the various sums of money received from the library fund, and from other sources, and how much moneys have been expended, and for what purpose; the number of books and periodicals on hand; the number added by purchases, gifts . or otherwise during the year; the number lost or missing, the number of books loaned out, and the general character and kind of such books, with other statistics, information and suggestions as they may deem of general interest. 1888, April 12; 85 v. 209, 211; Rev. Stat. 1880; 70 v. 142.)

(4002-30) **Sec. 7.** [Penalty for injuring library property.] The city council of such city shall have power to pass ordinances imposing suitable penalties for the punishment of any and all persons committing injury upon such library buildings, grounds or other property thereof. (1888, April 12; 85 v. 209, 211; Rev. Stat. 1880; 70 v. 142.)

(4002-31 **Sec. 8.** [Power of trustees to accept donations, etc.] Any person or persons desiring to make, devise or bequest, donation or gift of either books, personal property, money or real estate, to and for the use and benefit of such library, may vest the same or title thereto in the said trustees created under this act; to be held and controlled by said board, its successors, when accepted, according to the terms of such devise, bequest or deed of gift of such property; and as to such property the said board of trustees shall be held and considered special trustees thereof. (1888, April 12; 85 v. 209, 212; Rev. Stat. 1880; 70 v. 142.)

### IN DAYTON.

(4002-32) **Sec. 1.** [Dayton Public library board; election of.] In any city of the second grade of the second class the city board of education may elect by ballot, a special board of six competent persons, residents and electors of said city or school district, to be called the library board, which board shall have the sole custody, control and management of the public library of such city and of any reading rooms, branch libraries or library stations by said library board established in connection with such public library. (89 v. 229; 84 v. 171.)

(4002-33) **Sec. 2.** [Political composition of; terms; vote required to elect.] The six members of said library board shall be selected equally from the two political parties having the largest representation in the city board of education and shall be elected as follows: Two for a term of one year, two for a term of two years and two for a term of three years, one member from each of said political parties to be elected for each of said several terms; and at the end of the first year and of each year thereafter, two members of said library board, one from each of said political parties, shall be elected, by ballot, by said board of education for the term of three years. It shall require the affirmative vote of a majority of all the members elected to said board of education to elect the members of said library board. (89 v. 229; 84 v. 171.)

(4002-34) **Sec. 3.** [Powers and duties.] Said library board shall have power over and the exclusive control of the library fund hereinafter provided for, and of the expenditure of all moneys collected to the credit thereof. They shall have power to establish in said city reading rooms, branch libraries and library stations in connection with such public library, and to lease and furnish such rooms, buildings or parts thereof as are required for such purposes, and to pay all necessary expenses connected therewith. They shall have power and it shall be their duty to purchase and pay for all books, periodicals, magazines, and other literature, and supplies necessary, in their judgment, for said public library, reading rooms, branch libraries and library stations, and to incur the necessary expenditures for the encouragement and advancement of the best use of such public library, reading rooms, branches and stations, by the public; all of such purchases, payments and expenditures to be made out of said library fund hereinafter provided for. They shall have power and it shall be their duty to employ a librarian, assistant librarians, janitors and other necessary assistants for such public library, reading rooms, branches and stations, to fix the compensation of persons so employed and to pay same out of said library fund. Said library board may fix the term of any such persons employed by them for any period not to exceed one year. (89 v. 229; 84 v. 171.)

(4002-35) Sec. 4. [Expenses of library for ensuing year.] Said library board shall, annually, prior to the annual levy of taxes made by the city board of education, report and certify to such city board of education a statement of the amount by said library board deemed necessary for the expenses and expenditures of such library board for the ensuing fiscal year; and said city board of education shall annually levy a tax for such library purposes and for the use of such library board for such purposes for such ensuing year to the full amount so reported and certified by said library board; provided, however, that the amount so levied shall not exceed the amount hereinafter authorized to be levied for such purposes. The fiscal year of said library board shall be the same as that of the board of education. (89 v. 229; 84 v. 171.)

(4002-36) Sec. 5. [Tax for library fund; custodian; disbursements and balance.] The board of education of said city wherein a library board exists under the act to which this act is amendatory or shall hereafter be elected under this act, shall have the power and it shall be the duty of such board of education to levy annually for such public library purposes a tax not exceeding four-tenths of one mill on the dollar of the city valuation, to be called the library fund, which levy shall be certified by said board of education to the county auditor of the county in which said city is situate, within the time and in the manner fixed for the certifying of other levies made by said board of education; and [which levy shall be by said auditor placed on the tax duplicate of the county] and collected as other taxes. Such levy for library purposes shall not be a part of the general levy authorized to be made by such board of education for school purposes. The money realized from said levies and all moneys received or collected by the trustees for the library, shall be placed in the treasury of the county, subject to the order of the board of trustees of said library. Said funds shall be kept separate and apart from other funds and the treasurer shall be the custodian thereof, and no money shall be drawn therefrom except upon the requisition of the board of trustees of the library, certified by the president and secretary of said board and directed to said county treasurer. Any part of said fund unexpended during any year shall remain to the credit of said library fund. (94 v. 484; 89 v. 229; 84 v. 171.)

(4002-37) Sec. 6. [Provisions governing board.] Said library board shall, immediately after their election meet and organize by the election of a president, a secretary and other necessary officers from their number, and such election shall be held annually thereafter. Said board shall make and adopt such by-laws, rules and regulations for their own government and guidance and for the government and guidance of the public library, reading rooms, branch libraries, and stations, and of the employes of said board as may be expedient and not inconsistent with this act, and said board shall, by their by-laws, designate the officers authorized to draw orders upon said library fund. Any public library now established in any such city and which is maintained and in operation under and by virtue of the provisions of the act to which this act is amendatory, and the existing library board of such city and the officers thereof, shall be governed by the provisions of this act; and such library board shall succeed to and be vested with all the rights, powers and privileges, and charged with all the duties herein granted or imposed; and the members of such existing library board elected thereto by the board of education prior to the taking effect of this act shall continue as such until the expiration of their present terms, and their successors shall be elected pursuant to the provisions hereof. The present officers of such existing library board shall continue in office until the expiration of their present terms as such officers or until a vacancy occurs therein prior to such expiration when their successors shall be elected pursuant to the provisions hereof. Where such existing library board has heretofore reported to such board of education their estimate of the expenses of such library for the current year, pursuant to the provisions of the act to which this act is amendatory, such board of education shall forthwith, upon the taking effect of this act, set apart and pay over to the said county treasurer as the treasurer of such library fund the unexpended balance of the appropriation heretofore made by such board of education for such library expenses for the current year, which balance shall become and constitute a part of said library fund hereinbefore provided for and shall be expended by said library board for the maintenance, management and expenses of such public library, reading rooms, branch libraries and library stations, for the remainder of such current year. (89 v. 229; 84 v. 171.)

(4002-38) Sec. 1. [Museum may be established.] In any city of the second grade of the second class, wherein there now is or shall hereafter be a public library of such city, under the control, custody and management of a library board established pursuant to the provisions of an act entitled "An act to provide for competent and non-partisan public library boards in cities of the second class, second grade," passed March 21, 1887 (O. L., v. 84 p. 171), and of acts amendatory thereto, such library board shall have the power, and is hereby authorized to establish and maintain, in connection with such public library, a public museum for the benefit of the public of such city; and such board may appropriate and expend, out of the amount of the tax levy heretofore or hereafter annually made for library purposes and for the use of such board, such amounts as are in their judgment necessary for the establishment and maintenance of such public museum. Such library board is empowered to receive, by way of gift, loan or purchase, specimens and collections for such museum, to be accepted and held by such board and their successors in office, in trust for museum purposes, and under such conditions and regulations as they may from time to time establish. Such library board may make, from the funds arising from such tax levy, such purchases of specimens and collections for such museum, as shall not impair the proper and sufficient use of such funds for library purposes. (90 L. L., 377.)

### IN SMALLER CITIES AND VILLAGES.

(4002-39) Sec. 1. [Certain cities and villages may have libraries; tax.] The common council of every city not exceeding in population thirty thousand inhabitants and of every incorporated village shall have power to establish and maintain a public library and reading room, and for such purpose may annually levy and cause to be collected, as other general taxes are, a tax not exceeding one mill on each dollar of the taxable property of such city or village, to constitute the library fund, which shall be kept by the treasurer separate and apart from other money of the city or village, and be used exclusively for the purchase of books, periodicals, necessary furniture and fixtures and whatever is required for the proper maintenance of such library and reading room. (89 v. 98.)

**(4002-40) Sec. 2.** [Directors.] For the government of such library and reading room there shall be a board of six directors, appointed by the council of such city or village from among the citizens thereof at large, and not more than one member· of the council of such city or village shall at any one time be a member of said board. Such directors shall hold their office for three years from the date of appointment, and until their successors are appointed, but upon their first appointment they shall divide themselves at their first meeting by lot into three classes, one-third for one year, one-third for two years, and one-third for three years, and their terms shall expire accordingly. All vacancies shall be immediately reported by the directors to the proper council, and be filled by appointment in like manner; and if an unexpired term, for the residue of the term only. No compensation whatever shall be paid or allowed to any director. (89 v. 98.)

**(4002-41) Sec. 3.** [**Organization; by-laws, etc.; control of expenditures; custody of building; how money drawn from treasury; librarian and assistants.**] Said directors shall, immediately after their appointment, meet and organize by the election of one of their number president, and by the election of such other officers as they may deem necessary. They shall make and adopt such by-laws, rules and regulations for their own guidance, and for the government of the library and reading room, as may be expedient. They shall have the exclusive control of the expenditures of all moneys collected for the library fund, and the supervision, care and custody of the rooms or buildings constructed, leased or set apart for that purpose, and such money shall be drawn from the treasury by the proper officers, upon the properly authenticated voucher of the board of directors, without otherwise being audited. They may, with the approval of the common council, lease and occupy, or purchase, or erect on purchased ground, an appropriate building, provided that no more than half the income in any one year can be set apart in said year for such purpose or building. They may appoint a librarian and assistants, and prescribe rules for their conduct. (89 v. 98.)

**(4002-42) Sec. 4.** [**Who may use library.**] Every library and reading room established under this chapter shall be forever free for the use of the inhabitants of the city or village where located, always subject to such reasonable rules and regulations as the library board may find necessary to adopt and publish in order to render the use of said library and reading room of the greatest benefit to the greatest number; and they may exclude and cut off from the use of said library and reading room any and all persons who shall wilfully violate such rules. (89 v. 98.)

(4002-43) **Sec. 5.** [Annual report.] The said board of directors shall make an annual report to such council, stating the condition of their trust—the various sums of money received from the library fund, and from all other sources, and how much has been expended; the number of books and periodicals on hand; the number added by purchase, gift or otherwise during the year; the number lost or missing, the number of books loaned out, and the general character and kind of such books, with such other statistics, information and suggestions as they may deem of general interest. (89 v. 98.)

(4002-44) **Sec. 6.** [Donations.] All persons desirous of making donations of money, personal property or real estate, for the benefit of such library, shall have the right to vest the title of the same in the board of directors created under this law, to be held and controlled by said board, when accepted according to the terms of the deed of gift, devise or bequest of such property, and as to such property the said board shall be held and considered to be special trustees. (89 v. 98.)

(4002-45) **Sec. 7.** [Tax to assist existing library association.] In case a free public library has already been established in any city or incorporated village, and duly incorporated and organized, the council may levy a tax for its support as provided in this act, without change in the organization of such library association, and the sum so raised shall be paid to the officer or officers duly authorized to receive the same, and shall be under the control of the said library association; provided, that if at any time such library association ceases to exist or from any reason fails to provide a free circulating library as required by the provisions of this act, the books and other property accumulated from the proceeds of the levy herein authorized shall become the property of the city or village and be subject to the control of the council as herein provided. (89 v. 98.)

(4002-40) **Sec. 1.** [Library association in certain cities; levy.] In any city of the fourth grade of the second cláss, and in which city there is established and maintained by a public library association duly incorporated, but not organized for profit, a public library, free to all the inhabitants of such city, the board of education shall levy or cause to be levied an annual tax, in addition if need be to the annual amount of taxes limited by law for school purposes, of not less than three-tenths and not to exceed five-tenths of a mill on all the taxable property within such city and school district, to be called "a public library fund," which shall be certified to the .

county auditor of the county and placed on the tax duplicate of the county, and collected as other taxes. (93 v. 8.)

(4002-47) **Sec. 2.** [Disposition of tax.] Said tax when so levied and collected shall be paid over by the treasurer of the board of education to the treasurer of said library association, to be used only in the purchase of books, pamphlets, magazines or newspapers, and for general library expenses of said library association. (93 v. 8.)

(4002-48) **Sec. 3.** [Library association to render account; shall maintain free public library; city shall maintain library if association cease to exist; may levy tax.] Said board of education shall require said library association to render an account as often as it shall deem proper of all taxes so received by it, and how the same have been expended. Said association shall keep up and maintain in a public place in such city a public library free to all the inhabitants thereof, and to all persons residing within said school district. Provided, further, that if said public library association shall for any cause cease to exist then all property of said association, real and personal, shall immediately become vested in the city wherein said library association is established and maintained, and that had heretofore been taxed for the purpose of maintaining the same; and it shall become the duty of said city or municipality to have the charge of and care of such property in the same manner as other property of said city, and to carry out the educational purposes for which this act was originally intended, and may, if occasion require, levy taxes for said purposes upon the personal and real property of said city, and collect the same as other taxes are now levied and collected. (93 v. 9, § 3; 95 v. 417, § 4002-48.)

(4002-49) **Sec. 4.** [Tax in lieu of other taxes.] The tax so levied shall be in lieu of all other taxes levied for school library purposes, and no other levy shall be made for such purpose;

[Purchase of school apparatus; levy.] Provided, however, that nothing herein shall prohibit the board of education from purchasing all necessary philosophical or other apparatus for the schools and making necessary levies therefor. (93 v. 9.)

**Sec. 4003.** [Consolidation of libraries in Portsmouth authorized.| In all cities which at the last federal census had, or at any subsequent federal census may have, a population of ten thousand five hundred and ninety-two, it shall be lawful to merge any public library therein heretofore established with any other library or reading room therein existing; but the library formed by such consolidation shall be kept open for the use of the public at all reasonable hours (75 v. 541, § 1; 76 v. 97, § 1.)

**Sec. 4004.** [Board of Portsmouth to appoint library committee.] The board of education of every such city shall, at its first regular meeting after the second Monday in June, 1879, elect by ballot three suitable persons, residents of the city, but other than mem· bers of such board, who shall be known as the library committee of the city, one to serve for one year, one for two years, and one for three years, and until their successors are duly elected and qualified, and shall, annually thereafter, elect in like manner one person with the same qualifications to serve for three years, and until his successor is elected and qualified; and any vacancy in such committee shall be filled for the unexpired term at the first regular meeting of the board held after the same occurs. (75 v. 541, § 2; 76 v. 97, § 2.)

**Sec. 4005.** [Powers and duties of such committee.] Such committee shall report in writing to the board of education at least once each year, and oftener if required by the board, and shall have entire charge and control of the school library in the city with full power to make all rules and regulations for the government and regulation thereof, to employ a librarian, and such assistants and help as may be needed for its care and protection, and to require of the librarian such bond as they may deem proper for the faithful performance of his duties, and to attend to the drawing and return of books; but the salary of such librarian, and the rate of compensation of such assistants and help, shall be fixed by resolution prior to such employment. (76 v. 97, § 3.)

**Sec. 4006.** [Powers and duties of library committees in Portsmouth.] For the purpose of increasing and maintaining school libraries in cities mentioned in section *four thousand and three* of the Revised Statutes of Ohio, and the territory thereto attached for school purposes, such library committee in such cities is authorized to annually levy a tax of three-tenths of one mill on the dollar valuation of the taxable property of such cities aforesaid, and the territory thereto attached for school purposes, to be assessed, collected and paid in the same manner as are the school taxes of such cities, and all money appropriated or collected by tax for such library shall be expended under the direction of said library committee in the purchase of such books, pamphlets, papers, magazines, periodicals and journals, as may be deemed suitable for the public school library, and in payment of all other costs and charges, including the salaries of the librarian and assistants, that may be incurred in maintaining said libraries, the bills and payrolls for which said expenditures, shall, upon the order of the library committee, be certified by the chairman and secretary of such committee, and paid by the treasurer of the board of education of said city from such library fund. (92 v. 309; 78 v. 176; Rev. Stat. 1880; 75 v. 541, § 2; 76 v. 97, § 4.)

# AN ACT

To authorize the transfer of property by municipal corporations to trustees of libraries of school districts, and the acceptance of the same, and other property, for library purposes by said trustees.

*Be it enacted by the General Assembly of the State of Ohio:*

**Sec. 1.** That it shall be lawful for any municipal corporation in this state to transfer by ordinance duly passed, any property, real or personal, acquired or suitable for library purposes, to the trustees of any public library for the school district within which such municipal corporation is situate, upon such lawful terms and conditions as may be agreed to between said municipal corporation and said trustees.

**Sec. 2.** The trustees of any public library in any such school district are hereby authorized and empowered to receive and accept any such transfer, and to receive and accept from any other source or acquire in any other manner, any property, real or personal, for library purposes, and use and apply the same for such purposes, and to enter into any contract relating thereto. (Passed April 20, 1904. Approved April 21, 1904.)

# CHAPTER IX.

## SCHOOLS AND ATTENDANCE ENFORCED.

Sec. 4007. [Sufficient elementary schools must be provided; number of weeks to be continued; graded course of study required.] Each board of education shall establish a sufficient number of elementary schools to provide for the free education of the youth of school age within the district under its control, at such places as will be most convenient for the attendance of the largest number of such youth, and shall continue each and every elementary day school so established not less than thirty-two nor more than forty weeks in each school year, and all the elementary schools within the same school district shall be continued the same length of time. And boards of education are required ' to prescribe a graded course of study for all schools under their control in the branches named in section 4007-1 of the Revised Statutes of Ohio, subject to the approval of the state commissioner of common schools. Each township board of education shall establish and maintain at least one elementary school in each sub-district under its control, unless transportation is furnished to the pupils thereof as provided by law. (Passed and approved April 25, 1904.)

Sec. 4007-1. [Elementary school defined.] An elementary school is hereby defined as a school in which instruction and training are given in spelling, reading, writing, arithmetic, English language, English grammar and composition, geography, history of the United States, including civil government, physiology and hygiene; but nothing herein contained shall be construed as abridging the power of boards of education to cause instruction and training to be given in vocal music, drawing, elementary algebra, the elements of agriculture and other branches which they may deem advisable for the best interests of the schools under their charge. (Passed and approved April 25, 1904.)

**Sec. 4007-2.** [High school defined.] A high school is hereby defined as a school of higher grade than an elementary school, in which instruction and training are given in approved courses in the history of the United States and other countries; composition, rhetoric, English and American literature; algebra and geometry; natural science, political or mental science, ancient or modern foreign languages, or both, commercial and industrial branches, or such of the above named branches as the length of its curriculum may make possible, and such other branches of higher grade than those to be taught in the elementary schools, and such advanced studies and advanced reviews of the common branches as the board of education may direct. (95 v. 115.)

**Sec. 4007-3.** [College defined.] A college is hereby defined as a school of a higher grade than a high school, in which instruction in the high school branches is carried beyond the scope of the high school and other advanced studies are pursued, or a school in which special, technical or professional studies are pursued, and which may, when legally organized, have the right to confer degrees in agreement with the terms of the law regulating its practices or its charter; or in the want of legislative direction, in agreement with the practices of the better institutions of learning of their respective kinds in the United States. (95 v. 115.)

**Sec. 4007-4.** [High schools classified.] The high schools of the state of Ohio shall be classified into schools of the first, second, and third grades; and all courses of study offered in such high schools shall be in branches enumerated in section 4007-2 of the Revised Statutes of Ohio.

[First grade.] A high school of the first grade shall be a school in which the courses offered shall cover a period of not less than four years, of not less than thirty-two weeks each, in which not less than sixteen courses shall be required for graduation;

[Second grade.] A high school of the second grade shall cover a period of not less than three years, of not less than thirty-two weeks each, in which not less than twelve courses of study shall be required for graduation;

[Third grade.] A high school of the third grade shall cover a period of not less than two years, of not less than twenty-eight weeks each, in which not less than eight courses of study shall be required for graduation, and all public schools of a less grade shall be denominated as elementary schools. A course of study shall consist of not less than four recitations a week continued throughout the school year. (95 v. 116.)

Sec. 4007-5. [Diploma to be given to graduate of high school.] A diploma shall be granted by the board of education to any one completing the curriculum in any high school, which diploma shall state the grade of the high school issuing the said diploma as certified by the state commissioner of common schools, and shall be signed by the president and clerk of the board of education, the superintendent and the principal of the high school, if such there be, and shall bear the date of its issue.

[Certificate as to grade of school.] A certificate shall also be issued to the holder of each diploma in which shall be stated the grade of the high school, the names and extent of the studies pursued and the length of time given to each said study to be certified to in the same manner as set forth for a diploma.

[Admission without examination to professional school; exception.] And any holder of a diploma from a high school of the first grade shall be entitled to a certificate of admission without examination to any college of law, medicine, dentistry, or pharmacy in the state of Ohio, when the holder thereof shall have completed such courses in science and language as shall be prescribed by the legally constituted authorities regulating the entrance requirements of said college; except such privately endowed institutions which may require a higher standard for entrance examinations than herein provided.

[Who eligible to take examination for admission to bar or to enter professional school; exception.] And any holder of a diploma from any grade of high school or of a teacher's certificate from a county or city board of teachers' examiners, when such holder has pursued his studies under private tutorage or in an office shall be eligible to take the examination for admission to the practice of law or to take the examination prescribed to enter a college of law, medicine, dentistry or pharmacy; except such privately endowed institutions which may require a higher standard for entrance examinations than herein provided. (95 v. 116.)

**Sec. 4007-6.** [Information as to character of high school to be furnished state commissioner of common schools by clerk of board of education.] It shall be the duty of the clerk of the board of education of each district in which a high school is established and maintained to furnish to the state commissioner of common schools definite and accurate information concerning the length of time necessary for the completion of the high school curriculum or curriculums, the courses of instruction offered therein, and such other information as said commissioner may require in relation to the high school work of the district, and in the form and manner he may prescribe.

[Filed when.] Said information shall be filed not later than the first day of September, 1902, and as high schools are hereafter established or any changes made in curriculums, such establishment or changes with full information must be immediately reported as above provided.

[Certificate as to grade of school; withholding approval of curriculum.] And it shall be the duty of the said state commissioner of common schools, upon examination of the information thus filed, or after personal inspection of work done if he shall deem the same advisable, or both, to determine the grade of each such high school and to certify, under the seal of his office, to the clerk of the board of education his finding as to the grade of the high school maintained by such board of education. The said commissioner is also authorized to withhold his approval of any curriculum, when it shall appear to him that the same does not comply with the legal and reasonable requirements, and when it shall appear that any curriculum, which has already been approved, has been so modified as to change the grade of the high school, either by advancing or reducing the grade thereof, he shall certify his finding, and all diplomas issued thereafter shall bear the grade so designated by him.

[Penalty for failure to give information required by this section.] And after the first day of February, 1903, no school then maintained shall be considered a high school that has not furnished the information and received the certificate as provided above and shall not be entitled to the privileges and exceptions provided by law for high schools.. (95 v. 117.)

**Sec. 4008.** .Repealed February 22, 1887.

**Sec. 4009.** [Any board of education may establish a high school.] Any board of education may establish one or more high schools, whenever it deems the establishment of such school or schools proper or necessary for the convenience or progress of the pupils attending the same, or for the conduct and welfare of the educational interests of the district,

[Discontinuance thereof.] and such 'school or schools, when so established, shall not be discontinued under three years from the time of the establishment thereof, except by a vote of three-fourths of all the members of the board of education of the district, and at a regular meeting. (75 v. 513, § 50; R. S. of 1880; 79 v. 37; 95 v. 117.)

Sec. 4009-1. [Township high schools; management and control thereof.] Whenever a township board of education establishes and maintains a high school or high schools within the district under its control, it shall have the management and control of such school or schools with full power in respect to such school or schools to employ and dismiss teachers, and to give certificates of such employment, and for services rendered, directed to the township clerk.

[Schoolhouses, etc.] And the township board of education shall build, repair, add to and furnish the necessary schoolhouses, purchase or lease sites therefor, or rent suitable rooms, and make all other necessary provisions relative to such schools as may be deemed proper.

[Admission of pupils.] Said board of education shall have full power to regulate and control the admission of pupils from the elementary schools under its charge to such high school or high schools, according to age and attainments, and may admit adults over twenty-one years of age, and pupils from other districts on such terms and under such rules as it may adopt, and shall maintain such high school or high schools not less than twenty-eight nor more than forty weeks in any school year. (88 v. 484, § 1; 95 v. 117, § 4009-1.)

Sec. 4009-2. [Estimate of funds needed.] In townships where a high school or high schools are established, or may be established, by the township board of education, the board shall annually determine by estimate, as near as practicable, the entire amount of money necessary to be expended in the township for school and schoolhouse purposes, including the sustaining of teachers in such high schools, the prolonging of the terms of the several elementary schools of the township after the state funds shall have been exhausted, the erecting, repairing and furnishing of schoolhouses, and any other school purposes not exceeding in any one year ten mills on the dollar of the taxable property of the township, which amount shall be certified in writing to the county auditor, as required by section 3960 of the Revised Statutes of Ohio. (88 v. 484, § 2; 95 v. 117, § 4009-2.)

Sec. 4009-3. Repealed April 25, 1904.

Sec. 4009-4. Repealed April 25, 1904.

**Sec. 4009-5.** Repealed April 25, 1904.

**Sec. 4009-6.** Repealed April 25, 1904.

**Sec. 4009-7.** Repealed April 25, 1904.

**Sec. 4009-8.** Repealed April 25, 1904.

**Sec. 4009-9.** Repealed April 25, 1904.

**Sec. 4009-10.** Repealed April 25, 1904.

**Sec. 4009-11.** Repealed April 25, 1904.

**Sec. 4009-12.** Repealed April 25, 1904.

**Sec. 4009-13.** Repealed April 25, 1904.

**Sec. 4009-14.** Repealed April 25, 1904.

**(4009-15) Sec. 1.** [Joint township high schools; union of township and village or special districts for high school purposes; elections; control of high school; funds for maintenance of high school.] The boards of education of two adjoining township school districts, or of a township district and of a village or special school district situated partially or wholly within the township, may, by a majority vote of the full membership of each of said boards, unite said districts for· high school purposes and each board may submit the question of levying a tax on the property in their respective districts, for the purpose of purchasing a site and erecting a building, and may issue bonds, as is provided for in sections *thirty-nine hundred and sixty-one, thirty-nine hundred and sixty-two* and *thirty-nine hundred and sixty-three* of the Revised Statutes of Ohio, but said question of tax levy must carry in both districts before it shall become operative in either. If said boards of education have sufficient money in the treasury to purchase said site and erect said building, or if there is a suitable building in either district owned by the board of education that can be used for a high school building, it shall not be necessary to submit the proposition to a vote, and the boards are authorized to appropriate money from their funds for this purpose. Any high school so established shall be under the management of the board of education of the district in which the school house is located, and shall be free to all youth of school age within both districts, subject to such rules and regulations as may be adopted by the board of education having control of the school in regard to the qualifications in scholarship requisite for admission, such rules and regulations to be of uniform operation throughout both districts. The funds for the maintenance and support of such high school shall be provided by appropriations from the tuition or contingent funds, or both, of each district, in proportion to the total valuation of property in the respective districts, the same to be placed in a separate fund in the treasury of the board of education having control of the school and paid out by action of said board, but only for the purposes of maintaining said school. (Passed and approved April 25, 1904.)

(4009-16) Sec. 2. [Repeal of former laws relating to joint township and union high schools and substituting new law.] Joint township high school districts heretofore established as provided for in section 4009-15 to 4009-20 inclusive, of the Revised Statutes of Ohio, as they existed prior to the passage of this act, are hereby abolished and the schools in said districts shall be hereafter conducted as prov ᴜed in section 4009-15 of the Revised Statutes of Ohio, as contained herein. Boards of education of special districts for high school purposes, as provided in section 4009b of the Revised Statutes of Ohio, as it existed prior to the passage of this act, are hereby abolished and the high schools in said district shall hereafter be conducted and maintained as provided in section 4009-15 of the Revised Statutes of Ohio as herein contained. (Passed and approved April 25, 1904.)

Sec. 4010. [Schools at children's homes, orphans' asylums and infirmaries; how sustained; to be under control of trustees of institution.] The board of any district in which a children's home or orphans' asylum is or may be established by law, or in which a county infirmary is or may be established, shall, when requested by the board of trustees of such children's home, orphans' asylum or the directors of such infirmary, establish in such home, asylum or infirmary a separate school, so as to afford to the children therein, as far as practicable the advantages and privileges of a common school education; such schools at infirmaries shall be continued in operation each year until the full share of all the school funds of the district belonging to such children, on the basis of the enumeration, is expended, and at such homes and asylums not less than forty-four weeks, if the distributive share of school funds to which such school at any such home or asylum is entitled by the enumeration of children in the institution is not sufficient to continue the schools the length of time hereby required, the deficiency shall be paid out of the funds of the institution; all schools so established in any such home, asylum or infirmary, shall be under the control and management of the respective boards of trustees or directors of such institution, which boards of trustees or directors shall, in the control and management of such schools, as far as practicable, be subject to the same laws that boards of education and other school officers are who have charge of the common schools of such district; in the establishment of such schools the commissioners of the county in which such children's home, orphans' asylum or county infirmary is established, shall provide the necessary school room or rooms, furniture, fuel, apparatus and books, the cost of which furniture, fuel, apparatus and books for the schools of such homes, infirmaries and asylums, shall be paid out of the funds provided for such institutions; and the board of education shall incur no expense in supporting such schools. (1883, April 19; 80 v. 217; Rev. Stat. 1880; 75 v. 513, § 50; 76 v. 75, § 1.)

Sec. 4011. [Youth may be sent to charity school at Zanesville.] The board of education of the city of Zanesville may contract with the trustees having the management of any fund which has been provided by gift, devise, or bequest for the establishment or support of a school or schools for poor children therein, for the admission to any such school of children resident in the city, and pay to such trustees out of the school funds under its control, such tuition fee as may be agreed upon for each scholar so admitted, but not entitled to admission according to the terms of such gift, devise or bequest, and also provide for such right of visitation or control of such school or schools by the board as may be agreed upon; such school or schools shall be kept at the least equal in grade and efficiency to the corresponding public schools of the state, and every such contract shall expire in three years from the time of its execution, unless renewed or extended by agreement; but this section shall in no manner apply to any school or schools supported or controlled by any church, congregation, sect or religious denomination or association of any kind. (75 v. 530, § 1.)

Sec. 4012. [Evening schools.] In any township, special, village, or city district, or part thereof, parents or guardians of youth of school age may petition the board of education to organize an evening school. The petition shall contain the names of not less than twenty-five youth of school age who will attend such school, and who for reasons satisfactory to the board are prevented from attending day school. Upon receiving such petition the board of education shall provide and furnish a suitable room for the evening school and employ a competent person who holds a regularly issued teacher's certificate, to teach it. Such board may discontinue any such evening school, when the average evening attendance for any month falls below twelve. (90 v. 116; 72 v. 29, § 51; S. & C. 1359.)

Sec. 4012a. [Attendance by persons more than twenty-one years old.] Any person more than twenty-one years old may be permitted to attend evening school upon such terms and upon payment of such tuition as the board of education may prescribe. (90 v. 117.)

Sec. 4013. [Who may attend school free; crediting school tax on tuition of non-resident pupils; assignment of pupils.] The schools of each district shall be free to all youth between six and twenty-one years of age, who are children, wards or apprentices of actual residents of the district, including children of proper age who are or may ·be inmates of a county or district children's home located in any such school district, at the discretion of the board of education of said school district; provided that all youth of school age living apart from their parents or guardians and who work to support themselves by their own labor, shall be entitled to attend school free in the district in which they are employed. Each board of education may admit other persons upon such terms or upon the payment of such tuition as it may prescribe; provided, that when a youth between the age of six and twenty-one years or the parent of such youth owns property in a school district in which he does not reside and said youth attends the schools of said district, the amount of school tax paid on such property shall be credited on the tuition of said pupil. Boards of education are authorized to make such an assignment of the youth of their respective districts.to the schools established by them as will in their opinion best promote the interests of education in their districts. (Passed and approved April 25, 1904.)

Sec. 4014. [Suspension and expulsion of pupils.] No pupil shall be suspended from school by a superintendent or teacher except for such time as may be necessary to convene the board of education, and no pupil shall be expelled except by a vote of two-thirds of such board, and not until the parent or guardian of the offending pupil has been notified of the proposed expulsion, and permitted to be heard against the same; and no pupil shall be suspended or expelled from any school beyond the current term thereof. (89 v. 96; 70 v. 195, § 71.)

Sec. 4015. [Legal holidays; school may be dismissed on.] Teachers employed in the public schools may dismiss their schools, without forfeiture of pay, on the first day of January, the twenty-second day of February, the thirtieth day of May, the fourth day of July, the first Monday in September, the twenty-fifth day of December, and on the day set apart by proclamation of the President of the United States or Governor of this state as a day of fast, thanksgiving or mourning. (Passed and approved April 25, 1904.)

(4015-1) Sec. 1. [Arbor day.] That the governor of said state shall, not later than April appoint and set apart one day in the spring season of each year, as the day on which those in charge of the public schools and institutions of learning under state control, or state patronage, shall, for at least two hours, give information to the pupils and students concerning the value and interest of forestry, and the duty of the public to protect the birds thereof, and also for planting forest trees. Said day shall be known as Arbor day. (79 v. 243; 95 v. 38.)

**Sec. 4016.** [**School year, month, and week.**] The school year shall begin on the first day of September of each year, and close on the thirty-first day of August of the succeeding year; and a school week will consist of five days, and a school month of four school weeks. (70 v. 215, § 70; 72 v. 181, § 6.)

**Sec. 4017.** [**Control of schools vested in boards; appointees; salaries.**] Each board of education shall have the management and control of all of the public schools of whatever name or character in the district, with full power to appoint a superintendent of the public schools, truant officers, and janitors and fix their salaries; and, if deemed essential for the best interests of the schools of the district, the board may, under proper rules and regulations, appoint a superintendent of buildings, and such other employes as the board may deem necessary, and fix their salaries;

[**Salaries of teachers; paid during epidemic; appointments of former teachers.**] And each board shall fix the salaries of all teachers, which salaries may be increased, but shall not be diminished during the term for which the appointment is made, and teachers shall be paid for all time lost when the schools in which they are employed are closed owing to an epidemic or other public calamity, but no person shall be appointed as a teacher for a term longer than four school years, nor for a less term than one year except to fill an unexpired term, the term to begin within four months of the date of the appointment, provided that in making appointments teachers in the actual employ of the board shall be first considered before new teachers are chosen in their stead.

[**School director in city districts; appointment; power; duties; salary; removal.**] A board of education in a city district may, at its discretion, elect a director of schools, who shall serve as such for the term of two years, unless earlier removed as hereinafter provided, and any vacancy in this office shall be filled for the unexpired term of such director of schools. As director of schools, he shall execute for the board of education, in the name of the school district, its contracts and obligations, except that bonds issued shall be signed by the president of the board, and attested by the clerk. He shall see that all contracts made by or with said board shall be fully and faithfully performed. Except teachers, assistant teachers, supervisors, principals, superintendent of instruction, clerk of the board of education, he shall have the appointment subject to the approval and confirmation of the board of all employes, and may discharge the same.

104     OHIO SCHOOL LAWS.

Ch. 9.    Schools and Attendance Enforced.

He shall have the care and custody of all property of the school district, real and personal, except moneys. He shall oversee the construction of buildings, in the process of erection, and the repairs of the same. He shall advertise for bids and purchase all supplies and equipments authorized by the board. He shall report to the board monthly, and oftener if required, as to all matters under his supervision, and report to the board a statement of its accounts, exhibiting the revenues, receipts, disbursements, assets and liabilities of the board, the sources from which the revenues and funds are derived, and in what manner the same have been disbursed. He shall keep accurate account of taxes levied for school purposes, and all moneys due to, received and disbursed by the board; also, of all assets and liabilities and all appropriations made by the board, and shall receive and preserve all vouchers for payments and disbursements made to or by the board. He shall issue all warrants for the payment of money from the school fund, but no warrant shall be issued for the payment of any claim until such claim has been approved by the board, and the pay-roll for teachers, assistant teachers and supervisors shall be counter-signed by the superintendent of instruction. He shall attend all meetings of the board, and perform all of its executive functions not hereinbefore excepted in defining the duties of the director of schools. He shall devote such portion of his time to the duties of his office as may be required by the board of education at or before his election, and shall give a bond for the faithful discharge of his duties as director of schools, in such sum as the board may determine, his sureties to be approved by the board, which bond shall be deposited with the president of the board within ten days after his appointment. He shall receive such compensation, not exceeding $5,000 per annum, as may be fixed by the board before his election, which compensation shall not be changed during his term of office. The board of education may, at any time, by a two-thirds vote for cause, suspend or remove the director of schools, but such suspension or removal shall not be made unless the charges are preferred in writing, and an opportunity afforded to bring all offered pertinent testimony in as a defense, which testimony shall be received and considered by the board and made a part of the records.

[Contract with employes; resignations; dismissals.] Upon the appointment of any person to any position under the control of the board of education, it shall be the duty of the clerk promptly to notify such person verbally or in writing of the appointment and the conditions thereof and request and secure from such person within a reasonable time to be determined by the board, his acceptance or rejection of the appointment thus made, and an acceptance of such appointment within the time thus determined shall constitute a contract binding both parties thereto until such time as it may be dissolved, shall expire, or the appointee be dismissed for cause. All resignations or requests for release from contract by teachers, superintendents, or employes, shall be promptly considered by the board, but no resignation or release shall become effective except by consent of the board. Each board may dismiss any appointee or teacher for inefficiency, neglect of duty, immorality, or improper conduct; but no teacher shall be dismissed by any board unless the charges are first reduced to writing and an opportunity be given for defence before the board, or a committee thereof, and a majority of the full membership of the board vote upon roll call in favor of such dismissal. (Passed and approved April 25, 1904.)

Sec. 4017a. [Superintendents and teachers in city districts; appointment and term of office; duties.] The board of education in each city school district shall appoint a suitable person to act as superintendent of the public schools of the district, for a term not longer than five school years, the term to begin within four months of such appointment. Provided, that the present board of education shall not employ a superintendent for a term to exceed[extend]beyond the school year ending August 31, 1905. Said superintendent shall, upon his acceptance of the appointment, become thereby empowered to appoint, subject to the approval and confirmation of the board, all the teachers, and he may for cause suspend any person thus appointed until the board or a committee of the board may consider such suspension, but no one shall be dismissed by the board except as provided in section 4017 of the Revised Statutes of Ohio; provided that any city board of education may, upon a three-fourths vote of its full membership, re-employ any teacher whom the superintendent refuses to appoint. Said superintendent shall visit the schools under his charge, direct and assist teachers in the performance of their duties, classify and control the promotion of pupils, and perform such other duties as the board may determine. He shall report to the board of education annually, and oftener if required, as to all matters under his supervision, and may be required by the board to attend any and all of its meetings and may take part in its deliberations but shall not vote.

[Superintendent and teachers in other districts; appointment and term of office; duties.] The board of education of each village, township and special school district may appoint a suitable person to act as superintendent, and to employ the teachers of the public schools of the district, for a term not longer than three school years, the term to begin within four months of the date of the appointment; but nothing herein shall be construed as preventing two or more districts uniting and appointing the same person as superintendent. Provided, that the present board of education shall not employ a superintendent or teacher for a term to extend beyond the school year ending August 31, 1905. The superintendent shall, upon his acceptance of the appointment, become thereby empowered to visit the schools under his charge, direct and assist teachers in the performance of their duties, classify and control the promotion of pupils, and perform such other duties as the board may determine. He shall report to the board of education annually, and oftener if required, as to all matters under his supervision, and may be required by the board to attend any and all of its meetings, and may take part in its deliberations, but shall not vote; provided, however, that any board may permit or require the superintendent to devote a portion of his time to teaching, subject to the rules and regulations of said board. (Passed and approved April 25, 1904.)

Sec. 4018. [Teachers, duties of; janitor work not required.] All teachers shall exercise reasonable care in regard to all school property, apparatus, and supplies intrusted to their keeping. They shall strive to guard the health and physical welfare of the pupils in their schools, give efficient instruction in the studies pursued, and endeavor to maintain and preserve good discipline over all the pupils under their charge. Provided, however, that no teacher shall be required by any board to do the janitor work of any school room or building, except as mutually agreed by special contract, and for compensation in addition to that received by him for his services as teacher. (Passed and approved April 25, 1904.)

Sec. 4019. [Teachers dismissed for insufficient cause may institute suit.] If the board of education of any district dismiss any teacher for any frivolous or insufficient reason, such teacher may bring suit against such district, and if, on the trial of the cause, a judgment be obtained against the district, the board thereof shall direct the clerk to issue an order upon the treasurer for the sum so found due to the person entitled thereto, to pay the same out of any money in his hands belonging to such district, and applicable to the payment of teachers; and in such suits process may be served on the clerk of the district, and service upon his [him] shall be sufficient. (Passed and approved April 25, 1904.)

Sec. 4020.     Repealed, 88 v. 568, § 10.

(4020-1) Sec. 1. (Superseded by sec. 4020-10—4020-14, but not repealed. Enacted, 88 v. 568.)

(4020-2) Sec. 2. (Superseded by sec. 4020-10—4020-14, but not repealed.)

**(4020-3) Sec. 3.** (Superseded by sec. 4020-10—4020-14, but not repealed.)

**(4020-4) Sec. 4.** (Superseded by sec. 4020-10—4020-14, but not repealed.)

**(4020-5) Sec. 5.** (Superseded by sec. 4020-10—4020-14, but not repealed.)

**(4020-6) Sec. 6.** (Superseded by sec. 4020-10—4020-14, but not repealed.)

**(4020-7) Sec. 7.** (Superseded by sec. 4020-10—4020-14, but not repealed.)

**(4020-8) Sec. 8.** (Superseded by sec. 4020-10—4020-14, but not repealed.)

**(4020-9) Sec. 9.** (Superseded by sec. 4020-10—4020-14, but not repealed. Enacted, 88 v. 568.)

TEXT-BOOK LAW.

**(4020-10) Sec. 1.** [Filing and preservation of copies and prices of school books.] Any publisher or publishers of school books in the United States desiring to offer school books for use by pupils in the common schools of Ohio as hereinafter provided, shall, before such books may be lawfully adopted and purchased by any school board in this state, file in the office of the state commissioner of common schools a copy of each book proposed to be so offered, together with the published list wholesale price thereof, and no revised edition of any such book shall be used in the common schools until a copy of such revised edition shall have been filed in the office of the said commissioner together with the published list wholesale price thereof. The said commissioner shall carefully preserve in his office all such copies of books and the prices thereof so filed. (92 v. 282.)

**(4020-11) Sec. 2.** [Maximum price; notification of publisher.] Whenever and so often as any book and the price thereof shall be so filed in the commissioner's office as provided in section 1, a commission consisting of the governor, the secretary of state and the state commissioner of common schools shall immediately fix the maximum price at which such books may be sold to or purchased by boards of education as hereinafter provided, which maximum price so fixed on any book shall not exceed seventy-five per cent. of the published list wholesale price thereof, and the state commissioner of common schools shall immediately notify the publisher of such books so filed, of the maximum price so fixed. If the publisher so notified, shall notify the commissioner in writing that he accepts the price so fixed, and shall agree in writing to furnish such book during a period of five years at the price so fixed, such written acceptance and agreement shall entitle said publisher to offer said book so filed for sale to said board of education for use by the pupil under the terms of this act. (92 v. 282.)

(4020-12) **Sec. 3.** [Notices to boards; legality dependent on compliance.] The said commissioner shall during the first half of the month of June, 1896, and during the first half of the month of June in each year thereafter, furnish to each board of education the names and addresses of all publishers who shall have during the year ending on the first day of said month of June in each year, agreed in writing to furnish their publications upon the terms provided in this act. And it shall not be lawful for any board of education to adopt or cause to be used in the common schools any book whose publisher shall not have complied, as to said book, with the provisions of this act. (92 v. 282.)

(4020-13) **Sec. 4.** [Procedure upon violation of agreement by publisher.] If any publisher who shall have agreed in writing to furnish books as provided in this act, shall fail or refuse to furnish such books adopted as herein provided to any board of education or its authorized agent upon the terms as herein provided, it shall be the duty of said board at once to notify the said commission of such failure or refusal, and the commission shall at once cause an investigation of such charge to be made, and if the same is found to be true the commission shall at once notify said publisher and each board of education in the state that said book shall not hereafter be adopted and purchased by boards of education; and said publisher shall forfeit and pay to the state of Ohio five hundred dollars for each failure, to be recovered in the name of the state, in an action to be brought by the attorney general, in the court of common pleas of Franklin county, or in any other proper court or in any other place where service can be made, and the amount, when collected, shall be paid into the state treasury to the credit of the common school fund of the state. (92 v. 282.)

(4020-14) **Sec. 5.** [Studies, etc.; shipment of books, etc.; sale to pupils; purchase from pupils; free books.] Each board of education on receiving the statements, above mentioned, from said commissioner, shall on the third Monday in August thereafter meet, and at such meeting, or at an adjourned meeting within two weeks after said Monday, determine by a majority vote of all members elected the studies to be pursued and which of said text-books so filed shall be used in the schools under its control, but no text-books so adopted shall be changed, nor any part thereof altered or revised, nor shall any other text-book be substituted therefor for five years after the date of the selection and adoption thereof without the consent of three-fourths of all the members elected, given at a regular meeting; and each board of education shall cause it to be ascertained, and at regular meetings in April and August shall determine which, and the number of each of said books the schools under its charge shall require, until the next regular meetings in April and August, and shall cause an order to be drawn for the amount in favor of the clerk of the board of education, payable out of the contingent fund; and said clerk shall at once order said books so agreed upon by the board, of the publisher, and the publisher, on the receipt of such order, shall ship such books to said clerk without delay, and the clerk shall forthwith examine such books, and, if found right and, in accordance with said order, remit the amount to said publisher, and the board of education shall pay all charges for the transportation of such books, out of the school contingent fund; but if said boards of education can, at any time, secure of the publishers books at a price less than said maximum price, it shall be its duty so to do, and may without unnecessary delay, make effort to secure such lower price before adopting any particular text-book. Each board of education shall have power to, and shall make all necessary provisions and arrangements to place the books so purchased within easy reach of and accessible to all the pupils in their district, and for that purpose may make such contracts, and take such security as they may deem necessary, for the custody, care and sale of such books and accounting for the proceeds; but not to exceed ten per cent. of the cost price shall be paid therefor, and said books shall be sold to the pupils of school age in the district, at the price paid the publisher, and not to exceed ten per cent. therefor added, and the proceeds of such sale shall be paid into the contingent fund of such district, and whoever receives said books from the board of education for sale as aforesaid to the pupils, and fails to account honestly and fully for the same, or for the proceeds to the board of education when required, shall be guilty of embezzlement and punished accordingly. Provided, however, boards of education may contract with local retail dealers to furnish said books at prices above specified, the said board being still responsible to the publishers for all books purchased by the said board of education. And when pupils remove from any district, and have text-books of the kind adopted in such district, and not being of the kind adopted in the district to which they remove, and wish to dispose of the same, the board of the district from which they remove, when requested, shall purchase the same at the fair value thereof, and resell the same as other books; and nothing in this act shall prevent the board of education from furnishing free books to pupils as provided by law. That for the purpose of carrying into effect the foregoing provisions of this act, and paying the expenses incident thereto, there be and is hereby appropriated out of any money in the state treasury, to the credit of the general revenue fund, not otherwise appropriated, the sum of five hundred dollars, to be disbursed and paid on the allowance and order of said commissioner. (92 v. 282.)

(4020-15) **Sec. 1.** [Purchase of Howe's Historical Collections of Ohio for schools; payment.] The boards of education of city, village, township and special school districts in the state be and are hereby authorized to purchase for each school in either of said districts one copy of "Howe's Historical Collections of Ohio," to be used as a reference book in the study of the history of the state; provided that said book shall be in quality, style, binding and finish equal to the present published edition of said work, bound in half Russia leather, and shall cost not to exceed three dollars per volume, for each set of three volumes; provided further, that the price of the books and cost of transportation shall be paid out of the contingent fund of such district. (89 v. 241.)

(4020-16) **Sec. 2.** [Care and preservation of books.] Said books, during the vacations of schools, or when the schools are not in session, shall be taken care of in the same manner that maps, globes, dictionaries and other school apparatus are cared for and preserved. (89 v. 241.)

(4020-17) **Sec. 1.** [Physical training in city schools.] Physical training shall be included in the branches to be regularly taught in public schools in city school districts, and in all educational institutions supported wholly or in part by money received from the state, and it shall be the duty of the boards of education of city school districts, and boards of such educational institutions to make provisions in the schools and institutions under their jurisdiction for teaching of physical training, and to adopt such methods as shall adapt the same to the capacity of the pupils in the various grades therein; and other boards may make such provisions. The curriculum in all normal schools of this state shall contain a regular course on physical education. (Passed and approved April 25, 1904.)

(4020-18) **Sec. 1.** [Manual training departments, commercial departments and kindergartens authorized.] Any board of education may establish and maintain manual training and commercial departments and kindergartens in connection with the public school system and pay the expenses of establishing and maintaining said schools from the public school funds, in the same manner and from the same funds as other school expenses are paid. (Passed and approved April 25, 1904.)

(4020-19) Sec. 1.    Repealed April 25, 1904.

(4020-20) Sec. 2.    Repealed April 25, 1904.

(4020-21) Sec. 1.    Repealed April 25, 1904.

(4020-22) Sec. 2.    Repealed April 25, 1904.`

(4020-23) Sec. 1.    [Instruction in the effects of alcholic drinks and other narcotics; made a regular branch of study.]    The nature of alcoholic drinks and other narcotics, and their effects on the human system, in connection with the various divisions of physiology and hygiene, shall be included in the branches to be regularly taught in the common schools of' the state, and in all educational institutions supported wholly, or in part, by money from the state; and it shall be the duty of boards of education, and boards of such educational institutions to make suitable provisions for this instruction in the schools and institutions under their respective jurisdiction, giving definite time and place for this branch in the regular course of study; and to adopt such methods as will adapt the same to the capacity of pupils in the various grades; and to corresponding classes as found in ungraded schools; the same tests for promotion shall be required in this as in other branches.    (94 v. 396; 85 v. 213.)

(4020-24) Sec. 2.    [Instruction required in teachers' institutes and teachers' training schools; teachers' certificate must contain; enforcement of law.]    In all teachers' institutes, also in all normal schools and teachers' training classes which shall hereafter be established by the state, adequate time and attention shall be given to instruction in the best methods of teaching this branch.    No certificate shall be granted to any person to teach in the common schools or in any educational institution supported as aforesaid who does not pass a satisfactory examination on this subject, and the best methods of teaching the same.    It shall be the duty of the state commissioner of common schools to see that the provisions in this section relating to county teachers' institutes, and schools and classes by whatever name hereafter established for training teachers, and the examination of teachers, are carried out; and said commissioner shall, each year, make full report of the enforcement of said section in connection with his annual report.    (94 v. 396; 85 v. 213.)

(4020-25) **Sec. 3.** [Penalty for failure to enforce law; jurisdic-. tion of courts.] Any school official, or any employe in any way concerned, in the enforcement of the act, who wilfully refuses or neglects to provide for, or to give the instruction required by this act, shall be fined, and shall pay for each offense the sum of twenty-five dollars. Mayors, justices of the peace and probate judges shall have concurrent jurisdiction with the common pleas court to try the offenses described in this act and all fines, or penalties, collected under this act shall be paid into the general county school fund of the county in which such fine or penalty was collected. (94 v. 396; 85 v. 213.)

**Sec. 4021.** [German language taught, ·how.] Boards of education are authorized to provide for the teaching of the German language in the elementary and high schools of the district over which they have control, but said language shall only be taught in addition to, and as auxiliary to, the English language; all the common branches in the public schools shall be taught in the English language. (Passed and approved April 25, 1904.)

**Sec. 4022.** [Pupils may be sent from one district to another.] The board of any district may contract with the board of any other district for the admission of pupils into any school in such other district, on such terms as may be agreed upon by such boards; and the expense so incurred shall be paid out of the school funds of the district sending such pupils. (73 v. 243, § 64.)

**Sec. 4022a.** [Attendance when pupils live over one and one-half miles from school; payment of tuition, how computed.] When pupils live more than one and one-half miles from the school to which they are assigned in the district in which they reside, they are entitled to attend a nearer school in the same district, or if there be no nearer school in said district, they may attend the nearest school in another school district, in all grades below the high school, and in such cases the board of education of the district in which they reside shall be compelled to pay the tuition of such pupils without an agreement to that effect, but a board of education shall not collect tuition for attendance as provided herein until after notice of such attendance shall have been given to the board of education of the district where the pupils reside, but nothing contained herein shall be construed to require the consent of the board of education of the district where the pupils reside, to such attendance; said tuition shall be paid from either the tuition or the contingent funds and the amount per capita shall be ascertained by dividing the total expenses of conducting the elementary schools of the district attended, exclusive of permanent improvements and repairs, by the total enrollment in the elementary schools of the district, said amount to be computed by the month and an attendance any part of a month shall create a liability for the whole month. When the schools of a district are centralized or transportation of pupils provided, the provisions of this section shall not apply. (Passed and approved April 25, 1904.)

COMPULSORY EDUCATION.

**Sec. 4022-1.** [In what branches children must be taught; necessary time of attendance; excuse; appeal in case of refusal to excuse.] All parents, guardians and other persons who have care of children, shall instruct them, or cause them to be instructed in reading, spelling, writing, English grammar, geography and arithmetic. Every parent, guardian or other person having charge of any child between the ages of eight and fourteen years shall send such child to a public, private or parochial school, for the full time that the school attended is in session, which shall in no case be for less than twenty-four weeks, and said attendance shall begin within the first week of the school term, unless the child is excused from such attendance by the superintendent of the public schools, in city or other districts having such superintendent, or by the clerk of the board of education in village, special and township districts not having such superintendent, or by the principal of the private or parochial school, upon satisfactory showing, either that the bodily or mental condition of the child does not permit of its attendance at school, or that the child is being instructed at home by a person qualified, in the opinion of the superintendent of schools in city or other districts having such superintendent, or the clerk of the board of education in special, village and township districts not having such superintendent, to teach the branches named in this section. In case such superintendent, principal or clerk refuse to excuse a child from attendance at school, an appeal may be taken from such decision to the probate judge of the county, upon the giving of a bond, within ten days after such refusal, to the approval of said judge, to pay all the cost of the appeal, and the decision of the probate judge in the matter shall be final. All children between the ages of fourteen and sixteen years, not engaged in some regular employment, shall attend school for the full term the schools of the district in which they reside are in session during the school year, unless excused for [the] reasons above named. Any parent, guardian, or other person, having care of a child between the ages of eight and fourteen years, who shall, in violation of the provisions of this section, fail to place such child in school at the commencement of the annual school term within the time prescribed in this section, shall upon conviction, be fined not less than five dollars nor more than twenty dollars. And upon the failure or refusal of any such parent, guardian, or other person to pay said fine, then said parent, guardian, or other person shall be imprisoned in the county jail not less than ten days nor more than thirty days. (95 v. 615; 90 v. 285; 86 v. 333; 89 v. 389; 87 v. 316, 143.)

Sec. 4022-2. [Employment of children under sixteen years of age; penalty.] No child under sixteen years of age shall be employed or be in the employment of any person, company or corporation during the school term and while the public schools are in session, unless such child shall present to such person, company or corporation an age and schooling certificate herein provided for. An age and schooling certificate shall be approved only by the superintendent of schools, or by a person authorized by him, in city or other districts having such superintendent, or by the clerk of the board of education in village, special and township districts not having such superintendent, upon a satisfactory proof of the age of such minor and that he has successfully completed the studies enumerated in section 4022-1 of the Revised Statutes of Ohio; or if between the ages of fourteen and sixteen years, a knowledge of his or her ability to read and write legibly the English language. The age and schooling certificate shall be formulated by the state commissioner of common schools and the same furnished, in blank, by the clerk of the board of education. Every person, company or corporation employing any child under sixteen years of age, shall exact the age and schooling certificate prescribed in this section, as a condition of employment and shall keep the same on file, and shall upon request of the truant officer herein provided for, permit him to examine such age and schooling certificate. Any person, company or corporation, employing any minor contrary to the provisions of this section shall be fined not less than twenty-five nor more than fifty dollars. (April 25, 1904; 95 v. 616; 90 v. 285; 86 v. 334, § 2.)

Sec. 4022-3. [Attendance of minors in certain cases; employment of such minors; penalty.] All minors over the age of fourteen and under the age of sixteen years, who cannot read and write the English language shall be required to attend school as provided in section 4022-1 of the Revised Statutes of Ohio and all the provisions of said section shall apply to said minors; provided, that such attendance shall not be required of such minors after they have secured a certificate from the superintendent of schools, in districts having superintendents or the clerk of the board of education in districts not having superintendents, that they can read and write the English language. No person, company or corporation shall employ any such minor during the time schools are in session, or having such minor in their employ shall immediately cease such employment, upon notice from the truant officer who is hereinafter provided for. Every person, company or corporation violating the provisions of this section shall be fined not less than twenty-five nor more than fifty dollars. (95 v. 617; 90 v. 286; 86 v. 334; §§ 3, 4; 87 v. 143.)

Sec. 4022-4. [Juvenile disorderly persons.] Every child between the ages of eight and fourteen years, and every child between the ages of fourteen and sixteen years unable to read and write the English language, or not engaged in some regular employment, who is an habitual truant from school, or who absents itself habitually from school, or who, while in attendance at any public, private or parochial school, is incorrigible, vicious or immoral in conduct, or who habitually wanders about the streets and public places during school hours having no business or lawful occupation, shall be deemed a juvenile disorderly person, and be subject to the provisions of this act. (95 v. 617; 90 v. 286; 86 v. 335, § 5; 90 v. 57; 88 v. 136.)

Sec. 4022-5. [Truant officers; powers and duties.] To aid in the enforcement of this act, truant officers shall be appointed and employed as follows: In city districts the board of education shall appoint and employ one or more truant officers; in special, village and township districts the board of education shall appoint a constable or other person as truant officer. The compensation of the truant officer shall be fixed and paid by the board appointing him. The truant officer shall be vested with police powers, the authority to serve warrants, and shall have authority to enter workshops, factories, stores and all other places where children may be employed, and do whatever may be necessary, in the way of investigation or otherwise, to enforce this act; he is also authorized to take into custody the person of any youth between eight and fourteen years of age, or between fourteen and sixteen years of age when not regularly employed or when unable to read and write the English language, who is not attending school, and shall conduct said youth to the school he has been attending, or which he should rightfully attend. The truant officer shall institute proceedings against any officer, parent, guardian, person or corporation violating any provisions of this act, and shall otherwise discharge the duties described in this act, and perform such other services as the superintendent of schools or the board of education may deem necessary to preserve the morals and secure the good conduct of school children, and to enforce this act. The truant officer shall keep a record of his transactions for the inspection and information of the superintendent of the schools and the board of education; and he shall make daily reports to the superintendent of schools during the school term in districts having superintendents, and to the clerk of the board of education in districts not having superintendents, as often as required by him. Suitable blanks for the use of the truant officer shall be provided by the clerk of the board of education. (95 v. 617; 90 v. 286; 86 v. 335, § 6; 87 v. 325, 144.)

Sec. 4022-6. [Report of principal and teachers.] It shall be the duty of all principals and teachers of all schools, public, private and parochial, to report to the clerk of the board of education of the city, special, village or township district in which the schools are situated, the names, ages and residences of all pupils in attendance at their schools, together with such other facts as said clerk may require in order to facilitate the carrying out of the provisions of this act, and the clerk shall furnish blanks for such purpose, and such report shall be made during the last week of each month from September to June inclusive of each year. It shall be the further duty of such principals and teachers to report to the truant officer, the superintendent of public schools, or the clerk of the board of education, all cases of truancy or incorrigibility in their respective schools as soon after these offenses have been committed as practicable. (95 v. 618; 90 v. 287.)

Sec. 4022-7. [Proceedings in case of truancy; penalties.] On the request of the superintendent of schools or the board of education, or when it otherwise comes to his notice, the truant officer shall examine into any case of truancy within his district, and warn the truant and his parents, guardian or other person in charge, in writing, of the final consequences of truancy if persisted in. When any child between the ages of eight and fourteen years, or any child between the ages of fourteen and sixteen years who cannot read and write the English language or who is not regularly employed, is not attending school, in violation of the provisions of this act, the truant officer shall notify the parent, guardian or other person in charge of such child, of the fact, and require such parent, guardian or other person in charge, to cause the child to attend some recognized school within two days from the date of the notice; and it shall be the duty of the parent, guardian or other person in charge of the child, so to cause its attendance at some recognized school. Upon failure to do so, the truant officer shall make complaint against the parent, guardian or other person in charge of the child, in any court of competent jurisdiction in the city, special, village or township district in which the offense occurs, for such failure, and upon conviction, the parent, guardian or other person in charge, shall be fined not less than five dollars nor more than twenty dollars, or the court may in its discretion, require the person so convicted to give a bond in the penal sum of one hundred dollars, with sureties to the approval of the court, conditioned that he or she will cause the child under his or her charge to attend some recognized school within two days, thereafter and to remain at such school during the term prescribed by law; and upon the failure or refusal of any such parent, guardian or other person to pay said fine and costs or furnish said bond according to the order of the court, then said parent, guardian or other person shall be imprisoned in the county jail not less than ten days nor more than thirty days. (95 v. 618; 90 v. 287; 86 v. 336, § § 8, 9.)

**Sec. 4022-8.** [Proceedings against juvenile disorderly persons.] If the parent, guardian or other person in charge of any child shall, upon the complaint under the last section for failure to cause the child to attend a recognized school prove inability to do so, then he or she shall be discharged, and thereupon the truant officer shall make complaint that the child is a juvenile disorderly person within the meaning of section 4022-4 of the Revised Statutes of Ohio. If such complaint be made before any mayor, justice of the peace, or police judge, it shall be certified by such magistrate to the probate judge. The probate judge shall hear such complaint, and if he determine that the child is a juvenile disorderly person within the meaning of section 4022-4 of the Revised Statutes of Ohio he shall commit the child if under ten years of age, and eligible for admission thereto, to a children's home, or if not eligible, then to a house of refuge if there be one in the county or to the boys' industrial school or the girls' industrial home, or to some other juvenile reformatory. No child over ten years of age shall be committed to a county children's home, and any child committed to a children's home, may on request of the trustees of such home and it being shown that it is vicious and incorrigible, be transferred by the probate judge to the boys' industrial school or the girls' industrial home. A child committed to any juvenile reformatory under this section, shall not be detained there beyond the age of sixteen years and may be discharged sooner by the trustees under the restrictions applicable to other inmates. Any order of commitment to a juvenile reformatory may be suspended, in the discretion of the probate judge, for such time as the child may regularly attend school and properly conduct itself. The expense incurred in the transportation of a child to a juvenile reformatory and the costs in the case in which the order of commitment is made, or the child discharged, or in which judgment is suspended, shall be paid by the county where the offense was committed, after the manner provided in section 759 of the Revised Statutes of Ohio. Provided, further, that if for any cause the parent, guardian or other person in charge of any juvenile disorderly person as defined in section 4022-4 of the Revised Statutes of Ohio shall fail to cause such juvenile disorderly person to attend a school, then complaint against such juvenile disorderly person shall be made, heard and determined in like manner as provided in case the parent proves inability to cause such juvenile disorderly person to attend school. (95 v. 619; 90 v. 288; 86 v. 337, § 8; 87 v. 325, 144.)

Sec. 4022-9. [Relief to enable child to attend school required time.] When any truant officer is satisfied that any child, compelled to attend school by the provisions of this act, is unable to attend school because absolutely required to work, at home or elsewhere, in order to support itself or help support or care for others legally entitled to its services, who are unable to support or care for themselves, the truant officer shall report the case to the authorities charged with the relief of the poor, and it shall be the duty of said officers to afford such relief as will enable the child to attend school the time each year required under this act. Such child shall not be considered or declared a pauper by reason of the acceptance of the relief herein provided for. In case the child, or its parents or guardian, refuse or neglect to take advantage of the provisions thus made for its instruction, such child may be committed to a children's home or a juvenile reformatory, as provided for in section 4022-8 of the Revised Statutes of Ohio. In all cases where relief is necessary it shall be the duty of the board of education to furnish text books free of charge and said board may furnish any further relief it may deem necessary, the expenses incident to furnishing said books and the relief to be paid from the contingent funds of the school district. (95 v. 620; 90 v. 289; 86 v. 337, § 8.)

Sec. 4022-10. [As to institution of deaf and dumb or institution for blind.] The provisions of this act shall apply to children entitled under existing statutes, to attend school at the institution for the deaf and dumb or the institution for the blind, so far as the same are properly enforcible. Truant officers shall, within sixty days after the passage of this act, and annually between the first day of July and the first day of August, report to the probate judge of their respective counties the names, ages and residence of all such children between the ages of eight and eighteen years, with the names and postoffice address of their parents, guardians or the persons in charge of them; also a statement whether the parents, guardians or person in charge of each child is able to educate and is educating the child, or whether the interests of the child will be promoted by sending it to one of the state institutions mentioned. Upon information thus or otherwise obtained, the probate judge may fix a time when he will hear the question whether any such child shall be required to be sent for instruction to one of the state institutions mentioned, and he shall thereupon issue a warrant to the proper truant officer or some other suitable person, to bring the child before such judge at his office at the time fixed for the hearing; and shall also issue an order on the parents, guardian or person in charge of the child to appear before him at such hearing, a copy of which order, in writing, shall be served personally on the proper person by the truant officer or other person ordered to bring the child before the judge. If, on the hearing, the probate judge is satisfied that the child is not being properly educated at home, and will be benefited by attendance at one of the state institutions mentioned, and is a suitable person to receive instruction therein, he may send or commit such child to such institution. The cost of such hearing, and the transportation of the child to such institution shall be paid by the county after the manner provided, where a child is committed to a state reformatory under section 4022-8 of the Revised Statutes of Ohio; provided nothing in this section contained shall be construed to require the trustees of either of the state institutions mentioned, to receive any child not a suitable subject to be received and instructed therein, under the laws, rules and regulations governing such institutions. (95 v. 620; 90 v. 289; 86 v. 337, § 8.)

Sec. 4022-11. [Penalties; jurisdiction; violations by corporations; disposition of fines collected; employment of attorney; compensation.] Any officer, principal, teacher or other person mentioned in this act, neglecting to perform any duty imposed upon him by this act, shall be fined not less than twenty-five dollars nor more than fifty dollars for each offense. Any officer or agent of any corporation violating any provision of this act, who participates or acquiesces in or is cognizant of such violation, shall be fined not less than twenty-five dollars nor more than fifty dollars. Any person who violates any provision of this act for which a penalty is not elsewhere in this act provided, shall be fined not more than fifty dollars. Mayors, justices of the peace, police judges, and probate judges shall have jurisdiction to try the offenses described in this act, and their judgment

shall be final.  When complaint is made, information filed, or indict-
ment found against any corporation for violating this act, summons
shall be served, appearance made, or plea entered, as provided in
section 7231, Revised Statutes of Ohio, except that in complaints before magistrates, service shall be made by the constable.  In all
other cases process shall be served and proceedings had, as in cases
of misdemeanor.  In every case of complaint against a child involving commitment to any children's home or juvenile reformatory, the
board of county visitors shall be notified and must attend and protect
the interest of the child on the hearing, as provided in section 633-18
of the Revised Statutes of Ohio; and the order of commitment of
the child to a state reformatory must show that the county visitors
were so notified and attended the hearing.  All fines collected under
the provisions of this act shall be paid into the funds of the school
district in which the offense was committed.  Boards of education
are authorized to employ legal counsel to prosecute any case arising under the provisions of this act when it shall deem. the same
necessary, and the services of such counsel shall be paid for from
the contingent fund of the district.  (95 v. 621; 90 v. 290; 86 v.
338, §§ 11, 12, 13; 87 v. 326, 145.)

Sec. 4022-12.  [Repeated violations.]  Every person who, after
being once convicted for violating any of the provisions of this
act, shall be convicted of again violating any of the provisions of this
act, may, in addition to the punishment by way of a fine elsewhere
provided for, be imprisoned not less than ten days nor more than
thirty days.  On complaint, before a mayor, justice of the peace, or
police judge of a second violation of this act involving punishment
by imprisonment, if a trial by jury be not waived, a jury shall be
chosen and the case tried, after the manner provided in section
3718a, of the Revised Statutes of Ohio.  (95 v. 622; 90 v. 290.)

Sec. 4022-13.  [Sufficient school accommodations to be provided.]
It is hereby made the duty of every board of education in this state,
to provide sufficient accommodations in the public schools for all children in their district compelled to attend the public schools under the
provisions of this act.  Authority to levy the tax and raise the money
necessary for such purpose, is hereby given the proper officers charged
with such duty under the law.  (95 v. 622; 90 v. 291.)

Sec. 4022-14.  [Costs in prosecution under this act.]  No person
or officer instituting pro eedings under this act shall be required to
advance, or give security for costs; and if a defendant is acquitted
or discharged, or if convicted and committed to jail in default of
payment of fine and costs, the justice, mayor, police judge or probate

judge, before whom such case was brought shall certify such costs to the county auditor, who shall examine and, if necessary, correct the account, and issue his warrant to the county treasurer in favor of the respective persons to whom such costs are due for the amount due to each. (95 v. 622; 90 v. 291.)

**Sec. 4023.**   Repealed April 15, 1889.

**Sec. 4024.**   Repealed April 15, 1889.

**Sec. 4025.**   Repealed May 12, 1902.

**Sec. 4026.**   [Free school books.]   That each board of education may furnish the necessary school books free of charge, to enable the parent or guardian, without expense therefor, to comply with the requirements of this chapter, the same to be paid for out of the contingent fund at the disposal of the board; and such levy each year, in addition if necessary to that otherwise authorized by law, is hereby authorized, as shall be necessary to furnish such school books free of charge to all the pupils attending the public schools; but such pupils as are already wholly or in part supplied with necessary school books shall be supplied free of charge only as other or new books are needed; and all school books furnished as herein provided, shall be considered and be the property of the district and loaned to the pupils on such terms and conditions as such board may prescribe. (91 v. 260; 87 v. 317; 74 v. 57, § 4.)

**Sec. 4027.**   Repealed May 12, 1902.

**Sec. 4028.**   Repealed April 15, 1889.

**Sec. 4029.**   Repealed May 12, 1902.

**Sec. 4029-1.**   [Examination for entering high school.]   Each board of county school examiners shall hold examinations of pupils of township, special and joint sub-districts in the subjects of orthography, reading, writing, arithmetic, English grammar and composition, geography, history of the United States including civil government, and physiology.

[Number of examinations; when and where.]   Two such examinations shall be held annually, one on the third Saturday in April, and one on the second Saturday in May, at such place or places as the county board of examiners may designate.

[Preparation of questions.]   The questions for all such examinations, throughout the state, shall be uniform and be prepared under the direction of the state commissioner of common schools, and sample lists shall be mailed, under seal, to the clerks of the said boards of examiners not less than ten days before each examination. Upon receipt of said lists, the said boards are authorized and required to have a sufficient number of copies of the same printed for use at the examination. Only such applicants as receive an average grade of seventy per cent., with no grade less than fifty per cent. in any branch shall be passed.

[Township commencement.] It shall be the duty of the township boards of education upon written notice, filed by a successful applicant, with the clerk of the board of education, to provide for holding a township commencement not later than the month of June, at some place within the civil township, and to appoint some suitable person to have charge of the same. At this commencement each successful applicant residing in the township school distict or any special or joint sub-district having its schoolhouse located within the civil township of which the township district forms a part, shall be required to deliver an oration or declamation, or read an essay; thereupon said board of education shall issue a certificate to each successful applicant, stating that said applicant has taken part in said commencement.

[County commencement; diploma.] The board of county school examiners shall provide for the holding of a county commencement not later than August fifteenth, at such place as it may determine. At this commencement there shall be delivered an annual address, at the conclusion of which a diploma shall be presented to each successful applicant who has complied with the provisions of this act; said diploma shall entitle the holder thereof to enter any high school in the state. (89 v. 123, §§ 1, 2; 91 v. 67; 92 v. 198; 94 v. 175, § 4029-1; 95 v. 71, 95 v. 218.)

Sec. 4029-2. [Compensation of examiners and contingent expenses.] The compensation of county examiners shall be the same as that fixed in section 4075 of the Revised Statutes of Ohio for the examination of teachers, and each member of the said board of examiners shall be allowed the minimum fee provided for holding examinations for teachers as remuneration for his services incident to the county commencement, and such compensation and the necessary expenses incident to the examination and county commencement shall be paid out of the county treasury as provided in said section 4075; no other compensation shall be allowed county examiners for holding the county commencement. The expenses incident to the township commencement shall be paid by the township board of education from the contingent fund of the township district, and when the pupils of special districts take part in such commencements the boards of education of such districts shall pay, from their contingent funds, to the township board of education their share of such expenses, such share to be based on the proportion of pupils, from each district, taking part in such commencements; a proportional share for pupils from joint sub-districts, taking part in such commencements, shall be paid from the contingent fund of said joint sub-districts. (89 v. 123, § 4; 91 v. 67; 92 v. 198; 95 v. 72; § 4029-2; 95 v. 218.)

Sec. 4029-3. [Tuition.] The tuition of pupils holding diplomas and residing in township, special, or joint sub-districts, in which no high school is maintained, shall be paid by the board of education of the district in which they have legal school residence, such tuition to be computed by the month and an attendance any part of the month shall create a liability for the entire month; but a board of education maintaining a high school shall charge no more tuition than it charges for other nonresident pupils, and no board of education shall be required to pay the tuition of any pupil for more than four school years; provided the board of education shall be required to pay the tuition of all successful applicants, who have complied with the provisions of this act, residing more than three miles from the high school provided by said board, when said applicants attend a nearer high school. The tuition of pupils residing in joint sub-districts shall be paid by the boards of education, having control of such districts, from the contingent funds of said districts. A board of education not maintaining a high school may enter into an agreement with one or more boards of education maintaining such school for the schooling of all its high school pupils and when such agreement is entered into the board making the same shall be exempt from the payment of tuition at other high schools; provided the school or schools selected are located in the same civil township, or some adjoining township, as that of the board making the agreement. Where no such agreement is entered into the school to be attended can be selected by the pupil holding a diploma; provided, due notice in writing, is given to the clerk of the board of education of the name of the school to be attended and the date the attendance is to begin, said notice to be filed not less than five days previous to said beginning of attendance. Said tuition can be paid from either the tuition or contingent funds, and in case the board of education deems it necessary it may levy a tax of not to exceed two mills on each dollar of taxable property in the district or joint sub-district in excess of that allowed by section 3959 of the Revised Statutes of Ohio; the proceeds of said levy shall be kept in a separate fund and applied only to the payment of such tuition. (89 v. 123, § 3; 95 v. 72; § 4029-3; 95 v. 218.)

**Sec. 4029-4.** [What shall constitute a high school.] No board of education shall be entitled to collect tuition under this act unless said board shall be maintaining a regularly organized high school with a course of study extending over not less than two years and consisting mainly of branches higher than those in which the pupil is examined. Should the question arise as to the standing or grade of any particular high school, the state commissioner of common schools is hereby authorized to determine the grade of such school and his finding in the case shall be final. (95 v. 73, § 4029-4; 95 v. 218.)

## CHAPTER X.

### ENUMERATION, TREASURER AND CLERK.

### ENUMERATION.

**Sec. 4030. [Yearly enumeration of school youth.]** There shall be taken in each district, annually, during the two weeks ending on the fourth Saturday of May, an enumeration of all unmarried youth, noting sex, between six and twenty-one years of age, resident within the district, and not temporarily there, designating also the number between six and eight years of age, the number between eight and fourteen years of age, the number between fourteen and sixteen years of age, the number between sixteen and twenty-one years of age, and the number residing in the Western Reserve, the Virginia Military district, the United States Military district, and in any original surveyed township or fractional township to which belongs section sixteen, or other land in lieu thereof, or any other lands for the use of public schools, or any interest in the proceeds of such lands. (93 v. 312; 87 v. 80; 85 v. 192; Rev. Stat. 1880; 71 v. 15, § 77.)

**Sec. 4031. [Appointment of enumerators; oath and duties.]** The board of education of each school district, shall, on or before the second Saturday in May, appoint one or more persons to take the enumeration provided for in section *forty hundred and thirty* of the Revised Statutes of Ohio. Each person appointed to take such enumeration shall take an oath or affirmation to take the same accurately and truly to the best of his skill and ability. When making return thereof to the clerk of the board of education, he shall accompany the same with a list of the names of all the youth enumerated, noting the age of each, and with his affidavit duly certified that he has taken and returned the enumeration accurately and truly to the best of his knowledge and belief, and that such list contains the names of all such youth so enumerated and none others. The clerk of the board of education or any officer authorized to administer oaths, may administer such oath or affirmation, take and certify such affidavit, and the clerk shall keep in his office for the period of five years such report and the list of names, and each person so taking and returning the enumeration shall be allowed by the proper board of education reasonable compensation for his services. (Passed and approved April 25, 1904.)

Sec. 4032. [Enumeration in districts in two or more counties.] When a school district including territory attached for school purposes, is situated in two or more counties, it shall be the duty of the person or persons taking such enumeration to report the number of youth as provided in section *forty hundred and thirty* of the Revised Statutes of Ohio, residing in each county and the clerk of the board shall make returns to the auditors of the respective counties in which such youth reside as provided in section *forty hundred and thirty-five* of the Revised Statutes of Ohio. (Passed and approved April 25, 1904.)

Sec. 4033. .Repealed 90 v. 76.

Sec. 4034. Repealed April 25, 1904.

Sec. 4035. [Clerk to transmit abstract of enumeration to county auditor.] The clerk of each board shall, annually, on or before the first Saturday in July make, and transmit to the county auditor, an abstract of the enumeration by this chapter required to be returned by him, according to the form prescribed by the commissioner of common schools, with an oath or affirmation endorsed thereon that it is a correct abstract of the returns made to him under oath or affirmation; and the oath or affirmation of the clerk may be administered and certified by any member of the board of education, or by the county auditor. (Passed and approved April 25, 1904.)

Sec. 4036. [When the clerk fails, auditor to act.] If the clerk of any district fail to transmit such abstract of enumeration on or before the first Saturday in July, the auditor shall at once demand the same from such clerk; and in case the enumeration has not been taken as required by this chapter, or the abstract required be not furnished without delay, the auditor shall employ competent persons to take such enumeration, who shall be subject to the legal requirements already specified, except that the return shall be made directly to the auditor, who may administer to each person employed the oath or affirmation required; and the auditor shall allow the person employed by him, a reasonable compensation, to be paid out of the general county fund, and shall proceed to recover the amount so paid in civil action before any court having competent jurisdiction, in the name of the state, against such clerk on his bond, and the amount so collected shall be paid into the school funds of the district. (Passed and approved April 25, 1904.)

Sec. 4037. [When county line divides original surveyed township.] If parts of an original surveyed township or fractional township are situate in two counties, the auditor of the county in which the smallest part is situate shall, so soon as the abstracts of enumeration are received by him from the clerks of the boards of education, certify to the auditor of the county in which the largest part is situate the enumeration of youth residing in the part of the township situate in his county; if parts of such township or fractional township are situate in more than two counties, like certificates of enumeration shall be transmitted to the auditor of the county containing the greatest relative portion of such township, by the auditors of the other counties containing portions thereof; when it is uncertain which county contains the greatest relative portion of such township, such certificates shall be transmitted to the auditor of the oldest county, by the other auditor or auditors; and if the land granted by congress to such township or fractional township for the support of public schools has been sold, the auditor to whom such certificates are transmitted shall notify the auditor of state, without delay, that such enumeration has been certified to him. (70 v. 195, §§ 121, 130.)

Sec. 4038. [When enumeration not taken, district not entitled to school funds.] If an enumeration of the youth of a district be not taken and returned in any year, such district shall not be entitled to receive any portion of the school funds distributable in that year on the basis of enumeration; and if such loss to a district occur through the failure of the clerk of the board of education of a district to perform the duty required of him under section *forty hundred and thirty-five* of the Revised Statutes of Ohio, he shall be liable to the district for the loss, which may be recovered in an action in the name of the state; and the money so recovered shall be paid into the county treasury, and apportioned in the same manner as the school funds so lost would have been apportioned. (Passed and approved April 25, 1904.)

Sec. 4039. [Auditor to furnish abstract to state commissioner.] The auditor of each county shall make and transmit to the state commissioner of common schools, on or before the third Saturday in July in each year, on blanks to be furnished by the commissioner, an abstract of the enumeration returns made to him, duly certified.   (Passed and approved April 25, 1904.)

**Sec. 4040.**   [Duty of state commissioner when enumeration excessive, etc.]   When the state commissioner of common schools on examination of the enumeration returns of any district, is of opinion that the enumeration is excessive in number, or in any other way incorrect, he may require the same to be retaken and returned, and if he think it necessary he may for this purpose appoint persons to perform the service, who shall take the same oath, perform the same duties, and receive the same compensation, out of the same funds, as the person or persons who took the enumeration in the first instance, and the school fund distributable in proportion to enumeration shall be distributed upon the corrected returns.   (70 v. 195, § 75.)

**Sec. 4041.**   [Penalty for making fraudulent returns.]   An officer through whose hands the enumeration required by this chapter to be returned passes, who, by percentage or otherwise, adds to or takes from the number actually enumerated, shall be deemed guilty of a misdemeanor, and, upon conviction of such offense, shall be fined in any sum not less than five nor more than one thousand dollars, or imprisoned in the county jail not less than ten nor more than thirty days, at the discretion of the court.   (70 v. 175, § 75.)

TREASURER AND CLERK.

**Sec. 4042.**   [Treasurer of school funds.]   In each city, village and township school district, the treasurer of the city, village and township funds, shall be respectively the treasurer of the school funds; in each special district the board of education shall choose its own treasurer, whose term of office shall be for one year beginning on the first day of September.   (Passed and approved April 25, 1904.)

**Sec. 4043.**   [Bond of treasurer; additional sureties or new bond.] Each school district treasurer shall, before entering upon the duties of his office, execute a bond, with sufficient sureties, in an amount at least equal to the amount of school funds that may come into his hands, payable to the state of Ohio, to be approved by the board of education, conditioned for the faithful disbursement, according to law, of all funds which come into his hands; and he may at any time thereafter be required to give additional sureties on his accepted bond, or to excute a new bond with sufficient sureties to the approval of the board of education whenever the said board of education deem it necessary, and if said treasurer shall fail for ten days after service of notice in writing of such requisition, to give bond or additional sureties as aforesaid as required by said board, the office shall be considered and declared vacant and shall be filed[filled] as in other cases. Every bond when so executed and approved shall be filed with the clerk of the board of education of the district, and recorded, who shall cause a certified copy thereof or the names of additional sureties, to be filed with the county auditor without delay, and such board at the time of the approval of any bond or sureties, shall require the treasurer of the school funds to produce all money, bonds or other securities in his hands as such treasurer, and the same shall be then counted by the board or a committee thereof, in the presence of the clerk of the board, who shall thereupon enter upon the records of the board, a certificate, setting forth the exact amount of money or securities so found in the hands of such treasurer, which record shall be signed by the president and clerk of the board and shall be prima facie evidence that the amount therein stated was actually in the treasury at that date. (Passed and approved April 25, 1904.)

Sec. 4044. [Annual settlement by treasurer with county auditor.] The treasurer shall, annually, within the first ten days of September, settle with the county auditor for the preceding school year, and for that purpose shall make a certified statement showing the amount of money received, from whom, and on what account, and the amount paid out, and for what purpose; he shall produce vouchers for all payments made; if the auditor, on examination, find the statement and vouchers to be correct, he shall give the treasurer a certificate of the fact, which shall, prima facie, be a discharge of the treasurer for the money paid; and for making such settlement he shall be entitled to receive the sum of one dollar, and also five cents per mile for traveling to and from the county seat, to be paid out of the county treasury, on the order of the county auditor. When the treasurer's term begins on the first day of September the annual settlement shall be made by the outgoing treasurer. (92 v. 58; 85 v. 192, 194; Rev. Stat. 1880; 71 v. 9, § 47.)

Sec. 4045. [Penalty for failure to make such settlement.] If the treasurer of any school district willfully or negligently fail to make such annual settlement within the time prescribed in the preceding section, he shall be liable to pay a fine of fifty dollars, to be recovered in a civil action in the name of the state; which amount, when collected, shall be paid into the county treasury, and shall be applied to the use of common schools in his district; and the county auditor shall proceed forthwith, in case of such failure, to recover the penalty, by suit against such treasurer, before any justice of the peace of his county. (71 v. 9, § 47.)

**Sec. 4046.** Repealed April 11, 1888.

**Sec. 4047.** [When treasurer **may receive or pay money.**] No treasurer of a school district shall pay out any school money except on an order signed by the president and countersigned by the clerk of the board of education; and no money shall be paid to the treasurer of a district, other than that received from the county treasurer, except upon the order of the clerk of the board, who shall report the amount of such miscellaneous receipts to the county auditor each year, immediately preceding such treasurer's settlement with the auditor. (Passed and approved April 25, 1904.)

**Sec. 4047a.** Repealed April 25, 1904.

**Sec. 4048.** [**Maximum amount** of funds which treasurer may hold.] The clerk of a board of education or the county auditor shall pay no money into the hands of the treasurer of a school district in excess of the amount of his bond and should said clerk or auditor violate this provision, he and his bondsmen shall be liable for any loss occasioned thereby; and before giving said treasurer any warrant or order for any school funds the auditor may require the treasurer to file with him a statement showing the amount of such funds in his possession, signed by the clerk of the board of education. (Passed and approved April 25, 1904.)

**Sec. 4049.** [**Treasurer to deliver money, etc., to successor.**] At the expiration of his term of service each treasurer shall deliver to his successor in office all books, papers, money, and other property in his hands belonging to the district, and take duplicate receipts of his successor therefor, one of which he shall deposit with the clerk of the board of education within three days thereafter. (1888, April 11; 85 v. 192, 194; Rev. Stat. 1880; 71 v. 9, § 47.)

**Sec. 4050.** [**Bond of clerk.**] The clerk of each board of education shall execute a bond, in an amount and with surety to be approved by the board, payable to the state of Ohio, conditioned that he shall perform faithfully all the official duties required of him; which bond shall be deposited with the president of the board, and a copy thereof, certified by the president of the board, shall be filed with the county auditor. (70 v. 195, § 45.)

**Sec. 4051.** [**When orders of clerk for teachers' pay illegal.**] It shall be unlawful for the clerk of a board to draw an order on the treasurer for the payment of a teacher for services until the teacher files with him such reports as are required by the state commissioner of common schools and the board of education, a legal certificate of qualification, or a true copy thereof, covering the entire time of the service, and a statement of the branches taught; but orders may be drawn for the payment of special teachers of drawing, painting, penmanship, music, gymnastics, or a foreign language, on presentation of a certificate to the clerk, signed by a majority of the examiners, and the filing with him of a true copy thereof, covering the time for which a special teacher has been employed, and the specialty taught. (70 v. 195, §§ 53, 94.)

**Sec. 4052.** [Annual statistical report of the board of education; by whom prepared.] The clerk of each board shall prepare the annual report of the receipts and expenditures of school money, and the statistical statement in reference to the schools, required of the board by section *forty hundred and fifty-seven* of the Revised Statutes of Ohio, and transmit the same to the county auditor on or before the first day of September; provided, that in each school district having a superintendent of schools, the annual report, except the receipts and expenditures of money, shall be made by the superintendent. (Passed and approved April 25, 1904.)

**Sec. 4053.** [Publication of receipts and disbursements by clerk.] The board of education of each district, except city districts, shall require the clerk of the board annually, ten days prior to the election for members of the board of education, to prepare and post at the place or places of holding such elections, or publish in some newspaper of general circulation in the district, an itemized statement of all money received and disbursed by the treasurer of the board within the school year last preceding. (Passed and approved April 25, 1904.)

**Sec. 4054.** [Clerk to deliver books, etc., to successor.] Each clerk shall, at the expiration of his term of office, deliver to his successor all books and papers in his hands relating to the affairs of his district, including certificates, and copies thereof, and reports of school statistics, filed by teachers. (70 v. 195, § 84.)

**Sec. 4055.** [How treasurer and clerk to keep accounts.] The auditor of each county shall furnish to the clerk and treasurer of each school district in his county a suitable blank book, made according to the form prescribed by the bureau of inspection and supervision of public offices, in which each shall keep an account of the school funds of his district; the clerk's account shall show the amounts certified by the county auditor to be due the district, all sums paid to the treasurer from other sources on his order, and all orders drawn by him on the treasurer, and upon what funds and for what purposes drawn; the treasurer's accounts shall show the amounts received from the county treasurer, all sums received from other sources on the order of the clerk, and the amounts paid out, and from what funds and for what purposes paid; and a separate account of each fund shall be kept, and each account shall be balanced at the close of the school year, and the balance in the treasurer's hands belonging to each fund shown. (Passed and approved April 25, 1904.)

**Sec. 4056.** [Compensation of treasurer and clerk.] The board of education of each school district shall fix the compensation of its clerk and treasurer, which shall be paid from the contingent fund of the district; if the clerk and treasurer are paid annually the order for the payment of their salaries shall not be drawn until said clerk and treasurer shall present to the board of education a certificate from the county auditor stating that all reports required by law have been filed in his office; if the clerk and treasurer are paid semi-annually, quarterly, or monthly, the last payment on their salaries previous to August 31, shall not be made until all reports required by law have been filed with the county auditor and his certificate presented to the board of education as required herein. (Passed and approved April 25, 1904.)

# CHAPTER XI. '

## REPORTS.

**Sec. 4057.** [Annual report of board of education; its contents.] The board of education of each district shall make a report to the county auditor, on or before the first day of September in each year, containing a statement of the receipts and expenditures of the board, the number of schools sustained, the length of time such schools were sustained, the enrollment of pupils, the average monthly enrollment, and average daily attendance, the number of teachers employed, and their salaries, the number of school houses and school rooms, and such other items as the commissioner of common schools may require. (1888, April 11; 85 v. 192, 195; Rev. Stat. 1880; 70 v. 195, § 75; S. & C. 1353.)

**Sec. 4058.** [In what form to be made, etc.] The report shall be made on blanks which shall be furnished by the commissioner of common schools to the auditor of each county, and by the auditor to each school clerk in his county; and each board of education, or officer or employe thereof, or other school officer in any district or county, shall, whenever the commissioner so requires, report to him direct, upon such blanks as he shall furnish, any statements or items of information that he may deem important or necessary. (70 v. 195, § 75.)

**Sec. 4059.** [Reports by superintendents and teachers.] Boards of education shall require all teachers and superintendents to keep the school records in such manner that they may be enabled to report annually to the county auditor and state commissioner of common schools, as required by the provisions of this title and shall withhold the pay of such teachers and superintendents as fail to file the reports required of them; the records of each school shall, in addition to all other requirements, be so kept as to exhibit the names of all pupils enrolled therein, the studies pursued, shall indicate the character of the work done, the standing of each pupil, and shall be as near uniform throughout the state as may be practicable; said boards may require superintendents and teachers to report such matters as they deem important or necessary for information in regard to the management and conduct of the schools and to make such suggestions and recommendations as they may deem advisable relative to methods of instruction, school management, or other matters of educational interest; and the board of education of each city district shall prepare and publish annually a report of the condition and administration of the schools under its charge, and include therein a complete exhibit of the financial affairs of the district. (Passed and approved April 25, 1904.)

Sec. 4060. [Duties of county auditor as to school statistics, etc.] The auditor of each county shall, on or before the twentieth day of September, annually, prepare, and transmit to the commissioner of common schools an abstract of all the returns of school statistics made to him from the several districts in his county, according to the form prescribed by the commissioner, and a statement of the condition of the institute fund, and such other facts relating to schools and school funds as the commissioner may require; he shall also cause to be distributed all such circulars, blanks and other papers, including school laws and documents, in the several school districts in the county, as the commissioner may lawfully require; and if the auditor neglect to prepare and return any of the abstracts or reports herein required the county commissioners shall withhold from him all compensation for his services under this title. (1888, April 11; 85 v. 192, 195; Rev. Stat. 1880; 70 v. 195, § 123; S. & S. 705.)

Sec. 4061. [Penalties against auditor and clerk.] The auditor shall also be liable on his bond for any such neglect, in a sum not less than three hundred nor more than one thousand dollars, on complaint of the commissioner of common schools; and if the clerk of the board of education of any district fail to make the annual returns of school statistics required by this title, to the county auditor, he shall be liable on his bond in a sum not less than fifty nor more than three hundred dollars, on complaint of the county auditor, or of the board of education, to be recovered in a civil action in the name of the state, and when collected to be paid into the county treasury, and applied to the use of common schools in such district. (70 v. 195, § 123; S. & S. 706.)

Sec. 4062. [When auditor to appoint person to make report.] Upon the neglect or failure of the clerk of the board of education of any district to make the reports required in this title, and by the time specified, the county auditor shall appoint some suitable person, resident of the district, to make such reports, who shall receive the same compensation therefor, and in the same manner, as is allowed by law for like services. (70 v. 195, § 123; S. & S. 706.)

**Sec. 4063.** [**Further penalties against auditor.**] A county auditor who willfully or negligently fails, in any year, to transmit to the commissioner of common schools the abstract of enumeration required by section *forty hundred and thirty-nine*, or to perform any other duty required of him under this title, shall be liable on his bond to the extent of twice the sum lost to the school districts of his county in consequence of such failure, which sum shall be recovered in a civil action against him, on his bond, in the name of the state, before any court of competent jurisdiction; and the money so recovered shall be paid into the county treasury, for the benefit of such districts, and apportioned in the same manner as the school funds so lost would have been apportioned. (70 v. 195, §§ 81, 124.)

**Sec. 4064.** [**Compensation of auditor.**] The commissioners of each county shall allow the county auditor, annually, a reasonable compensation for his services under this title, not to exceed five dollars for each city, village, special, and township school district in his county to be paid out of the county treasury; but before such allowance shall be made for any year the auditor shall present to the commissioners a statement, officially certified and signed by the commissioner of common schools, that he has transmitted to the commissioner all reports and returns of statistics for that year required by this title. (70 v. 195, § 125.)

## CHAPTER XII.

### BOARDS OF EXAMINERS.

### STATE BOARD OF EXAMINERS.

**Sec. 4065.** [State board; appointment; term; vacancies.] There shall be a state board of examiners, which shall consist of five competent persons, resident of the state, to be appointed by the state commissioner of common schools; not more than three of whom shall belong to the same political party. The term of office of such examiners shall be five years; the term of one of the examiners shall expire on the 31st day of August, each year, [and when one of which shall expire on the 31st of August every year,] and when a vacancy occurs in the board, whether from expiration of the term of office, refusal to serve, or other cause, the commissioner shall fill the same by appointment for the full or unexpired term, as the case demands. (1888, April 16; 85 v. 330; 81 v. 95; Rev. Stat., 1880; 70 v. 195, § 85; S. & S., 709.)

**Sec. 4066.** [Power to issue three grades of life certificates; record thereof.] The board thus constituted may issue three grades of life certificates to such as are found to possess the requisite scholarship, and who exhibit satisfactory evidence of good moral character and of professional experience and ability; the certificates shall be for different grades of schools according to branches taught, and shall be valid in the schools specified therein. The clerk of the board shall keep a record of the proceedings, showing the number, date and grade of each certificate, to whom granted, and for what branches of study, and shall report such statistics to the commissioner, annually, on or before the 31st day of August. (1888, April 16; 85 v. 330; 78 v. 39; Rev. Stat., 1880; 70 v. 195, § 86; S. & S., 709.)

Sec. 4067. [Effect thereof; may be revoked for cause.] All certificates issued by such board shall be countersigned by the commissioner of common schools; and such certificates shall supersede the necessity of any and all other examinations of the persons holding them, by any board of examiners, and shall be valid in any school district in the state, unless revoked by the state board for good cause. (70 v. 195, § 87; S. & S., 709.)

Sec. 4068. [Examination fees; their disposition; compensation of members; stationery.] Each applicant for a certificate shall pay to the board of examiners a fee of five dollars; and the clerk of the board shall pay to the state treasurer, all fees received, and file with the state auditor a written statement of the amount. Each member of the board shall be entitled to receive five dollars for each day he is necessarily engaged in official service, and also six cents per mile each way for traveling from and to his place of residence, by the most direct route of public travel to and from the places of meetings of the board, to be paid out of the state treasury on the order of the state auditor; all books, blanks and stationery required by the board shall be furnished by the secretary of state. (1888, April 16; 85 v. 330; 82 v. 100; Rev. Stat., 1880; 70 v. 195, § 88; S. & S., 709.)

COUNTY EXAMINERS.

Sec. 4069. [County boards; appointment, term, and vacancies; removals; notice of appointment; disqualifications.] There shall be a county board of school examiners for each county, which shall consist of three competent persons to be appointed by the probate judge. Two of such persons shall have had at least two years' experience as teachers or superintendents, and shall have been within five years, actual teachers in the public schools. Each person so appointed shall be a legal resident of the county for which he is appointed, and, should he remove from the county during his term, his office shall be thereby vacated and his successor be appointed. No examiner shall teach in, be connected with, or be financially interested in any school which is not supported wholly or in part by the state, or be employed as an instructor in any teachers' institute in his own county; nor shall any person be appointed to the position, or exercise the office of examiner who is agent of or is financially interested in any book publishing or book-selling firm, company or business, or in any educational journal or magazine. If an examiner becomes connected with or interested in any school not under state control, or is employed in any such institute in his own county, or becomes an agent of or interested in any book company or journal, or fails to hold the necessary teacher's certificate, or removes from the county, the probate judge shall forthwith, upon being apprised of such fact, remove such examiner and appoint his successor. The term of office of such examiner shall be three years. The term of one of the examiners shall expire on the thirty-first day of August, each year; but the probate judge shall revoke the appointment of any examiner, upon satisfactory proof that he is inefficient, intemperate, negligent, guilty of immoral conduct, or that he is using his office for personal or private gain. When a vacancy occurs in the board, whether from expiration of the term of office, refusal to serve, or other cause, the probate judge shall promptly fill the same by appointment for the full or unexpired term, and said judge shall, within ten days, report the same to the state commissioner of common schools, together with the names of the other members of the board and the date of the expiration of their several terms of office. The members of county boards of examiners, as now constituted, shall serve for the full term for which they were appointed unless removed for cause as provided for in section *forty hundred and sixty-nine* as it existed previous to this enactment. (Passed and approved April 25, 1904.)

**Sec. 4070.** [Organization of county boards of examiners; reports of clerk; compensation of clerk.] The board of county school examiners shall annually in the month of September organize by choosing from its members a president, a vice-president, and a clerk; the president shall preside at all the meetings of the board, and in his absence the vice-president shall preside; the clerk shall keep a full and accurate record of the proceedings of the board, showing the number and date and character of each certificate issued, and to whom, for what term, and for what branches of study, and such other statistics relating to the examination and the proceedings of the board as the state commissioner of common schools may require, and in the form and manner he may require, and shall make a report of all such items annually on or before the first day of September; the clerk shall receive for his services as clerk four dollars for each examination of sixty applicants or less, six dollars for each examination of more than sixty applicants and less than one hundred, eight dollars for each examination of one hundred applicants or more, to be paid out of the county treasury on the order of the county auditor, but no order shall be drawn for the month of August until the clerk produce a receipt from the state commissioner of common schools that he has filed all the reports for the year required by said commissioner. The board shall make all needful rules and regulations for the proper discharge of its duties and the conduct of its work, subject to statutory provisions and the approval of the state commissioner of common schools.   (Passed and approved April 25, 1904.)

Sec. 4071. [Meetings for examinations; majority's power; examination fee.]   Each board shall hold public meetings for the examination of applicants for county teachers' certificates on the first Saturday of every month of the year, unless Saturday should fall on a legal holiday, in which case, said examination shall be held on the succeeding Saturday, at such place or places, within the county as will, in the opinion of the board, best accommodate the greatest number of applicants, notice of which shall be published in two weekly newspapers of different politics printed in the county, if there are two papers thus published, if not, then a publication in one only is required.   In no case shall the board hold any private examination or ante-date any certificate.   A majority of the board may examine applicants and grant certificates; and as a condition of any applicant being admitted to take the examination, each such applicant shall pay to the board for the use of the county institute a fee of fifty cents.   (Passed and approved April 25, 1904.)

Sec. 4071a.   [Uniform system of examinations; preparation and distribution of examination questions.]   After the first day of September, 1904, the questions for all county teachers' examinations, throughout the state, shall be prepared under the direction of the state commissioner of common schools, and sample lists shall be mailed, under seal, to the clerks of the said boards of examiners not less than ten days before each examination.   Upon the receipt of said lists, the boards are authorized and required to have a sufficient number of copies of the same printed for use in the examination.   Any person connected with the preparation, printing, distribution, or handling of said questions, who shall, prior to the examination in each branch of study, make the same public in any manner or give information in regard to the nature or character of the questions to any applicant for a certificate or other person, shall be guilty of a misdemeanor and upon conviction thereof shall be fined in a sum not less than fifty dollars nor more than one hundred dollars.   (Passed and approved April 25, 1904.)

**Sec. 4072.** [Disposition of fees.] The clerk of the board of county school examiners shall promptly collect all fees from applicants at each examination and pay the same into the county treasury quarterly, and he shall file with the county auditor a written statement of the amount, and the number of applicants, male and female, examined during the quarter; and all such money thus received shall be set apart by the auditor for the support of county teachers' institutes, to be applied as provided for in chapter thirteen of this title. (Passed and approved April 25, 1904.)

**Sec. 4073.** [Granting renewal and revocation of certificates; age limit; hearing on revocation of certificate; expenses.] The county board of school examiners may grant teachers' certificates for one, two, three, five, and eight years from the day of the examination; and said certificates shall be valid in all village, township, and special school districts of the county wherein they are issued, but in all school districts situated in two or more counties teachers' certificates obtained in either county shall be valid in such districts. All teachers' certificates granted for one, two or three years shall be regarded as provisional certificates and shall be issued only in compliance with such reasonable regulations and standards and upon such ratios as the board may adopt, but no such certificate shall be renewed except upon examination; provided, that when any teacher holding a two year certificate and having for the last five years preceding been continuously engaged in teaching in the same county, said teacher shall be entitled to have his or her certificate renewed by passing an examination in theory and practice; all certificates granted for five years, or eight years, shall be regarded as professional certificates and shall be renewable without examination at the discretion of the examining board, if for three years preceding the date of the application the holders thereof shall have been engaged in teaching, not less than twelve months of such time being spent in the same district and the board of examiners being satisfied as to the moral character and the professional attainments of the holders thereof. No certificate shall be issued to any person who is less than eighteen years of age; and if at any time the recipient of a certificate be found intemperate, immoral, incompetent, or negligent, the examiners, or any two of them, may revoke the certificate; but such revocation shall not prevent a teacher from receiving pay for services previously rendered; but before any hearing is had by a board of examiners on the question of the revocation of a teacher's certificate, the charges against the teacher shall be reduced to writing and placed upon the records of the board, and the teacher shall be notified in writing as to the nature of the charges and the time set for the hearing, such notice to be served personally or at his residence, and the teacher shall be entitled to produce witnesses and defend himself; the examining board shall have power to send for witnesses and examine them on oath or affirmation touching the matter under investigation, and said oath or affirmation may be administered by any member of the board of examiners. The fees and the per diem of examiners for conducting such investigation at three dollars a day each and other expenses of such trial shall be certified to the county auditor by the clerk and president of the examining board, and be paid out of the county treasury upon the order of the auditor. (Passed and approved April 25, 1904.)

Sec. 4074. [Certificates of different grades; prerequisites to employment; branches of study; value of certain life certificates.] From and after the first day of September, 1904, three kinds of teachers' certificates only shall be issued by county boards of school examiners; said kinds of teachers' certificates shall be styled respectively "Teacher's Elementary School Certificate," which shall be valid for all branches of study in schools below high school rank, "Teacher's High School Certificate," which shall be valid for all branches of study in recognized high schools and for superintendents, and "Teacher's Special Certificate," which shall be valid in schools of all grades, but only for the branch or branches of study named therein. From and after the first day of September, 1905, no person shall be employed or enter upon the performance of his duties as a teacher in any elementary school supported wholly or in part by the state in any village, township, or special school district who has not obtained from a board of school examiners having competent jurisdiction a certificate of good moral character and that he or she is qualified to teach orthography, reading, writing, arithmetic, English grammar and composition, geography, history of the United States, including civil government, physiology including narcotics, literature, and that he or she possesses an adequate knowledge of the theory and practice of teaching; and no person shall be employed or enter upon the performance of his duties as a teacher in any recognized high school supported wholly or in part by the state in any village, township, or special school district, or act as superintendent of school in such district, who has not obtained from a board of examiners having competent jurisdiction a certificate of good moral character and that he or she is qualified to teach literature, general history, algebra, physics, physiology including narcotics, and, in addition thereto, four branches elected from the following branches of study: Latin, German, rhetoric, civil government, geometry, physical geography, botany, and chemistry; and that he or she possesses an adequate knowledge of the theory and practice of teaching; and no person shall be employed and enter upon the performance of his duties as a special teacher of music, drawing, painting, penmanship, gymnastics, German, French, the commercial and industrial branches, or any one of them, in any elementary or high school supported wholly or in part by the state in any village, township or special school district, who has not obtained from the board of examiners having competent jurisdiction a certificate of good moral character and that he or she is qualified to teach the special branch or branches of study, and in addition thereto, that he or she possesses an adequate knowledge of the theory and practice of teaching; provided, that county boards of school examiners are authorized to recognize or renew, at their discretion, in the appropriate kind and for the same length of time any certificate or certificates, held by teachers who may apply for such recognition or renewal prior to the first day of September, 1905, and provided, further, that no person holding a common school life certificate issued by the board of state examiners shall be required to hold any other certificate to teach in the elementary schools of the state, nor shall any holder of said common school life certificate be required by any board to be examined in any of the branches covered by said certificate in order to be granted the teachers' high school certificate authorized herein. (Passed and approved April 25, 1904.)

Sec. 4075. [Compensation and expenses of board.] Each member of the county board of school examiners shall be entitled to receive ten dollars for each examination of sixty applicants or less, fourteen dollars for each examination of more than sixty applicants and less than one hundred, eighteen dollars for each examination of one hundred applicants or more, to be paid out of the county treasury on the order of the county auditor; all books, blanks and stationery required by the board shall be furnished by the county auditor; the board may contract for the use of suitable rooms in which to conduct examinations, for the printing of examination questions, may procure fuel and light, and employ janitors, to take charge of the rooms and keep them in order, and the expenses so incurred, together with the cost of advertising required by section *forty hundred and seventy-one*, shall be paid out of the county treasury on orders of the county auditor, who shall issue such orders upon the certificate of the president of the board, countersigned by the clerk. (Passed and approved April 25, 1904.)

Sec. 4076. [Annual report of clerk **and his bond.**] The clerk of the board shall prepare, and forward to the state commissioner of common schools, on or before the first day of September in each year, a statement of the number of examinations held by the board, the number of applicants examined, the total number of certificates granted, and the number for each term mentioned in section *forty hundred and seventy-three*, the amount of fees received and paid to the county treasurer, the amount received from the county treasury by the members of the board for their services, and such other statistics and information in relation to the duties of the board as said commissioner may require; and he shall deposit with the county auditor a bond, with surety to be approved by the auditor, in the sum of three hundred dollars, that he will pay into the county treasury, quarterly, the examination fees received by the board, and make the statistical returns required by this chapter. (Passed and approved April 25, 1904.)

CITY EXAMINERS.

**Sec. 4077.** [Boards of examiners in city districts; appointment and removal; filling of vacancy; village boards of examiners abolished.] There shall be a city board of school examiners for each city school district, to be appointed by the board of education of the district; such board shall consist of three persons, and the majority of the persons appointed shall have had at least two years' practical experience in teaching in the public schools and all persons appointed shall be otherwise competent for the position and residents of the district for which they are appointed; the term of office of such examiners shall be three years; the term of one-third of the examiners shall expire on the thirty-first day of August each year; but the board of education may revoke any appointment upon satisfactory proof that the appointee is inefficient, intemperate, negligent, or guilty of immoral conduct; when a vacancy occurs in the board, whether from expiration of term of office, refusal to serve, or other cause, the board of education shall fill the same by appointment for the full or unexpired term, as the case demands; and within ten days after an appointment, the clerk of the board of education shall report to the state commissioner of common schools the name of the appointee, and whether the appointment is for a full or an unexpired term; provided, that in city school districts that now have a board of city school examiners consisting of three members, the members of the same shall serve for the full term for which they were appointed; when the board does not consist of three members the same is hereby abolished and a new board shall be appointed, the members to serve for one, two and three years from the thirty-first day of August succeeding the passage of this act. All village boards of examiners are hereby abolished, but certificates issued by said boards shall continue in force within the village school district, for the full time for which they were issued. (Passed and approved April 25, 1904.)

Sec. 4078. [Standard of qualification for teachers; examination of schools; law governing board in examining teachers; special examiners; their oath; duty of school superintendents.] Each city board of school examiners shall determine the standard of qualification for teachers, and may examine any school in the district when such examination is deemed necessary to ascertain a teacher's qualifications, but in the examination of applicants and the granting of certificates the board shall be governed by the provisions of section *forty hundred and seventy-four*, and to secure a thorough examination of applicants in difficult branches, or special studies, the board may secure the assistance, temporarily, of persons of sufficient knowledge in such branches or studies, who shall promise on oath or affirmation, to be administered by the clerk of the board of examiners, to perform the duties of examiner faithfully and impartially, and superintendents of schools shall give to the board all necessary information in reference to branches and special studies to be taught, and the branches of study and grades of school which teachers will be required to teach. (Passed and approved April 25, 1904.)

Sec. 4079. [Organization of board; bond of clerk.] Each city board of school examiners shall organize during the month of September each year by choosing from its members a president, a vice-president, and a clerk; the president shall preside at all the meetings of the board, and in his absence the vice-president shall preside; the clerk shall perform all the duties required in this chapter of the clerk of the board of county school examiners in so far as said duties apply, and shall give bond, in the sum of three hundred dollars with surety to be approved by the board of education, conditioned that he will perform faithfully the duties required of him by this chapter, which bond shall be deposited with the clerk of the board of education. (Passed and approved April 25, 1904.)

Sec. 4080. [Meetings for examinations; notice.] Each board of city school examiners shall hold not less than two meetings each year, notice of which shall be published in some newspaper of general circulation in the district, and the expense of such publication shall be paid as provided in section *forty hundred and eighty-three*, and all examinations of applicants shall be conducted at the meetings of the boards thus called, and the examination of each and every applicant shall be in the presence of at least two members of the board. (Passed and approved April 25, 1904.)

**Sec. 4081.** [Granting, renewal and revocation of certificates; age limit; hearing on revocation of certificate.] Each city board of school examiners may grant teachers' certificates for one, two, three, five, and eight years from the day of examination; and said certificates shall be valid within the district wherein they are issued. All teachers' certificates granted for one, two, or three years, shall be regarded as provisional certificates and shall be issued only in compliance with such reasonable regulations and standard and upon such ratios as the board may adopt, but no such certificate shall be renewed except upon examination; provided, that when any teacher holding a two year certificate and having for the last five years preceding been continuously engaged in teaching in the same county, said teacher shall be entitled to have his or her certificate renewed by passing an examination in theory and practice; all certificates granted for five years, or eight years, shall be regarded as professional certificates and shall be renewable without examination at the discretion of the examining board, if for three years next preceding the date of the application of the holders thereof shall have been engaged in teaching, not less than twelve months of such time being spent in the same district and the board being satisfied as to the moral character and the professional attainments of the holders thereof. No certificate shall be issued to any person who is less than eighteen years of age; and if at any time the recipient of a certificate be found intemperate, immoral, incompetent, or negligent, the examiners, or any two of them, may revoke the certificate; but such revocation shall not prevent a teacher from receiving pay for services previously rendered; and before any hearing is had by a board of examiners on the question of the revocation of a teacher's certificate, the charges against the teacher shall be reduced to writing and placed upon the records of the board, and the teacher shall be notified in writing as to the nature of the charges and the time set for the hearing, such notice to be served either personally or at his residence, and the teacher shall be entitled to produce witnesses and defend himself; the examining board shall have power to send for witnesses and examine them on oath touching the matter under investigation, and said oath or affirmation may be administered by any member of the board of examiners. (Passed and approved April 25, 1904.)

**Sec. 4082.** [Nature of certificates to be granted; branches of study.] The provisions of section *forty hundred and seventy-four* of the Revised Statutes of Ohio relating to the kinds of certificates authorized to be issued by the county boards of school examiners for teachers in elementary schools and high schools, and for superintendents shall apply to city boards of school examiners; provided,

10—S. L.

that city boards of school examiners may, in their discretion, require teachers in elementary schools to be examined in drawing, music, or German if such subjects are a part of the regular work of such teachers. (Passed and approved April 25, 1904.)

Sec. 4083. [Compensation of examiners; incidental expenses.] Each city board of education shall fix the compensation of the members of the city board of school examiners and the additional compensation of the .clerk of the board, and the person or persons called to their assistance, furnish the necessary books, blanks and stationery for their use, and designate a school building within the district in which they shall conduct examinations, and to cause such building to be lighted and heated if necessary; and such compensation, and the incidental expenses incurred on account of the city board of school examiners, shall be paid, by order of the board of education, from the contingent fund of the district. (Passed and approved April 25, 1904.)

Sec. 4084. [Records and reports; duties of the clerk; disposition of fees.] The clerk of the city board of school examiners shall keep a record of the proceedings of the board, and such statistics as the state commissioner of common schools may require, and in the form and manner he may require, and shall report such statistics to the commissioner annually, on or before the first day of September; he shall pay the examination fees received by him to the treasurer of the district within ten days after each meeting, and at the same time file with the clerk of the board of education a written statement of the amount, and also a statement of the number of applicants, male and female, examined, and the number of certificates granted, and for what terms; and the fees paid to the treasurer of the district shall be applied to the support of teachers' institutes, as provided in chapter thirteen. (Passed and approved April 25, 1904.)

Sec. 4085. [Applicants who fail may appeal to the state commissioner of common schools; method of procedure.] All manuscripts filed as answers to questions propounded to any applicant appearing before any county or city board of school examiners, shall be promptly considered and passed upon by said board together with the results of oral tests if any and such other information which may come to said board touching the fitness of any applicant for teaching in the public schools; and said board shall promptly issue all certificates granted to successful applicants and send notices of failure to those who fail in .the examination, if such there be. All such manuscripts shall be kept on file for sixty days by the members of the examining board propounding the questions, and if within the sixty days any applicant after receiving his returns from the examination has cause to and does believe that he has been discriminated against and his manuscripts unfairly graded, it shall be his right to review his manuscripts with the member or members of the board having the same in charge, and if after such inspection and review of the manuscripts, he is still of the opinion that said board will not correct the error, if any, and issue his certificate, he shall have the right to appeal his case to the state commissioner of common schools for final review. Such appeal shall be in the form of an affidavit setting forth the facts as he believes them, accompanied by a fee of one dollar to cover the expenses incident to said appeal, and requesting that the matter be inquired into; thereupon the said commissioner shall require the clerk of said board to procure and forward said manuscripts, together with a full explanation of the reasons for the board's action, and if upon his examination of all the facts, together with the manuscripts, he finds that said applicant was denied a certificate when he should have been granted one and has been discriminated against by the board, he shall order the board forthwith to issue a certificate of the date of the teachers' examination attended by said applicant and indicate the length of time said certificate shall be valid, but if upon inspection of the manuscripts and reviewing the facts submitted he shall conclude that no injustice has been done, he shall so notify the applicant and the clerk of the board of examiners. (Passed and approved April 25, 1904.)

## CHAPTER XIII.

### TEACHERS' INSTITUTES.

**Sec. 4086.** [Organization of county teachers' institute; elections, term, duties and bond of officers.] A teachers' institute may be organized in any county, by the association of not less than thirty practical teachers of the common schools residing therein, who shall declare their intention in writing to attend such institute, the purpose of which shall be the improvement of such teachers in their profession; such institute shall elect annually, by ballot, a president, secretary, and one member of an executive committee, said member of the executive committee to serve for a term of three years; provided, that at the first annual election held after the organization of any institute, there shall be elected three members of the executive committee, the one receiving the highest number of votes to serve for three years; the one receiving the next highest number of votes to serve two years; and the one receiving the next highest number of votes to serve one year. The president and secretary of the institute shall be ex-officio members of the executive committee and shall act as chairman and secretary of said committee. Any vacancy in the office of president, secretary, or member of the executive committee caused by death, resignation, removal from the county or other cause, may be filled by the executive committee, the person elected to fill such vacancy to serve until the next annual meeting of the institute. It shall be the duty of this executive committee to manage the affairs of the institute; which committee shall enter into a bond, payable to the state of Ohio, with sufficient surety, to be approved by the county auditor in double the amount of the institute fund in the county treasury, for the benefit of the institute fund of the county, and conditioned that the committee shall account faithfully for the money which will come into its possession, and make the report to the commissioner of common schools, required by section *four thousand and eighty-eight*, and such election of officers shall be held during the session of such institute and at time fixed by the executive committee thereof, of which election at least three days' notice shall be given the members of such institute by posting conspicuously in a room, where such institute is held, a notice of the time and place of holding such election and of the officers to be voted for at such election. (95 v. 237; 92 v. 10; 84 v. 230; Rev. Stat. 1880; 70 v. 195, § 112.)

**Sec. 4087.** [Payment of institute fund to committee.] The declaration and bond mentioned in section *forty hundred and eighty-six* shall be filed with the county auditor, whereupon the auditor shall give to the institute committee an order on the county treasurer for the amount of the institute fund in the treasury; and any portion of said fund not disbursed by the committee shall be returned to the county treasury, on the certificate of the county auditor. (70 v. 195, § 112; S. & S. 709.)

**Sec. 4088.** [Report of secretary; his compensation.] The secretary shall, within five days after the adjournment of the institute, report to the state commissioner of common schools the number of teachers in attendance at the institute, the names of instructors and lecturers attending said institute, the amount of money received and disbursed by the committee and such other information relating to the institute as the commissioner may require; the secretary may be allowed compensation not to exceed ten dollars for making such report and for his services as secretary, to be paid out of the institute fund of the county, but no other compensation shall be allowed any officer or member of the executive committee; on failure to make such report, the secretary shall forfeit and pay to the state the sum of fifty dollars. (95 v. 238; 1888, April 11; 85 v. 192, 196; Rev. Stat. 1880; 70 v. 195, § 112; S. & S. 709.)

**Sec. 4089.** [Forfeiture of committee's bond.] Upon the forfeiture of the committee's bond, the prosecuting attorney of the county shall prosecute an action thereon, in the name of the state, and collect any money which the committee may have failed to disburse according to law, and any penalty to which the committee may be liable under this chapter, and pay the same into the county treasury to the credit of the institute fund. (70 v. 195, § 112.)

**Sec. 4090.** [When school commissioner may hold institute.] When a teachers' institute has not been held within two years in any county, the commissioner of common schools may hold or cause to be held therein such institute; and the management thereof and all proceedings in relation thereto, shall be the same as hereinbefore provided, except that the written declaration required shall not be necessary. (70 v. 195, § 114.)

**Sec. 4091.** [Teachers may dismiss school to attend institute; compensation for time, when allowed.] All teachers of the public schools within any county in which a county institute is held may dismiss their schools for one week for the purpose of attending such institute, and when such institute is held while the schools are in session the boards of education of all school districts are required to pay the teachers of their respective districts their regular salary for the week they attend the institute upon the teachers presenting a certificate of full regular daily attendance at said institute signed by the president and secretary thereof; the same to be paid as an addition to the first month's salary after said institute by the board of education by which said teacher is then, employed, or in case he is unemployed at the time of the institute, then by the board next employing said teacher, provided the term of said employment begins within three months after said institute closes.  (Passed and approved April 25, 1904.)

**Sec. 4092.** [Institutes for city districts; number of days; payment of expenses; appropriation by board of education.] The board of education of each city school district may provide for holding an institute yearly, for the improvement of the teachers of the common schools therein; and general meetings of the teachers of any such city district held upon not less than four days in any year, whether consecutive days or not, for the purpose of instruction, shall be deemed to constitute a teachers' institute for said city district within the meaning of this section; the expenses of such institute shall be paid from the institute fund provided for by section *forty hundred and eighty-four*; and in addition to this fund the board of education of any district may expend annually, for the instruction of the teachers of said district in an institute or in such other manner as it may prescribe, a sum not to exceed five hundred dollars, the same to be paid from its contingent fund; if the board of any district do not provide for such institute in any year, it shall cause the institute fund in the hands of the district treasurer for the year to be paid to the treasurer of the county wherein the district is situated, who shall place the same to the credit of the county institute fund, and the teachers of the schools of such district shall be entitled, in such case, to the advantages of the county institute, subject to the provisions of the preceding section; and the clerk of the board shall make the report of the institute required by section *forty hundred and ninety-four*. (Passed and approved April 25, 1904.)

**Sec. 4093.**    Repealed April 25, 1904.

Sec. 4094. [Number of days institutes must continue; reports.] All institutes held under the provisions of this chapter shall continue at least four days; and a report of the institute held in pursuance of the provisions of section *forty hundred and ninety-two* shall be made to the state commissioner of common schools within five days after the adjournment thereof, which shall state the number of teachers in attendance, the names of the instructors and lecturers, the total expenses of the institute, and the portion thereof paid from institute funds, and such other information relating to the institute as the commissioner may require. (Passed and approved April 25, 1904.)

## CHAPTER XIIIa.

### STATE NORMAL SCHOOLS.

(4094-1) **Sec. 1.** [State normal schools; location.] That there be and are hereby created and established two state normal schools to be located as follows: One in connection with the Ohio university, at Athens, and one in connection with the Miami university, at Oxford. (95 v. 45, March 12, 1902.)

(4094-2) **Sec. 2.** [Organization, control, instruction.] The boards of trustees of said universities shall, not later than September, 1903, organize at their respective institutions a normal school which shall be co-ordinate with existing courses of instruction, and shall be maintained in such a state of efficiency as to provide proper theoretical and practical training for all students desiring to prepare themselves for the work of teaching; said normal schools, in each case, being under the general charge and management of the respective boards of trustees of said universities. (95 v. 45, March 12, 1902.)

(4094-3) **Sec. 3.** [Tax levy for "Ohio and Miami university fund".] To enable the Ohio university and the Miami university to organize and support said normal schools there shall be levied annually a tax on the grand list of the taxable property of the state of Ohio, which shall be collected in the same manner as other state taxes and the proceeds of which shall be made a part of the "Ohio and Miami university fund," as already provided for (O. L., Vol. 92, pp. 40-41). The rate of such levy shall be designated by the general assembly at least once in two years, and if the general assembly shall fail to designate the rate for any year, the same shall be for the said "Ohio and Miami university fund," one thirtieth (1-30) of one mill upon each dollar of the valuation of such taxable property. (95 v. 45, March 12, 1902.)

(4094-4) **Sec. 4.** [How fund distributed.] The said "Ohio and Miami university fund," as herein described, shall be distributed and paid annually, seven-twelfths (7-12) thereof to the treasurer of the Ohio university upon the order of the president of the board of trustees of the said Ohio university and five-twelfths (5-12) thereof to the treasurer of the Miami university upon the order of the president of the board of trustees of said Miami university. (95 v. 45, March 12, 1902.)

(4094-5) Sec. 5. [State normal school commission, governor to appoint.] The governor is hereby authorized and required, within ninety days after the passage of this act, to appoint a board, to be known as the state normal school commission, consisting of four judicious citizens of the state, not more than two of whom shall be of the same political party, who shall serve without compensation,

[Duties.] and whose duty it shall be to make investigation upon the need and advisability of the future establishment by the state of one or more additional normal schools, and to consider in what manner and to what extent existing educational institutions other than those now supported by the state can be made more active and effective in the better training of persons for service in the public schools. (95 v. 45, March 12, 1902.)

(4094-6) Sec. 6. [Commission to make report to governor.] The state normal school commission shall, prior to the meeting of the seventy-sixth general assembly, make full report of its findings and investigations to the governor, who shall upon the organization of the general assembly transmit to it said report with such recommendations as he may deem proper. (95 v. 46, March 12, 1902.)

# CHAPTER XIV.

## COLLEGES AND UNIVERSITIES.

**Sec. 4095.** [Common council of any municipal corporation may accept educational trusts.] The board of directors of the university, college or other educational institution of any municipal corporation, in the name and on behalf of such corporation, may accept and take any property or funds heretofore or hereafter given to such corporation for the purpose of founding, maintaining or aiding a university, college or institution for the promotion of education, and upon such terms, conditions and trusts not inconsistent with law as the said board of directors may deem expedient and proper for that end. (Passed April 23, 1904. Approved May 3, 1904.)

**Sec. 4096.** [How trust funds to be applied.] For the further endowment, maintenance and aid of any such university, college or institution heretofore or hereafter founded, the board of directors thereof may, in the name and in behalf of such municipal corporation, accept and take as trustee and in trust for the purposes aforesaid any estate, property or funds which may have been or may be lawfully transferred to the municipal corporation for such use by any person, persons or body corporate having the same, or any annuity or endowment in the nature of income which may be covenanted or pledged to the municipal corporation, towards such use by any person, persons or body corporate; and any person, persons or body corporate having and holding any estate, property or funds in trust or applicable for the promotion of education, or the advancement of any of the arts or sciences, may convey, assign and deliver the same to such municipal corporation as trustee in his, their or its place, or covenant or pledge its income or any part thereof to the same; and any such estate, property, funds or income shall be held and applied by such municipal corporation in trust for the further endowment, maintenance and aid of such university, college or institution, in accordance nevertheless with the terms and true intent of any trust or condition upon which the same was originally given or held. (Passed April 23, 1904. Approved May 3, 1904.)

**Sec. 4097.** [Trusteeship to vest in city, etc.] Upon such transfer and the acceptance thereof by the municipal corporation and its successors, as trustees shall become and be perpetually obligated and held to observe and execute such trust in all respects according to any other or further terms or conditions lawfully agreed upon at the time of such transfer and acceptance; and any court having jurisdiction of the appointment of trustees of such trust for educational purposes, may, in a proceeding for that purpose duly instituted and had, appoint and constitute such municipal corporation with the consent of its council, trustee of the estate, property and funds so transferred to it, and may dispense with bond and surety upon the part of the municipal corporation for the performance of such trust, unless the same is required by the original terms or conditions thereof, and shall upon the due transfer and acceptance of such trust by the municipal corporation, release and fully discharge the trustee, or trustees so transferring the same; and any acceptance or acceptances by such municipal corporation of any or all property, funds, rights, trust estate or trusts heretofore given, granted, assigned, or otherwise conveyed or transferred to, or bestowed upon any such municipal corporation or to or upon any such university, college or institution in good faith, and which are still held and retained by such municipal corporation, or any such university, college or institution, shall be held and deemed to be valid and binding as to all parties. (Passed April 23, 1904. Approved May 3, 1904.)

**Sec. 4098.** [Board of directors; how appointed.] The custody and management of any and all estates, property, or funds so given, or transferred in trust to said city, and the entire administration of any and all such trusts so accepted by the common council thereof, and any university, college, or institution for the promotion of education heretofore or hereafter so founded in or by said city, except the common and high schools thereof, shall be committed to a board of nineteen directors, of whom the mayor of the city shall be one, and the others shall be appointed by the common council from persons of approved learning, discretion, and fitness for the office, six of whom shall be appointed from persons nominated to the common council by the board of education of the city, and twelve from persons nominated to the common council by the superior court of said city, if there be such court; the term of office of each director shall be six years. Such directors shall serve until the election or qualification of their successors; and any vacancy in the board caused by expiration of term, resignation, removal, or any other cause, shall be filled by appointment herein provided for the unexpired term. The board of directors shall, at the first regular meeting in January, elect a chairman, who is hereby authorized to administer the oath of office to any director so appointed. (1889, April 13; 86 v. 292; 78 v. 178; Rev. Stat. 1880; 67 v. 86, § 3.)

(4098-1) [Appointment of trustees of universities in Cincinnati supported by taxation in whole or in part.] In cities of the first grade of the first class all vacancies in the board of directors or trustees of universities supported in whole or in part by public taxation upon the property of such city, shall be filled by appointment by the judge or judges of the superior court of such cities where the same have a court; otherwise by the judge or judges of the common pleas court of the county in which such cities are located. (89 v. 31.)

Sec. 4099. [Powers of board; duties of city solicitor.] As to all matters not herein or otherwise provided by law, such board of directors shall have all the authority, power and control vested in or belonging to such municipal corporation as to the management and control of the estate, property and funds, given, transferred, covenanted or pledged to the municipal corporation for the trusts and purposes aforesaid, and the government, conduct and control such university, college or institution; it may appoint a clerk and all agents proper and necessary for the care and administration of the trust property, and the collection of the income, rents and profits thereof; it may appoint the president, professors, tutors, instructors, agents and servants necessary and proper for such university, college or institution, and fix their compensation; it may provide all the necessary buildings, books, apparatus, means and appliances, and may pass all such by-laws, rules and regulations concerning the president, professors, tutors, instructors, agents, and servants, and the admission, government and tuition of students, as it may deem wise and proper, and it may, by suitable by-laws, delegate and commit the admission, government, management and control of the students, courses of studies, discipline and other internal affairs of such university, college or institution, to a faculty which the board of directors may appoint from among the professors.

The solicitor of such municipal corporation shall, whenever requested so to do by resolution of said board, prosecute and defend, as the case may be, for and in behalf of the corporation, all complaints, suits and controversies in which the corporation or such board is a party, and which relate to any property, funds, trusts, rights, claims, estate or affairs, which shall or may be under the control or direction of said board, or which shall, in any manner, relate to the conduct or government of such university, college or institution. (Passed April 23, 1904. Approved May 3, 1904.)

**Sec. 4100.** [Citizens not to be charged for admission of children; non-residents may be admitted.] Citizens of such municipality shall not be charged for instruction in the academic department, except in professional courses therein. Such board of directors may charge fees to students in other departments and to students in professional courses in the academic department, and shall have power in its discretion from time to time to make such university, college or institution free in any or all of its departments to citizens of such county in which such university, college or institution may be located. The board of directors may in their discretion receive other students on such terms as to tuition or otherwise as they may see fit. (Passed April 23, 1904. Approved May 3, 1904.)

**Sec. 4101.** [Accounts of receipts and expenditures of endowment fund; how said fund may be invested.] The accounts of such trust estate, property and funds, and of the income and expenditure thereof, shall be kept by the auditor of such municipal corporation entirely distinct from all other accounts or affairs of the municipal corporation, and the moneys shall be kept by the treasurer of the municipal corporation distinct from other moneys. And the said board of directors shall, at all times, confine their disbursements for current expenses within the income of the trust, estate, property and funds, and shall annually report to the mayor and council of such municipal corporation a full statement of the accounts of administration of such trust and other funds; and said board of directors is hereby authorized to invest any part of the funds belonging to, or set apart for the use of such university, college or institution, or to any department thereof, as it may, from time to time, deem proper, in bonds of the United States or of the State of Ohio, or of any municipal corporation in the State of Ohio, or any county or school district in the State of Ohio, or in any other bonds or first mortgage securities approved by the board of directors; and said board is further authorized to use any funds under its control for the improvement of real estate belonging to, or set apart for the use of, such university, college or institution. (Passed April 23, 1904. Approved May 3, 1904.)

**Sec. 4102.** [When board may confer degrees; certain universities defined.] The board of directors of such university, college or institution, may, upon the recommendation of the faculty thereof, confer such degrees and honors as are customary in universities and colleges in the United States, and such others as with reference to the course of studies and attainments of the graduates in special departments it may deem proper.

A university supported in whole or in part by municipal taxation, is hereby defined as an assemblage of colleges united under one organization or management, affording instruction in the arts, sciences and the learned professions, and conferring degrees. (Passed April 23, 1904. Approved May 3, 1904.)

**Sec. 4103.** [Site and grounds for universities.] The council of any such municipal corporation may set apart, or appropriate as a site for the buildings and grounds of any such university, college or institution, any public grounds of the city not especially appropriated or dedicated by ordinance to any other use, any other law to the contrary notwithstanding; and the board of education of any such municipal corporation may also, for a like purpose, set apart, convey or lease for a term of years, any grounds or building owned or controlled by such board of education. Any grant for the use of such grounds or buildings heretofore or hereafter made by any council or board of education, may be modified, changed or extended as to the time when the same shall take effect and be in force, or otherwise, by agreement between said council, or board of education, and the board of directors of such university, college or institution, and said council shall be taken and held to be the representative of such municipal corporation vested with the title, right of possession and entire control of such property for the purposes of a new grant. (Passed April 23, 1904. Approved May 3, 1904.)

**Sec. 4104.** [When and how tax may be levied for universities in municipal corporations; astronomical observatory.] The council may assess and levy annually taxes on all the taxable property of such municipal corporation to the amount of three-tenths of one mill on the dollar valuation thereof, to be applied by said board to the support of such university, college or institution, and may also levy and assess annually five one-hundredths of one mill on the dollar valuation thereof, for the establishment and maintenance of an astronomical observatory, or for other scientific purposes, to be determined by the board of directors and to be used in connection with such university, college or institution, the proceeds of which shall be applied by the board of directors for such purposes exclusively; provided, however, that the taxes specified in this section shall only be levied and assessed when the chief work of such university, college or institution, is the maintenance of courses of instruction, in advance of or supplementary to the instruction authorized to be maintained in high schools by boards of education. Said levies shall be made by council at the same time, and in the same manner as other levies for other municipal purposes, and shall be certified by council, and placed upon the tax duplicate in the same manner as other municipal levies. The funds of any such university, college or institution shall be paid out by the treasurer upon the orders of the board of directors and the warrant of the auditor. (Passed April 23, 1904. Approved May 3, 1904.)

**Sec. 4105.** [Trust funds, board of education to act as trustee in certain cases; tax levy.] The custody, management and administration of any and all estates or funds, given or transferred in trust to any municipality for the promotion of education, and accepted by the council thereof, and any institution for the promotion of education heretofore or hereafter so founded other than a university as defined by this act, shall be committed to, and exercised by, the board of education of the school district including such municipality, and such board of education shall be held the representative and trustee of such municipality in the management and control of such estates and funds so held in trust and in the administration of such institution, excepting always such funds and estates held by any municipality which are used to maintain a university as defined by this act. And for the uses and purposes of such board of education in administering such trusts, the council of such municipality may annually levy taxes on all the taxable property of such municipal corporation to the amount of three-tenths of one mill on the dollar valuation thereof. (Passed April 23, 1904. Approved May 3, 1904.)

### OHIO UNIVERSITY.

**(4105-1) Sec. 1.** [Providing for sale of university lands.] The owner of the lands or town lots held under leases from the president and trustees of the Ohio University, or held under sale-leases or assignments by or under the original lessees, may pay to the treasurer for the time being of said university, such sum of money, as being put at interest at six per cent. will yield the amount of rent reserved in the original lease, or in case of a division of the original tract or parcel leased, will equal the proper aliquot part thereof, or the part agreed upon by the several owners; providing, that such person so surrendering and releasing to said corporation shall pay the necessary expenses incident to such change of tenure, and procure the services of an agent to perform the necessary labor thereof; and upon payment of such sum and of all rents due upon the land, the treasurer aforesaid shall, on demand of such owner, give him a certificate of such payment. (80 v. 193.)

**(4105-2) Sec. 2.** [Owner to receive deed; form of.] That such owner, upon such payment, shall be entitled to receive a deed of conveyance for such land by him owned, to be signed by the president of said corporation, countersigned by its secretary, and sealed with the corporate seal of the university, conveying the premises in fee simple to such owner, or such owner may, at his option, demand and receive a certificate as aforesaid; and the governor of Ohio, upon presentation thereof, shall execute and deliver to such owner, a deed in due form of law conveying the premises in fee simple to such owner. (80 v. 193.)

(4105-3) Sec. 3. [Validity of such deed.] That either of such deeds, so made, shall have the effect in law and in fact to vest in the grantee an absolute estate in fee simple in the premises, subject, however, to all liens, equities, or rights of third persons in, to or upon the premises. (80 v. 193.)

(4105-4) Sec. 4. [Registry of deed, etc., to be kept.] It shall be the duty of such secretary to keep an accurate registry of all such payment, certificates and deeds, with an accurate description of the tract or lot of land so paid for or deeded; and thereafter, the lands so deeded shall be subject to taxation, in like manner as other freehold estates in said county; and the original leases therefor, in so far as regards the land so deeded, shall cease to have force or effect. (80 v. 193.)

(4105-5) Sec. 5. [Proceeds to be deposited in state treasury, and become irreducible trust fund.] That it shall be the duty of the treasurer of the Ohio University, on or before the first day of January, next, after said receipt of money, to deposit the same in the state treasury upon the certificate of the state auditor, and the sum so deposited shall be added to the irreducible trust funds held by the state for education purposes, and interest thereon shall be paid semi-annually to the treasurer of said university, upon the requisition of the state auditor. (80 v. 193.)

(4105-6) Sec. 1. [Levy and collection of state tax upon lands donated to Athens University for use of said university.] Hereafter a state tax or a tax equal to the state tax upon like property, shall be levied and collected upon all lands donated to the Ohio University, situated at Athens, Ohio, and held by lease from said university or by deed from the governor or the said university, including such parts of said lands as are or may be owned, occupied or used by railroad companies as roadbeds, roadways, station houses, or for other purposes; and the said taxes when collected shall be paid over by the treasurer of Athens county, upon the warrant of the auditor of said county, to the treasurer of the Ohio University, for its use. (82 v. 115.)

(4105-7) Sec. 2. [Tax in lieu of rents; tax collected from railroad companies not to include tax upon rolling stock.] That the tax so to be collected upon lands so held by lease, shall be in lieu of so much of the rents due to the university; and the tax so to be collected from railroad companies, and paid to the university, shall not include the tax upon rolling stock. (82 v. 115.)

(4105-8) Sec. 3. [Repeal.] That the act entitled "an act to re-fund to the Ohio University certain funds in the state treasury, and to provide for the future payment of the claims of said university," passed March 25, 1875, be and is hereby repealed, saving however, all rights vested or required under said act. (82 v. 115.)

### OHIO STATE UNIVERSITY.

(4105-9) Sec. 1. [Establishment and style of college.] A col-lege, to be styled the Ohio Agricultural and Mechanical College, is hereby established in this state, in accordance with the provisions of an act of congress of the United States, passed July 2d, 1862, entitled "an act donating public lands to the several states and terri-tories which may provide colleges for the benefit of agricultural and mechanic arts," and said college to be located and controlled as here-inafter provided. The leading object shall be, without excluding other scientific and classical studies, and including military tactics, to teach such branches of learning as are related to agricultural and mechanic arts. (67 v. 20.)

(4105-10) Sec. 4. [Style and powers of trustees.] The trustees and their successors in office shall be styled the "Board of trustees of the Ohio Agricultural and Mechanical College," with the right as such, of suing and being sued, of contracting and being contracted with, of making and using a common seal, and altering the same at pleasure. (67 v. 20.)

(4105-11) Sec. 5. [Further powers and duties.] The board of trustees shall have power to adopt by-laws, rules and regulations for the government of said college; to elect a president; to determine the number of professors and tutors, elect the same, and fix their salaries. They shall also have power to remove the president or any professor or tutor whenever the interests of the college, in their judgment, shall require; to fix and regulate the course of instruction, and to prescribe the extent and character of experiments to be made. (67 v. 20.)

(4105-12) Sec. 7. [Who shall be admitted as pupils.] The col-lege shall be open to all persons over fourteen years of age, subject to such rules and regulations and limitations, as to numbers from the several counties of the state, as may be prescribed by the board of trustees; provided, that each county shall be entitled to its just proportion, according to its population. The board may provide for courses of lectures, either at the seat of the college or elsewhere in the state, which shall be free to all. (67 v. 20.)

(4105-13) **Sec. 8.** [Prerogative of the trustees.] The board of trustees shall have the general supervision of all lands, buildings, and other property belonging to said college, and the control of all expenses therefor; provided, always, that said board shall not contract any debt not previously authorized by the general assembly of the state of Ohio. (67 v. 20.)

(4105-14) **Sec. 9.** [Officers of the board.] The board of trustees shall annually elect one of their number chairman, and in the absence of the chairman shall elect one of their number temporary chairman, and shall have power to appoint a secretary, treasurer, and librarian, and such other officers as the interests of the college may require, who may or may not be members of the board; and shall held their offices for such term as said board shall fix, subject to removal by said board, and shall receive such compensation as the board shall prescribe. The treasurer shall, before entering upon the duties of his office give bond to the state of Ohio in such sum as the board may determine, which bond shall not be for a less sum than the probable amount that will be under his control in any one year, conditioned for the faithful discharge of his duties and the payment of all moneys coming into his hands, said bond to be approved by the attorney general of the state. (67 v. 20.)

(4105-15) **Sec. 11.** [Board may receive devises of land, etc.] The board of trustees shall have power to receive, and hold in trust, for the use and benefit of the college, any grant or device of land, and any donation or bequest of money or other personal property, to be applied to the general or special use of the college; all donations or bequests of money shall be paid to the state treasurer, and invested in the same manner as the endowment fund of the college, unless otherwise directed in the donation or bequest. (67 v. 20.)

(4105-16) **Sec. 13.** [Title of lands to be vested in the state, etc.] The title for all lands for the use of said college, shall be made in fee simple to the state of Ohio, with covenants of seizin and warranty, and no title shall be taken to the state for the purposes aforesaid until the attorney general shall be satisfied that the same is free from all defects and incumbrances. (67 v. 20.)

(4105-17) **Sec. 15.** [Attorney general to be legal adviser of the board.] The attorney general of the state shall be the legal adviser of said board of trustees, and he shall institute and prosecute all suits in behalf of the same, and shall receive the same compensation therefor as he is entitled to by law for suits brought in behalf of the asylums of the state. (67 v. 20.)

(4105-18) **Sec. 17.** [Location of the college; sundry provisos.] It shall be the duty of the board of trustees to permanently locate said agricultural and mechanical college upon lands, not less than one hundred acres, which in their judgment is best suited to the wants and purposes of said institution, the same being reasonably central in the state, and accessible by railroad from different parts thereof, having regard to healthiness of location, and also regarding the best interests of the college in the receipt of moneys, lands, or other properties donated to said college by any county, town, or individual, in consideration of the location of said college at a given place; provided, it shall require a three-fifths vote of the trustees to make said location; and, provided further, that said location shall be made on or before the fifteenth day of October, 1870; provided, further, that any person acting as a trustee, who shall accept or receive, directly or indirectly, any sum or amounts from any person or persons, to use their influence in favor of the location of said college at any particular point or place, shall be held to be guilty of a misdemeanor, and on conviction thereof by any court of competent jurisdiction, shall be fined in any sum not less than one thousand nor more than ten thousand dollars; provided, further, that in the location of said college the said trustees shall not in any event incur any debt or obligation exceeding forty thousand dollars; and if, in their opinion, the interests of the college cannot be best promoted without a larger expenditure for the location than that sum, then they may delay the permanent location of the same until the third of Monday of January, 1871, and report their proceedings and conclusions to the general assembly; provided, further, that said college shall not be located until there are secured thereto for such location, donations in money, or unincumbered lands, at their cash valuation, whereon the college is to be located, or in both money and such lands, a sum equal to at least one hundred thousand dollars. (67 v. 120.)

(4105-19) Sec. 1. [Acceptance of ceded lands.] The unsurveyed and unsold lands ceded to the state of Ohio by a certain act of congress of the United States, approved February 18, 1871, situate and being in the Virginia Military district between the great Scioto and the Little Miami rivers in said state, be and the same are hereby accepted by the state of Ohio, subject to the provisions of said act. (70 v. 107.)

(4105-20) Sec. 2. [Compensation for damages to lands may be demanded, etc.] The trustees of the Ohio agricultural and mechanical college are hereby authorized to demand from all persons who have destroyed or converted any timber growing upon the lands ceded to the state of Ohio, as stated in the act to which this is supplementary, since the date of said act of Congress ceding said lands to the state of Ohio, full compensation for the timber so destroyed or converted, and for all damages, and if payment shall be refused, to institute proper proceedings in the name of said Ohio Agricultural and Mechanical College, in any court of competent jurisdiction, to recover the same with damages and costs of suit; provided, that the provisions of this section shall not apply to timber taken from the one hundred and sixty acres by any person who shall obtain the title to the same under section three of this act. (70 v. 107.)

(4105-21) Sec. 3. [Title of lands invested in trustees of agricultural college, etc.] The title of said lands is hereby vested in the trustees of the Ohio Agricultural and Mechanical College for the benefit of said college; and said trustees are hereby required to cause a complete survey of said lands to be immediately made, and a correct plat thereof to be returned to said trustees, and to ascertain and set off, in reasonably compact form, by accurate boundaries to each occupant who was in actual possession of and living upon any of said lands at the time of the passage of said act of Congress, as provided therein, or their heirs and assigns, a tract not exceeding forty acres; and upon the payment, by the claimant, of the cost of surveying and making the deed, the said trustees shall make and deliver to said claimant a deed for said tract; and if any such occupant shall have been in such actual possession of more than forty acres, and is desirous of holding the same, he shall be entitled to have in addition to said forty acres, any number of acres not exceeding, with said forty acres, the number of one hundred and sixty acres, to be in reasonably compact form, by paying for the said excess over forty acres, the sum of one dollar per acre; and if any claimant under the provisions of this act shall desire to purchase any tract of land adjoining said forty acres, not exceeding, including said forty acres, the amount of one hundred and sixty acres, of which said claimant shall have been in actual possession, but does not desire to purchase the same at one dollar per acre, said trustees, upon notice by said claimant, shall cause said tract or part of tract to be sold separate from other tracts of land at a valuation fixed upon by the appraisers named in this act, payable one-third at the date of the survey, and the residue in two equal annual installments, with interest at six per cent., payable annually, and upon full payment being made with the cost of survey and conveyance, said trustee shall make and deliver to such claimant, his or her heirs or assigns, a deed for said excess over said forty acres; provided, that any person claiming the benefit of the provisions of this section as occupant, shall comply in all respects with, and be subject to the provisions of the thirteenth section of the act of Congress, approved September 4, 1841, entitled an act to appropriate the proceeds of the sales of the public lands and to grant pre-emption rights, and to the rules and regulations of the general land office of the United States relating to proof for the establishment of pre-emptor's claims; provided, however, that the affidavit required by said thirteenth section of said act of Congress may be made before any justice of the peace or other officer authorized to administer oaths. (70 v. 107.)

(4105-22) Sec. 4. [Division of unsold lands into tracts, etc.; tracts to be numbered and appraised.] All the unsurveyed and unsold lands in said military district, not occupied as aforesaid, shall be divided by said trustees into such tracts, not exceeding five hundred acres in any one boundary, as will be most advantageous, reference being had to the quality of said lands and the uses to which they will be applied; the boundaries to all such tracts and divisions shall be accurately surveyed, and the lines of each tract plainly marked, and substantial stone monuments firmly placed at the principal corners. The character of the soil, water courses, elevation of hills, timber, ledges, or stratas of the Waverly building stone, iron ore, fire clay, and limestone, shall be fully noted by the surveyors on their plats and in their field books. All the tracts so divided and surveyed shall be numbered in consecutive order, commencing with the tracts in Adams county, and so continuing until all said lands in said district shall be platted and numbered; which number shall be shown upon the plats, and the said plats shall correctly indicate all township lines. The said lands, when so divided, surveyed and numbered, shall be appraised in separate tracts at their true value in money, by three qualified freehold residents in said state, to be summoned by said trustees, or any committee of theirs. Said appraisers before entering upon their duties, shall take and subscribe an oath before competent authority honestly and impartially to appraise all such lands, and to perform all other duties in relation thereto; they shall each be paid two dollars a day for their services, and their expenses allowed them; they shall make due return of all their appraisements to said trustees, which, with all said plats and surveys, shall be delivered by them to the auditor of state, and the same shall be recorded in the office of said auditor in suitable books to be provided for such purpose; which, with all such original plats, surveys, and papers, shall form a part of the public records of the state in the land department of said office. (70 v. 107.)

(4105-23) Sec. 5. [To be sold at private or public sale; contracts of sale to be recorded, etc.] And the said trustees are hereby authorized and required to sell all of said lands at public or private sale, at a price not less than the appraised value thereof, on such terms for cash and credit as may be agreed upon between the purchaser and said trustees, or any authorized agent of theirs; provided, that the first payment shall, in every case, be not less than one-third of the appraised value of such tract; all deferred payments shall bear six per cent. interest, to be paid annually, and said trustees may, in their discretion, extend subsequent annual payments through a period not exceeding five years. All public sales of said lands shall be by auction, at the front door of the court house of the county in which these lands so offered lie, after having been advertised five consecutive weeks in a newspaper published and generally circulated in such county; such notices of sale, shall contain a sufficient description of the premises to clearly identify the same, with a statement of the terms of payment and the amount of appraisement, and all such public sales shall be made at such times as said trustees shall deem expedient; and in case such land or any tract thereof shall not sell for the amount of the appraisement at such public sale, then upon the same being again offered as aforesaid at public sale, the same may be sold for any sum not less than three-fourths of the appraisement; provided, that no trustee of said college or appraiser of said land shall be the purchaser of any of said lands at any such sale or sales, either directly or indirectly. The said trustees shall cause all contracts for the sale of said lands to be printed or written in a book or books, stating the consideration and terms of all sales, which said contracts shall be signed in duplicate by the said trustees or any authorized agent of theirs, and by the purchaser or purchasers, one copy of which shall be preserved in said book, and the other shall be delivered to the purchaser at the time the same shall be signed; and every purchaser shall execute his promissory note or notes, with interest, payable as aforesaid, for all deferred payments, which notes shall be non-negotiable, and payable to said college at such place or places as may be directed by said trustees; and upon full payment being made by the purchaser, his heirs or assigns, for any such land, every such person shall be entitled to receive a conveyance therefor in fee simple by deed of said trustees, executed by the president of the board, under the corporate seal of said college; and all lands disposed of under the provisions of this act, shall be returned by said trustees to the auditor of the counties in which they are situate, and by them be placed on the duplicate for taxation. (70 v. 107.)

(4105-24.) [Trustees of Ohio State University may erect residences for faculty.] The proceeds of the sales of such lands, or so much thereof as may be necessary, after the payment out of the same of all the necessary expenses of survey and sale remaining uncertified into the treasury of said state, may be used by said trustees in building and maintaining upon the lands of said university a suitable

number of houses, adapted to use as family residences, for the use
of members of the faculty of said university, for which use a fair
and reasonable rent shall be paid to said university. Said buildings
shall be erected under the provisions of title six of the Revised
Statutes of Ohio; and the said trustees shall annually report to the governor a detailed statement of receipts and disbursements in the execution of the trusts under the provisions of this act. (1882, April
17; 79 v. 144; Rev. Stat. 1880; 70 v. 107.)

(4105-25) **Sec. 7.** [Acts repealed.]   The act entitled an act to
sell lands ceded to the state of Ohio by the Congress of the United
States by act of Congress, approved February 18, 1871, passed
March 26, 1872, and the act supplementary thereto and amendatory
thereof, passed April 29, 1872, be and they are hereby repealed; provided, that the passage of this act shall in no wise affect the validity
of the transactions of said board of trustees, or rights vested in any
person, under the provisions of said acts; and this act shall take
effect and be in force from and after its passage. (70 v. 107.)

(4105-26) **Sec. 1.** [Ohio **State** University; **establishment of a
school of mines; course of study; apparatus, etc.**]   The trustees of
the Ohio State University be and they are hereby required to establish in said university, a school of mines and mine engineering, in
which shall be provided the means for studying scientifically and
experimentally the survey, opening, ventilation, care and working of
mines; and said school shall be provided with a collection of draw-
ings, illustrating the manner of opening, working, and ventilating
mines, and with the necessary instruments for surveying, measuring
air, examining and testing the noxious and poisonous gases of mines,
and also with the models of the most improved machinery for ventilating and operating all the various [kinds] of mines with safety
to the lives and health of those engaged. Said school shall also be
provided with complete mining laboratories for the analysis of coals,
ores, fire clays and other minerals, and with all the necessary apparatus for testing the various coals, ores, fire clays, oils, gases, and
other minerals. (1888, April 4; 85 v. 155; Rev. Stat. 1880; 74 v. 216.)

(4105-27) **Sec. 2.** [Employment and duties of instructors; cabinet of specimens to be kept.]   Said trustees shall employ competent persons to give instruction in the most improved and successful methods of opening, [and operating] surveying and inspecting
mines, including the methods and machinery employed for extract-
ing coal, ore, fire clay, oil, gas and other minerals from the pit's
mouth and for facilitating the ascent and descent of workmen, the
draining and freeing of mines from water, the causes of the vitiation
of air, the quantities of fresh air required under various circumstances,

natural ventilation, mechanical ventilation by flues and fans, and other ventilating machinery, the use of air engines, air compressors and coal cutting machinery; also instruction in the various uses of coals, ores, fire clays, oils, gases and other minerals, and the methods of testing, analyzing and assaying such minerals; also the methods employed in metallurgical and other processes in the reduction of ores and in determining the qualities of metals, particularly iron and steel, as shown by practical and laboratory tests; and there shall be kept in a cabinet properly arranged for ready reference and examination, suitably connected with said school of mines samples of the specimens from the various mines in the state, which may be sent for analysis, together with the names of the mines and their localities in the counties from which they were sent, and the analysis and a statement of their properties attached (it shall also be his duty to furnish analysis of all minerals found in the state and sent to him for that purpose by residents of this state). (1888, April 4; 85 v. 155; Rev. Stat. 1880; 74 v. 216.)

(4105-28) **Sec. 3.** [**Appropriation.**] There is hereby appropriated out of the general revenue fund the sum of three thousand five hundred dollars to be expended in the equipment, support and maintenance of said school of mines as provided for in the first and second sections of this act. (1888, April 4; 85 v. 155; Rev. Stat. 1880; 74 v. 216.)

(4105-29) **Sec. 1.** [Support of Ohio State University law school.] The board of trustees of the Ohio State University are hereby authorized and empowered to appropriate annually, for the period of ten years, to the support and maintenance of the school of law of the Ohio State University, out of the fund derived under section 3951 of the Revised Statutes of Ohio, amended March 20, 1891 (88 O. L., 159), a sum not exceeding five thousand dollars, in addition to the sum derived from the tuition fees of the students in said school of law. (90 v. 253.)

(4105-30) **Sec. 1.** [Ohio State University department of ceramics.] The trustees of the Ohio State University be and they are hereby required to establish in said university a department of ceramics, equipped and designed for the technical education of clay, cement and glass workers, in all branches of the art which exist in this state, or which can be profitably introduced and maintained in this state from the mineral resources thereof, including the manufacture of earthenwares, stonewares, yellowwares, whitewares, china, porcelain and ornamental pottery, also the manufacture of sewer pipe, fireproofing, terracotta, sanitary claywares, electric conduits and specialties, firebricks and all refractory materials, glazed and enameled bricks, pressed bricks, vitrified paving material, as well as the most economic methods in the production of the coarser forms of bricks used for building purposes; also the manufacture of tiles used for paving, flooring, decorative wall-paneling, roofing and draining purposes, also the manufacture of cement, concrete, artificial stone and all kinds of glass products and all other clay industries represented in our limits. (91 v. 164.)

(4105-31) **Sec. 2. [Special instruction.]** Said department shall offer special instruction to clay workers on the origin, composition, properties and testing of clays, the selection of materials for different purposes, the mechanical and chemical preparation of clays, the laws of burning clays, the theory and practice of the formation of clay bodies, slips and glazes, and the laws which control the formation and fusion of silicates. (91 v. 164.)

(4105-32) **Sec. 3. [Laboratory.]** Said department shall be provided with an efficient laboratory designed especially for the practical instruction of clay workers in the list of subjects enumerated in the second section of this act, and also equipped to investigate into the various troubles and defects incident to every form of clay working, which cannot be understood or avoided except by use of such scientific investigation. Said laboratory shall be equipped with apparatus for chemical analysis, with furnaces and kilns for pyrometric and practical trials, with such machinery for the grinding, washing and preparation of clays for manufacture as is consistent with the character of the department. (91 v. 164.)

(4105-33) **Sec. 4. [Expert.]** Said trustees shall employ to conduct this department of ceramics a competent expert, who shall unite to the necessary education and scientific requirements, a thorough practical knowledge of clay working, and not less than two years' actual experience in some branch of the art. It shall be his duty to teach the theoretical part of the subject and to conduct the laboratory for the instruction of students, and also to prosecute such scientific investigation into the technology of the various clay industries as may be practicable, and from time to time to publish the results of his investigations in such form that they will be accessible to the clay workers of the state for the advancement of the art. (91 v. 164.)

(4105-34) **Sec. 5. [Appropriations.]** There shall be hereafter appropriated out of the general revenues of the state the sum of five thousand dollars, to be expended in the organization, equipment and maintenance of said department, as provided for in the first four sections of this act, for the current year, and there shall be appropriated from the same fund the sum of two thousand five hundred dollars annually for two years for the salary, supplies and all other expenses of maintenance of said department. (91 v. 164.)

**(4105-35) Sec. 2. [Written analysis to be furnished by professor of chemistry at agricultural college.]** It shall be the duty of the professor occupying the chair in the chemical and mechanical department of the Ohio agricultural and mechanical college, upon application, to make and give a written analysis of such artificial fertilizers as may be furnished to him for that purpose. (75 v. 91.)

**(4105-37) Sec. 1. [To be known as "The Ohio State University."]** The educational institution heretofore designated as the Ohio Agricultural and Mechanical College shall be known and designated hereafter as "The Ohio State University." (75 v. 126.)

**(4105-37) Sec. 2. [To be governed by board of seven trustees; how and by whom appointed.]** The government of said university shall be vested in a board of seven trustees, who shall be appointed by the governor of the state, with the advice and consent of the senate; but no trustee, or his relation by blood or marriage, shall be eligible to any professorship or position in the university, the compensation for which is payable out of the state treasury, or said college fund. (75 v. 126.)

**(4105-38) Sec. 3. [Their terms of office; to be paid their expenses while engaged in the discharge of duties.]** The members of said board of trustees and their successors shall hold their offices for the term of seven years each; provided, that the trustees first appointed under the provisions of this act shall hold their terms for one, two, three, four, five, six, and seven years, respectively, to be fixed by the governor in their commissions. In case a vacancy shall occur from death or other cause, the appointment shall be for the unexpired term. The trustees shall not receive any compensation for their services, but they shall be paid their reasonable and necessary expenses while engaged in the discharge of their official duties. (75 v. 126.)

**(4105-39) Sec. 4. [Powers and duties of board.]** The board of trustees shall have power, and it is made their duty, to collect, or cause to be collected, specimens of the various cereals, fruits, and other vegetable products, and to have experiments made in their reproduction upon the lands of the university, and to make report of the same, from year to year, together with such other facts as may tend to advance the interests of agriculture. (75 v. 126.)

**(4105-40) Sec. 5. [Collections of specimens.]** The board of trustees shall have power, and it is hereby made their duty to secure and keep in the said university a collection of specimens in mineralogy, geology, zoology, botany, and other specimens pertaining to natural history and the sciences; and it shall be the duty of the president of the university to collect and deposit in the said university, in such manner as shall be directed by the trustees, a full and complete set of specimens as collected by him and his assistants, together with a brief description of the character of the same, and where obtained; and the said specimens shall be properly classified and kept for the benefit of said university. (75 v. 126.)

(4105-41) **Sec. 6.** [Meetings of board of trustees.] The first meeting of the members of the board shall be called by the governor, as soon after the appointment of said board as convenient, to be held at said university, in Columbus, Ohio. All succeeding meetings shall be called in such manner, and at such times as the board may prescribe. The said board shall meet at least three times annually, and at such other times as they may think necessary for the best interests of the said university. A majority of the board of trustees present at any meeting shall constitute a quorum to do business; provided, a majority of all the board shall be required to elect or remove a president or professor. (75 v. 126.)

(4105-42) **Sec. 7.** [Annual report of trustees; fiscal year; printing and distribution of report.] The board of trustees shall cause to be made on or before the first of October of each year a report to the governor of the condition of said university; the amount of receipts and disbursements, and for what the disbursements were made; the number of professors, officers, teachers, and other employes and the position and compensation of. each; the number of students in the several departments and classes, and the course of instruction pursued in each; also an estimate of the expenses for the ensuing year; a statement showing the progress of the university, recording any improvements and experiments made, with their costs and the results, and such other matters as may be supposed useful. Said annual report shall be for the year ending June 30, and the said Ohio State University is hereby exempted from the provisions of section 172, Revised Statutes of Ohio. There shall be printed under the provision of section 58 of the Revised Statutes of Ohio, as amended May 1, 1891 (O. L. v. 88, p. 498), five thousand copies of the said annual report, to be distributed by the trustees in such manner as they shall deem best for the interest of said university. The president of said university shall transmit by mail one copy to the secretary of the interior, one copy to the secretary of agriculture, and one copy to each of the colleges which are, or may be endowed under the provisions of the act of congress of July 2, 1862. (90 v. 292; 75 v. 126.)

(4105-43) **Sec. 8.** [Funds from the sale of land script to form part of irreducible debt; and interest of same paid to university.] All funds derived from the sale of land script issued to the state of Ohio by the United States, in pursuance of the aforesaid act of congress, together with the interest accumulated thereon, shall constitute a part of the irreducible debt of this state, the interest upon which, as provided by the act of February 10, 1870 (O. L., vol. 67, p. 15), shall be paid to the university by the auditor of state, upon the requisition of the commissioners of the sinking fund, issued on the certificate of the secretary of the board of trustees, that the same has been appropriated by said trustees to the endowment, support, and maintenance of the university, as provided in the act of congress aforesaid. (75 v. 126.)

(4105-44) **Sec. 9.** [Compensation of president, professors, teachers, etc.] That said board of trustees shall fix the compensation for the president, professors, teachers and all other employes of the university; provided, that the compensation for the services of the professors shall not exceed twenty-five hundred dollars each per annum. (91 v. 74; 75 v. 126.)

(4105-45) **Sec. 10.** [Branches prescribed at Ohio State University.] It shall be the duty of the board of trustees, in connection with the faculty of the university, to provide for the teaching of such branches of learning as are related to agriculture and the mechanic arts, mines, and mine engineering, and military tactics, and such other scientific and classic studies as the resources of the fund will permit. (1880, April 15; 77 v. 227; Rev. Stat., 75 v. 126.)

(4105-46) **Sec. 1.** [Computation and investment of interest.] The auditor of state be and is required to compute the interest which has accrued and will accrue on the agricultural college scrip fund since the same has been sold, to July first, one thousand eight hundred and seventy, compounding the same by semi-annual rests on the first day of January and the first day of July in each year; and on the fifteenth day of June eighteen hundred and seventy to transfer the sum so arising to the said college fund, and invest the same in the interest-bearing bonds of the state, in the same manner as the principal of the said fund is now invested. (67 v. 15.)

(4105-47) **Sec. 2.** [How interest invested.] That on the first day of July, eighteen hundred and seventy, and every six months thereafter (viz: on the first day of January and July, respectively) the auditor of state shall invest the interest of said funds falling due in the same manner as the principal now invested. (67 v. 15.)

(4105-48) **Sec. 1.** [Trustees of Ohio State University authorized to make deeds.] As soon as the board of trustees of the Ohio State University accepts the provisions hereinafter made, it is hereby authorized and required to execute and deliver upon demand, a deed of conveyance to the parties in possession under claim of title of any unpatented survey or part thereof, in said Virginia Military District; provided, however, that all applicants for such deed must furnish said trustees with a certified copy of the deed under which they claim, and if required, a certified copy of the unpatented survey in which their lands are situate, as the necessary evidence to satisfy the board that the same has never been patented, but has been occupied and improved by the said parties in possession or those under whom they claim title, for more than twenty-one years. Provided, also, that each applicant shall pay the board of trustees the sum of two dollars, as the cost of preparing and executing such deed. (86 v. 92.)

(4105-49) **Sec. 2.** [Duty of auditor of state.] The auditor of state shall add the sum of one dollar per acre, reckoned by the number of acres of land in each actual survey for all conveyances so made to that part of the irreducible debt of the state, which forms the endowment of said Ohio State University; provided, that in cases where suit has been brought for the recovery of said lands, persons demanding deeds of release, shall pay all court costs of such suits. (86 v. 92.)

(4105-50) **Sec. 1.** [Relief of persons who wrongfully paid for lands in Virginia Military District; duty of auditor of state.] All persons who were in possession of lands in the Virginia Military District under claim of title of an unpatented survey or part thereof, said lands having been occupied and improved by said persons in possession or those under whom they claim title for more than twenty-one years and were compelled by suit, or the fear thereof, to pay the Ohio State University for said lands, are hereby authorized to present a statement of the amount of money so paid by them, together with all the facts relating to the land held by them and their title thereto, to a board composed of the secretary of state, auditor of state and attorney general, who are hereby authorized and empowered to examine such statements and call for and examine such other testimony as they see fit, and if upon such examination said board are satisfied 'that said persons are justly entitled to relief as those persons were who have obtained relief under the provisions of the aforesaid act, then said board shall determine how much said party has wrongfully paid and issue an order to the auditor of state directing him to draw his warrant on the treasurer of state for the said amount in behalf of the person filing said statement; provided, that where such claims have been heretofore as (or) shall hereafter be allowed by said board, the auditor of state shall add the amount thereof to that part of the irreducible debt of the state which constitutes the endowment fund of said Ohio State University. (91 v. 375; 90 v. 221.)

(4105-51) **Sec. 2.** [Appropriation.] That there be and is hereby appropriated, out of any money in the state treasury accredited to the fund of the Ohio State University, the sum of twelve hundred and ninety-six dollars to pay said warrants. (90 v. 221.)

(4105-52) **Sec. 3.** [Costs of obtaining evidence.] That persons filing such statements shall pay all the costs incurred in obtaining evidence. (90 v. 221.)

(4105-53) **Sec. 4.** [Report to general assembly.] Said board shall report all its proceedings to the general assembly. (90 v. 221.)

### WILBERFORCE UNIVERSITY

(4105-54) **Sec. 1.** [Normal and industrial department at Wilberforce University.] There shall be established and maintained at Wilberfore University, in Greene county, Ohio, a combined normal and industrial department. (84 v. 127.)

(4105-55) **Sec. 2.** [Board of trustees; appointment by governor, etc.] To carry out the purposes of this act, there shall be and hereby is created a board of nine trustees to be known as "the board of trustees of the combined normal and industrial department at Wilberforce University," five shall be appointed by the governor by and with the consent of the senate, and three shall be chosen by the board of trustees of said university. The president of the university shall be ex-officio a member of said board. The trustees so to be appointed by the governor, as aforesaid, shall be appointed, on or before the first day of May, 1896, and they shall hold their office respectively as follows: One for one year, two for two years, and two for four years the term of such to begin to run from July first, 1896; said term shall be designated by the governor in his message of appointment to the senate and in the commission issued to said trustees. At the session of the senate next preceding the expiration of the term of any trustee, the governor shall appoint his successor for the term of four years; and every appointment of the governor under this act shall be submitted to the senate for confirmation. (92 v. 275; 89 v. 368; 87 v. 215; 84 v. 127.)

(4105-56) **Sec. 3.** [Choosing of trustees by university board.] The three trustees to be chosen as aforesaid by the board of trustees of said university shall be chosen at the first regular meeting of said board in June, 1892, after the passage of this act; and the three so chosen at such meeting, shall hold their offices, respectively, as follows: One for one year, one for two years, and one for three years, and the term of each to begin to run from the third Thursday in June, 1892. In anticipation of the expiration of the term of any trustee so chosen, the said university board shall, annually thereafter at its regular meeting choose his successor, who shall hold his office for (the) term of three years. (89 v. 368; 84 v. 127.)

(4105-57) **Sec. 4.** [Vacancies.] In case a vacancy in that portion of the board so appointed by the governor or chosen by the university board shall occur from death, resignation, or other cause, the appointment or selection to fill such vacancy shall be made in the one case by the governor, and in the other by the executive board of said university for the unexpired term. (84 v. 127.)

**(4105-58) Sec. 5.** [Names of trustees chosen by university board to be certified to governor.] It shall be the duty of the secretary of the said university, immediately upon choice being made by the university board of three trustees as aforesaid, to certify to the governor, under the seal of said university, the names of the persons so chosen as trustees under this act, with their terms, respectively; and also the name of the person chosen by said executive board at any time to fill a vacancy. (84 v. 127.)

**(4105-59) Sec. 6.** [Meetings of trustees; their expenses.] The board of trustees created under this act shall meet in regular session at said university twice a year; the first meeting shall be on the third Thursday in June, and the second on the first Thursday in November of each year; but other meetings may be held at such places and times as a majority of the board may determine. The said trustees shall receive no compensation, but shall be reimbursed their traveling and other reasonable and necessary expenses out of appropriations under this act. (89 v. 368; 84 v. 127.)

**(4105-60) Sec. 7.** [Powers and duties of trustees.] It shall be the duty of said board of trustees created under this act to take, keep and maintain exclusive authority, directions, supervision and control over the operations and conduct of said normal and industrial department, so as to assure for it the best attainable results with the aid hereby secured to it from the state. Said board shall determine the branches of industry to be pursued, purchase, through a suitable and disinterested agent, the necessary means and appliances, select a superintendent for the industrial branch of the department, fix his salary and prescribe his duties and authority. The expenditures of all moneys appropriated under this act for carrying out its purposes and provisions, shall be made only under such regulations and for such specific purposes not herein provided for, as the board of trustees of said department shall establish; but no money hereby appropriated by the state shall be used at any time for any purpose not in direct furtherance and promotion of the objects of the department. (84 v. 127.)

**(4105-61) Sec. 8.** [Non-sectarian character of department.] No sectarian influence, direction or interference in the management or conduct of the affairs or education of said department shall be permitted by its board; but its benefits shall be open to all applicants of good moral character and within the limitations of age determined by said board. (84 v. 127.)

**(4105-62) Sec. 9.** [Payment to university of state appropriations; bond of treasurer.] Upon the certificate of the board of trustees of said department that the necessary steps have been taken by the board of trustees of said university to co-operate with the department trustees in carrying out the purposes of this act by granting the use of its buildings, grounds and educational facilities, there shall be paid to the treasurer of said department, semi-annually, one-half of such amounts as may be annually appropriated by the general assembly for the purposes therein named. The treasurer of said department shall give to the state of Ohio a bond to be approved by the attorney general in the sum of twenty thousand dollars, conditioned that he shall faithfully discharge his duties and account for any money coming into his hands from the state of Ohio. (92 v. 275; 84 v. 127.)

**(4105-63) Sec. 10.** [Annual report, and estimate of appropriations.] The board of trustees shall cause to be made on or before the first day of December, eighteen hundred and eighty-eight (and) each year thereafter, a report to the governor of the condition, progress and results of said department, with an estimate of what appropriation shall be required to secure the objects of this act. (84 v. 127.)

**(4105-64) Sec. 11.** [Designation of pupils by members of general assembly.] Each senator and representative of the general assembly of the state of Ohio may designate one or more youth resident of his district who shall be entitled to attend the said normal and industrial department free of tuition. (92 v. 275; 84 v. 127.)

**(4105-65) Sec. 12.** [Appropriations; application of revenues.] For the purpose of carrying out the provisions of this act there shall be levied annually a tax on the grand list of taxable property of the state, which shall be collected in the same manner as other state taxes, and the proceeds of which shall constitute "the fund of the combined normal and industrial department at Wilberforce university." The rate of such levy shall be designated by the general assembly at least once in two years, and if the general assembly shall fail to designate the rate for any year, the same shall be for the said fund of the "combined normal and industrial department of Wilberforce university" two-hundredths of one mill upon each dollar valuation of such taxable property for the year 1900 and one-hundredth of one mill thereafter. The same shall be paid to the treasurer of the normal and industrial department at Wilberforce university in accordance with the provisions of section twelve of said act. All revenue arising from tuitions, sales of products or otherwise under the aforesaid department shall be applied by its board of trustees to defray its expenses, or to increase its efficiency, a strict account of which shall be kept by the department board, and accompany the report to the governor. (94 v. 598; 92 v. 156; 84 v. 127.)

(4105-66) **Sec. 1.** [Additional appropriations for Wilberforce University.] There is hereby appropriated out of any moneys in the treasury to the credit of the general revenue fund not otherwise appropriated, for combined normal and industrial department at Wilberforce University, two thousand dollars, the same being the balance due said institution under the provisions of an act passed March 19, 1887. And this amount shall be in full of all claims against the state by said university. (86 v. 392.)

## CHAPTER XV.

### SCHOOLS SPECIALLY ENDOWED.

(4105-67) **Sec. 1.** [Courts of common pleas to appoint trustees for schools specially endowed; powers.] Whenever any person shall, by deed, devise, gift or otherwise, set apart any lands, moneys or effects, as an endowment of a school or academy, not previously established, and shall not provide for the management of such school or academy, the court of common pleas of the proper county shall appoint five trustees, who shall have the control and management of the property, moneys, and effects, so set apart, and of the school or academy thus endowed, and shall hold their offices for five years, and until their successors are elected and qualified; but in making the first appointment the court shall appoint one trustee for one year, one for two years, one for three years, one for four years, and one for five years. The trustees shall be a body corporate, with perpetual succession, and by such name as may be ordered by the court making the first appointment; may sue and be sued; have a corporate seal and the same alter or change at pleasure, and may hold all kinds of estates, real and personal, and mixed, which they may acquire by purchase, donation, devise or otherwise. (53 v. 33; S. & C. 1383.)

(4105-68) **Sec. 2.** [Filling vacancies; removal.] The said court shall annually appoint one trustee, to fill the vacancy then occurring; and at any other time fill vacancies that may occur from any cause, for the unexpired term; said court shall also have power upon sufficient cause shown, reasonable notice of the time and place of hearing having been given to the party interested, remove any trustee, and may, until a hearing be had, suspend a trustee in the exercise of his office. (53 v. 33; S. & C., 1383.)

(4105-69) **Sec. 3.** [Duties of trustees.] The trustees shall have power to establish, from time to time, rules and regulations for the management and safekeeping of the property, moneys, and effects, belonging to the trust, and the expenditure of the income thereof, and also for the management and government of the school or academy; which rules and regulations shall not be inconsistent with the terms of the deed, devise or gift, creating the endowment, or with the laws of this state; they shall not, at any time, or for any cause, incur any debt or liability, beyond the net income of the trust property, moneys, and effects, or use or appropriate the same, otherwise than to invest for the purpose of income, any part of the principal thereof, unless expressly authorized so to do by the terms of the deed, devise or gift, creating the endowment of trust. (53 v. 33; S. & C. 1383.)

(4105-70) **Sec. 4.** [Same; oath; bond.] The trustees shall, immediately after their appointment, organize by appointing a president, secretary, and treasurer, from their own number, and shall severally take and subscribe an oath to faithfully discharge the duties of trustees, and deposit the same with the county auditor. They shall, also, before taking possession of the property, moneys, or effects, constituting the endowment or trust, severally give bond, in such sum as the court may require, with two or more sufficient sureties, to be approved by a judge of said court, whose approval shall be endorsed on the bonds, conditioned for the faithful management of the property, moneys, and effects, intrusted to them and accountability therefor in such form as the court or judge may require; and the court may, from time to time, require additional bonds and surety, as may appear necessary for the preservation of the trust estate. The bonds required shall be payable to the state of Ohio, and deposited in the office of the county auditor for safe keeping. (53 v. 33; S. & C. 1383.)

(4105-71) **Sec. 5.** [Accounts to be rendered.] The trustees shall, on the second Monday of September, in each year, and at such other times as the court may require, render a full and accurate account, statement, and exhibit, of the condition of the 'school or academy under their management, and the condition of the trust estate and funds; and shall cause the same to be published in such form as the court may direct; which account, statement, and exhibit, shall be sworn to by the president, secretary, and treasurer, or some two of them. (53 v. 33; S. & C. 1383.)

(4105-72) **Sec. 6.** [Visitors.] The court of common pleas of the proper county shall, annually, at the first session after the second Monday in September, appoint three competent and disinterested persons, who shall have authority to visit any such school or academy and examine the same, together with the condition of the trust estate or endowment, and shall report thereon to the court making the appointment. The court shall also authorize such other visitations and examinations as may appear to be necessary. (53 v. 33; S. & C. 1383.)

(4105-73) **Sec. 7.** [When to take effect.] This act shall apply to endowments heretofore created, as well as to those hereafter created, and shall take effect from and after its passage. (53 v. 33; S. & C. 1383.)

# TITLE II.

---

## CHAPTER XIV.

### COLLEGES, AND INSTITUTIONS OF LEARNING.

**Sec. 3726.** [Certain corporations may appoint a faculty and confer degrees.] The trustees of a college, university, or other institution of learning, incorporated for the purpose of promoting education, religion, morality, or the fine arts, which has acquired real or personal property of the value of five thousand dollars, and which has filed in the office of the secretary of state a schedule of the kind and value of such property, verified by the oaths of the trustees, may appoint a president, professors, and tutors, and any other necessary agents and officers, and fix the compensation of each, and may enact such by-laws, not inconsistent with the laws of this state or of the United States, for the government of the institution, and for conducting the affairs of the corporation, as they may deem necessary; and may, on the recommendation of the faculty, confer all such degrees and honors as are conferred by colleges and universities of the United States, and such others having reference to the course of study, and the accomplishments of the student, as they may deem proper. (50 v. 128, § 1; 51 v. 403, §§ 2, 3; S. & C. 266, 270.)

**Sec. 3727.** [May hold donated property in trust.] Any university, college, or academy, or the trustees thereof, may hold in trust any property devised, bequeathed, or donated to such institution, upon any specific trust consistent with the objects of the corporation. (50 v. 128, § 5; S. & C. 267.)

**Sec. 3728.** [Who constitute the faculty; its powers.] The president and professors shall constitute the faculty of any incorporated literary college or university, and may enforce the rules and regulations enacted by its trustees for the government and discipline of the students, and suspend and expel offenders, as may be deemed necessary. (50 v. 128, § 6; S. & C. 267.)

**Sec. 3729.** [May teach mechanics and agriculture.] Any incorporated university, college, or academy may connect therewith, to be used as a part of its course of education, any mechanical shops and machinery, or lands for agricultural purposes not exceeding three hundred acres, to which may be attached all necessary buildings for carrying on the mechanical or agricultural operations of such institution. (50 v. 128, § 8; S. & C. 267.)

**Sec. 3730.** [May change stock into scholarships.] Any company formed in pursuance of this title, or which now exists by virtue of any special act of incorporation, the property of which is held as stock, and not derived by donation, gift, devise, or gratuitous subscription, may change its capital stock into scholarships, when it becomes necessary for the purpose of carrying out the object for which it was formed, in the manner provided in section *thirty-two hundred and sixty-two.* (50 v. 128, §§ 9, 10; S. & C. 268.)

**Sec. 3731.** [Location may be changed and how.] A college, university, or other institution of learning, now existing by virtue of any act of incorporation, or that may hereafter become incorporated for any of the purposes specified in this chapter, may, if three-fourths of the trustees or directors thereof deem the same proper, or if the institution is owned in shares, or by stock subscribed or taken, by a vote of the holders of three-fourths of the stock or shares, change the location of such institution, convey its real estate, and transfer the effects thereof, and invest the same at the place to which such institution may be removed; but no removal shall be ordered, and no vote taken thereon, until after publication in the manner provided in the last section, in which notice shall be fully set forth the place to which it is proposed to remove such institution and, in case of removal, a copy of the proceedings of such meeting shall be filed with the secretary of state. (52 v. 77, § 12; S. & C. 268.)

**Sec. 3732.** [When and how college endowment fund diverted.] The trustees of a corporation incorporated for the purpose of creating, holding, and managing a college endowment fund, the articles of incorporation of which provide that the fund may be applied to any object not inconsistent with the purposes of education different from that particularly specified therein, may apply to the court of common pleas in the county where the corporation is located for permission to make such change, designating particularly the purposes to which it is proposed to apply the funds; and the court, on being satisfied that such change is not inconsistent with the object of the original creation and institution of the fund, shall authorize and sanction the change. (51 v. 393, § 2; S. & C. 269.)

**Sec. 3733.** [How vacancies in boards filled in certain cases.] Whenever there occurs a vacancy, in whole or in part, in the board of trustees of an incorporated college, seminary, or academy, by reason of an amendment of the charter in such corporation, or from any other cause, and there is no provision of law for filling such vacancy, the governor shall, within three months after receiving information thereof, appoint the required number of trustees, one-third thereof to serve for one year, one-third to serve for two years, and one-third for three years. (75 v. 25, § 2.)

**Sec. 3734.** [Certain corporations may increase their property; bonds.] A college, university, academy, seminary, or other institution devoted to the promotion of education, now existing by virtue of any special act of incorporation, or organized under the provisions of any law, whose property is derived and held by donation, gift, purchase, devise or gratuitous subscription, and the amount of which, or the income arising therefrom, is limited by such special act, or by the articles of association adopted by such institution, may receive, acquire, possess and hold hereafter any amount of property, real, personal or mixed, which its board of directors or trustees shall deem it advisable for the institution to accept, and may, by its trustees, sell, dispose of and convey the same, but such property shall not be diverted from the express will of the donor, devisor or subscriber. The board of trustees of any such college, university, academy, seminary, or other institution devoted to the promotion of education, in anticipation of donations to be received and collections to be made, may, for the purpose of constructing, enlarging or adding to any college buildings or improvements, borrow such sum of money as they may determine necessary for such purpose, and may issue bonds therefor and secure the same by mortgage upon the property upon which such improvement is to be made, provided such property is not held by them under some specific trust.   (90 v. 71; 53 v. 170, § 1; S. & C., 368.)

Sec. 3735. [Statement to be made and filed.] Before any such institution shall be authorized to acquire and hold such additional property, the trustees thereof, at a regular meeting of their board, or at a special meeting called for that purpose, shall, from time to time, make and sign a statement specifying the amount of such additional property which they seek to acquire and hold, and shall set forth therein the purposes to which it is to be devoted, which statements shall be entered at large upon the record book of the trustees and be filed in the office of the secretary of state.   (90 v. 72; 53 v. 170, § 2; S. & C., 368.)

Sec. 3736. [How certain boards may be constituted and governed.] The board of trustees of any university or college heretofore incorporated, and now under the patronage of four or more conferences or other religious bodies of any religious denomination, may accept the provisions of this and the nine succeeding sections, by resolution adopted at any regular meeting of the board and entered upon the record of its proceedings; and after such acceptance the board shall in all respects be organized, constituted, regulated, and perpetuated, pursuant to and under said provisions; but no right acquired by any such board, or any such university or college under its charter, or any law of this state, shall in any way, be affected by said provisions.   (65 v. 188, § 1; S. & S., 106.)

Sec. 3737. [Trustees to be divided into classes.] At a meeting of such board held after a vacancy occurs therein it shall fill such vacancy, or if more than one vacancy has occurred, then one of them, by appointing the president of the university or college a trustee, and the president of such university or college shall, ex-officio, be a trustee perpetually thereafter; the board shall also, at such meeting, divide its number, excluding the said president, and including all vacancies except the one he is so appointed to fill, into classes, corresponding in number to the number of conferences or other religious bodies at the time patronizing such university or college, such classes to have in each an equal number of trustees, as near as may be; and the board shall assign one of such classes to each of the conferences or other religious bodies, and thereafter each may fill any and all vacancies in the class so assigned to it. (65 v. 188, § 2; S. & S., 106.)

**Sec. 3738.** [Term of office of trustees; how vacancies filled.] When the classes of trustees are formed, as provided in the preceding section, the term of office of one of the trustees in each of the classes, to be selected by lot in open session of the board of trustees, shall expire each year, and the persons thereafter elected as trustees shall act as such for a term of years equal in number to the number of trustees in any class, except as hereinafter provided; but the term of office of a trustee shall not expire during any meeting of the board which does not continue for more than two weeks; and vacancies which occur in any class of trustees otherwise than by the expiration of term of office shall be filled only for the remainder of the term. (65 v. 188, § 3; 70 v. 157, § 1; S. & S., 107.)

**Sec. 3739.** [When the board is to be enlarged.] If the number of the conferences or other religious bodies patronizing any such university or college, the board of trustees of which has been divided into classes as hereinbefore provided, be increased to not exceeding six, the board of trustees shall be enlarged to the extent of one additional class of trustees for each of such additional conferences or other religious bodies, such additional classes to have in each a number of trustees equal to the number in any one of the former classes; and each of such additional conferences or other religious bodies may elect, as members of the board, the number in its class, one for one year, one for two years and one for three years, and so on to the extent of the number; and each of such additional conferences or other religious bodies may fill any vacancy in its class. And such board of trustees composed according to the foregoing provisions and the provisions of section *thirty-seven hundred and forty-seven* of this chapter, without regard to the number of members so composing it, may increase its own numbers by the election of trustees at large, not exceeding the number of conferences or other religious bodies co-operating with or patronizing such university or college, and may divide such trustees at large into classes, at its discretion. (89 v. 119; 65 v. 188, § 4; S. & S., 107.)

**Sec. 3740.** [When the number in a class is to be reduced.] If the number of such patronizing conferences or other religious bodies at any time exceeds six, the representation of each shall be reduced by lot, in open session of the board of trustees, to a class of three trustees, if they exceed that number, who shall thereafter be elected to serve as trustees for the term of six years, and in that case the term of office of one trustee in each class shall expire every second year. (65 v. 188, § 5; S. & S., 107.)

**Sec. 3741.** [A conference may become a patron by consent of other bodies.] Any conference or other religious body, not patronizing any particular university or college, may become such patronizing conference or religious body, by and with the consent of the conferences or other religious bodies at the time patronizing such university or college. (65 v. 188, § 6; S. & S., 107.)

**Sec. 3742.** [Patronizing bodies may appoint visitors.] Each conference or other religious body patronizing any particular university or college may, annually, appoint two visitors, and the board of trustees of a college or university may provide, at the time of its organization, by resolution adopted and entered on its records, for the appointment of two visitors by each conference or other religious body patronizing such college or university; and such visitors shall attend the meetings of the board of trustees of such university or college, and, with the trustees, constitute a joint board for the appointment and removal of all officers, professors, and instructors of the university or college. (73 v. 163, § 7; S. & S., 107.)

**Sec. 3743.** [When the right of representation shall cease.] If a a conference or other religious body patronizing any university or college, and having a representation in its board of trustees, cease to exist, or cease to patronize such university or college, the right of such conference or other religious body to such representation shall cease, and its board of trustees shall be thereby and to that extent reduced in numbers. (65 v. 188, § 8; 73 v. 163; S. & S., 107.)

**Sec. 3744.** [What action the board must first take.] Before a conference or other religious body not represented in the board of trustees of any university or college shall be entitled to be represented therein, and before any conference or other religious body represented therein shall be deprived of such representation as provided in the preceding section, the board shall declare, and cause to be entered in the record of its proceedings, that the conditions and contingencies hereinbefore provided for in that behalf have taken place. (65 v. 188, § 9; S. & S., 107.)

**Sec. 3745.** [Quorum; how constituted.] Eleven trustees shall constitute a quorum of the board of any such university or college, whatever the number of trustees constituting the board is or may become, if the number is more than twenty; and if the number is twenty or less, a majority thereof shall constitute a quorum. (65 v. 188, § 10; S. & S., 108.)

Sec. 3746. [Certain corporations may have benefit of subsequent provisions.] The board of trustees of any university or college which has accepted or hereafter accepts the provisions of the ten preceding sections, may accept the provisions of the three succeeding sections by resolution adopted at any regular meeting of the board, and entered upon the record of its proceedings, and thereafter the board, and the university or college, shall be subject to (the) provisions thereof. (69 v. 71, § 1.)

Sec. 3747. [Alumni may elect trustees and appoint visitors.] After such acceptance by the board of any university or college, the alumni thereof (composing the alumnal association thereof) may elect as members of the board of trustees of such college or university members of such alumnal association, in numbers equaling the numbers of the conferences co-operating with or patronizing such university or college, and may divide such alumnal trustees into classes, and perpetuate the same; and such alumnal may, at the same time elect as visitors members of their association equaling in numbers one-half of the numbers of the conferences or other religious bodies co-operating with or patronizing such university or college, and such visitors shall have the same powers and duties as visitors appointed by any conference or other religious body aforesaid; provided, that when women are members of the alumnal association so electing, they shall be eligible as visitors; provided, further, that the board of trustees shall be judge of the validity of the election and the returns thereof, of trustees and visitors elected under this section. (89 v. 120; 81 v. 174; Rev. Stat. 1880; 69 v. 71, § 2; 76 v. 87, § 1.)

Sec. 3748. [Conduct of elections.] The election of trustees and visitors by the alumni shall be by ballot, and held each year, beginning the year after such acceptance, on the secular day next before the day of commencement of such university or college, at such place in a building on its grounds as may be designated by the president of the alumnal association by written notice posted the day before the election in at least two public places on such grounds; and the polls shall be opened at the hour named in said notice, which shall not be later than three o'clock p. m., and shall be kept open for two hours thereafter. The election shall be conducted by three judges and two clerks, who shall be members of said association and be chosen by the members present at the place of voting at the time for opening the polls, and they shall certify to the board of trustees the result of such election,

with a list of the members voting thereat; each ballot shall contain
the names of the persons voted for, the office which each is to fill and
a designation of the term for which he is to serve. At such election
all members of the alumnal association of such university or college
shall be entitled to vote, and members not in attendance may exercise
their right by sending ballots conformable to the foregoing provisions,
with their names thereon endorsed, and addressed under seal to the
president of such association. (89 v. 120; 69 v. 71, § 3.)

Sec. 3749. [Returns of the election, and certificates.] After the
polls are closed the result shall be ascertained and certified to by
the judges and clerks, and the person or persons, not exceeding
the number to be elected as trustees, having received the highest
number of votes for trustee or trustees, shall be declared elected
as trustee or trustees as designated on the ballot, and the two persons who receive the highest number of votes for visitors shall be
declared elected, but their terms of office shall not begin until after
the final adjournment of the regular meeting of the trustees for
that year; if any two or more persons receive an equal number of
votes for the same office of trustee or visitor, one of them, as may
be determined by lot by the judges, in the presence of all the electors
who may wish to be present, shall be the trustee or visitor, and shall be
so declared; and duplicate certificates of election shall be signed by the
judges and clerks, and delivered by them, one to each of the persons
elected, and the other, with the poll books duly certified by the judges
and clerks, to the secretary of the board of trustees of the university
or college, the next day after the election, which certificate he shall
enter of record in the book containing the proceedings of the board of
trustees. (69 v. 71, § 3.)

Sec. 3750. [Endowment fund corporations.] The trustees of
a corporation incorporated for the purpose of creating a fund, the
income of which is to be applied to the promotion of education,
may receive subscriptions for membership in the corporation, and
they, or a majority of them, by giving ten days' notice, by publication in the county where the corporation is located, may call a
meeting of members to adopt by-laws, and elect not more than nine
directors; each member shall have a vote for every amount by
him subscribed equal to that in the articles of incorporation specified as necessary for membership, which may be cast in person or
by proxy, but at no subsequent meeting may a member vote for or be
eligible as a director who is in arrears to the corporation; and the
trustees shall control the funds and disburse the income of the corporation as may be provided by its by-laws. (69 v. 173, §§ 1, 2, 3, 4, 5.)

Sec. 3751. [How certain board may be constituted and governed.] The board of trustees of any university, college, or other institution of learning, incorporated, and acting under the patronage of one annual conference or other religious body of any religious denomination, may accept the provisions of this and the succeeding section, by resolution adopted at any meeting of the board, and entered upon the record or journal of its proceedings; and after such acceptance the board shall be organized, constituted, regulated, and perpetuated as therein provided; but no right acquired by any such board, university, or other institution of learning, under its charter, or any law of this state, shall in any way be impaired or affected thereby. (69 v. 180, § 1.)

Sec. 3751a. [Increase in number of trustees of certain corporations.] The board of trustees of any university or college, heretofore incorporated, and now under the patronage of one annual conference or synod or other religious body of any religious denomination, may increase the number of its trustees, not exceeding six; said additional trustees to be nominated by the collegiate alumni of such university or college from the collegiate alumni of three years' standing, for appointment or election by such patronizing conference or synod, under such regulations as may be prescribed by such board of trustees; provided, that the board of trustees of such university or college shall so determine to increase the number of its trustees and adopt such regulations for their nomination, by resolution adopted at any regular meeting of such board, and duly entered on the record of its proceedings; and, provided further, that such patronizing or governing conference or synod shall consent to such increase of said board of trustees and the rules and regulations for the nomination of the same. And after such board of trustees is so increased by the election of any additional trustees, not exceeding six, the board of trustees shall in all respects be organized, constituted, regulated and perpetuated pursuant to and under the provisions of the charter and said provisions; but no rights acquired by any such board or any such university or college, under its charter or any law of this state, shall in any way be affected or impaired thereby. (91 v. 155.)

Sec. 3751b. [Incorporation of colleges under ecclesiastical patronage; what articles shall contain.] A corporation may be formed for the promotion of academic, collegiate or university education, under religious influences, and is hereby authorized and empowered to set forth in its articles, or certificate of corporation, as a part of the same, the name of the religious sect, association or denomination with which it proposes to be connected, and it is further authorized and empowered to grant any ecclesiastical body of such religious sect, association or, denomination, whether the same be

a conference, association, presbytery, synod, general assembly, convocation or otherwise, the right to appoint its trustees or directors,
or any number thereof; and it is further authorized and empowered
to set forth in its articles or certificate of corporation, such other
rights as to the administration of the purpose for which it is organized,
and not inconsistent with the laws of this state or of the United States,
as said incorporation may desire to confer upon said ecclesiastical body
of such religious sect, association or denomination and the said ecclesiastical body of such religious sect, association or denomination shall
possess and exercise all rights and powers to set forth in said articles
or certificate of corporation.   (94 v. 331.)

Sec. 3751c.  [Existing corporations may avail themselves of provisions of act; how.]   Any corporation formed for the promotion of
academic, collegiate or university education, under religious influences, which has been incorporated under the laws of this state,
whether by special act of the legislature or otherwise, may avail
itself of the provisions of the preceding section, as a part of its
articles or certificate of incorporation, and may confer on any ecclesiastical body of such religious sect, association or denomination, as
it is now, or proposes to be connected with, whether the same be a
conference, association, presbytery, synod, general assembly, convocation or otherwise, any or all the rights, powers or privileges provided by the preceding section to be conferred on corporations hereafter organized, and may accept the provisions of such preceding
section by a vote of the majority of the trustees of such corporation
at any regular meeting; and when so accepted, a copy of said acceptance, certified by the secretary or clerk of its board of trustees or
directors, shall be sent to the ecclesiastical body with which it is now
or proposes to be connected; if such ecclesiastical body agree to
accept the powers proposed to be conferred upon it, it shall certify
its approval upon such certified copy sent to it, and the same shall
thereupon be filled in the office of the secretary of state; and, when
so filed, the same shall become and be a part of the charter of said
corporation; and said ecclesiastical body of such religious sect, association or denomination, whether the same be a conference, association, presbytery, synod, general assembly, convocation or otherwise,
shall possess and exercise all the rights and powers so set forth in said
articles or certificate of corporation.   (94 v. 331.)

Sec. 3752.  [Classes and election of trustees; president ex-officio
a member of the board; term; vacancies; increase in board.]   After
such acceptance the board shall certify the same to the patronizing
conference or other religious body having the right to elect or appoint trustees of such university or other institution of learning, at

the next meeting of such conference or other religious body; and thereafter the board shall consist of twenty-one trustees elected or appointed, and the president of such university or other institution of learning, who shall be ex-officio a member of the board; such elected or appointed trustees shall be divided into three classes of seven members each. At the first election or appointment after such acceptance, one of such classes shall be elected or appointed for one year, one for two years and one for three years, and in all subsequent elections or appointments each of the classes of trustees shall be elected or appointed for three years, but no term of office of any such trustee shall expire during any meeting of the board which does not continue more than two weeks. Ten members of the board shall constitute a quorum, and all vacancies which occur in any class of trustees otherwise than by expiration of the term of office, shall be filled only for the remainder of the term; provided, that any such university or other institution of learning, having heretofore accepted the provisions of orignal sections 3751 and 3752, may increase its board of trustees by electing or appointing two additional members in each of the classes of trustees herein provided for. (1888, March 30; 85 v. 140, 141; Rev. Stat..1880; 69 v. 180, §§ 2, 3; 70 v. 157, § 1.)

**Sec. 3753.** [Assessments may be made against stockholders.] The proportion that each stockholder of any college, academy, university, seminary, or other institution for the promotion of education, shall be required to pay to meet the debts and liabilities of the corporation, may be determined and collected in the manner provided by the three succeeding sections. (58 v. 20, § 1; S. & S. 108.)

**Sec. 3754.** [Meeting of the stockholders, and notice thereof.] The trustees of any such corporation desiring to avail themselves of such provisions shall call a meeting of the stockholders for the purpose of determining what amount of the indebtedness of the corporation shall be paid by each stockholder; and they shall give thirty days' notice to the stockholders, in writing, or by publication in some newspaper of general circulation in the county where the corporation is located, of the time, place, and purpose of the meeting, at which the trustees shall submit a detailed statement showing the assets and indebtedness of the corporation. (58 v. 20, §§ 2, 3; S. & S., 108.)

**Sec. 3755.** [Meeting may fix amount of assessment.] A majority in interest of the stockholders present at such meeting may determine what amount of the indebtedness of the corporation shall be paid by each stockholder, and fix the time or times, and the mode, for the payment of the amount of money assessed against each stockholder; but these provisions shall not interfere with or abridge the right of any creditor of the corporation to institute any proceedings authorized by law to enforce the liability of stockholders. (58 v. 20, § 4; S. & S., 108.)

**Sec. 3756. [How much may be assessed, and collection thereof.]** The assessments shall be pro rata upon the stock subscribed or otherwise acquired by each stockholder, and in no case shall exceed the amount for which each stockholder is or may be liable by law; and a stockholder who fails to pay, as required by the assessment, the amount so assessed against him, shall be liable in a civil action, to be brought in the name of the corporation, for the recovery thereof, as in other cases of indebtedness. (58 v. 20, §§ 5, 6; S. & S. 108, 109.)

**Sec. 3757. [The board of military academies; how constituted, etc.]** The academic board of an institution incorporated for military and polytechnic education shall consist of the superintendent of the institution, the commandant of cadets, and the professors, and may make and enforce rules and regulations for the government of cadets; but such rules and regulations must be first submitted to and approved by the governor of the state. (64 v. 239, §§ 1, 2; S. & S., 109.)

**Sec. 3758. [Board of visitors; how constituted.]** The board of visitors of such institution shall consist of the governor who shall be ex-officio a member and the president of the board, of two other persons to be named by the governor, and such other persons as the superintendent of the institution may appoint. (64 v. 239, § 3 ; S. & S. 110.)

**Sec. 3759. [Duties of board of visitors.]** The board of visitors shall meet annually at the institution, on the first day of the annual commencement exercises, and examine into the condition of the classes, quarters, and commons, and the discipline, drill, records of standing in study, and conduct of the cadets, and shall report on same to the legislature at its next annual session; but the board of visitors, or any member thereof, may visit and inspect the institution at any time. (64 v. 239, § 4; S. & S. 110.)

**Sec. 3760. [How the term of office of trustees and visitors may be fixed.]** At a regular meeting for the election of directors or trustees of any college or other institution of learning, the authorized voters may determine, by vote, whether the election of directors or trustees shall be held annually, if the term of their election is for a longer period than one year, and also what proportion of the entire board shall be elected annually; at the first election held under the provisions of this section the voters shall designate upon their ballots who shall serve for one year, who for two years, and who for three years; and vacancies caused by expiration of term of office shall be filled by election annually thereafter. (70 v. 125, § 1.)

Sec. 3761. [Certain corporations may change location.] The trustees of colleges and other institutions of learning not endowed by voluntary contributions, which have been established under special acts of incorporation, and which by the provisions of such acts are located at particular places, may change the location thereof to such other places as they may deem proper, and erect and maintain academies and other schools auxiliary thereto. (70 v. 248, § 1.)

Sec. 3762. [Sale and distribution of the property of certain corporations.] The trustees of any university, college, or other institution of learning, incorporated hy the authority of this state under special charter, owned in shares or stock subscribed or taken, may dispose of its property at public sale, upon such terms as to payment as the stockholders thereof, by a vote of three-fourths of the shares or stock of the institution, may direct, after giving public notice of the same, by publication, for six consecutive weeks in some newspaper published in the county where the institution is located, if one is published therein, and if not, then in some newspaper published in this state, and of general circulation in such county, which notice shall contain a full statement of the terms, time, and place of sale, and the action of the trustees as aforesaid; and the trustees may close up the corporate existence of such institution, and make an equitable division and distribution of the proceeds of the sale among all the holders of shares or stock, after- the payment of the just debts of the corporation. (67 v. 24, § 1.)

Sec. 3762a. [Certain colleges, whose articles of incorporation are not on file in the office of the secretary of state, may file same there and amend.] The trustees of any university, college or institution of learning, incorporated by the authority of this state, or under the general corporation laws thereof, owned in shares of stock subscribed and paid up in full, by a majority of the owners of such stock, for the sole purpose of promoting education, religion and morality, or the fine arts, exclusively among males or females, may, on the written petition of the owners of the majority of such stock filed before them, or on the vote of the owners of the majority of such shares of paid up stock at any general meeting of the stockholders called for such purpose, after thirty days' notice published in some newspaper published and of general circulation in the county, by the board of trustees, may change the name and enlarge the purposes and objects of any such university, college or institution, by amendments to its charter, approved by the owners of the majority of such stock for the change of the name and the enlargement of the purpose and object of such university, college or institution of learning, so that all the educational rights and privileges thereof may be bestowed in the co-equal and co-ordinate education of both sexes. When such amendment is adopted and the original articles of incorporation of said corporation have not been filed and recorded in the office of the secretary of state, a copy of such amendment and copy of the original articles of incorporation of said corporation, with a certificate to each of them thereto affixed, signed by the president and secretary of said corporation, and sealed with the corporate seal, if any there be, stating the fact and date of the adoption of such amendment, and that such copy of said amendment, and that such copy of said original articles of incorporation of said corporation are and is a true copy of the originals, shall be recorded in the office of the secretary of state, and when so recorded, and not until then, said amendment shall become and be in law the sole articles of incorporation of said corporation; and all the property, real and personal and the title thereunto, and all the rights and credits, shares of stock, and rights of stockholders, corporate franchises, and all endowment fund or funds, or gift or bequest, or legacies or mortgage securities and promissory notes, and rights of every kind belonging to, vested in or claimed, or possessed by the said original corporation, shall by said amendment pass to, be assigned and transferred and vested in and held, enjoyed and exercised by the said corporation named, created and organized by said amendment for the promotion of all the objects and purposes of its creation and organization. For recording such amendments and copies of such original articles of incorporation, and for furnishing a certified copy or copies thereof, the secretary of state shall receive a fee of twenty cents per hundred words, to be in no case less than five dollars. (1888, April 14; 85 v. 270.)

Sec. 3762b. [Colleges may change name and purpose, when; procedure; fees.] That the board of trustees of any university, college or institution of learning, incorporated by the authority of this state, or under the general corporation laws thereof, for the sole purposes of promoting education, religion and morality, or the fine arts, may, at any regular or special meeting of such board of trustees, called for such purpose, after thirty days' actual notice to each and all of such trustees, change the name and enlarge the purposes and objects of any such university, college or institution of learning, by amendment to its charter, approved by a majority of such board of trustees at such regular or special meeting, so called and so notified, for the change of such name and the enlargement of the purposes and objects of such university, college or institution of learning. When such amendment is so adopted by the board of trustees of any university, college or institution of learning, already incorporated by the authority of this state, or under the general corporation laws thereof, a copy thereof, with a certificate thereto affixed, signed by the president and secretary of such board of trustees, and sealed with the corporate seal, if any there be, stating the fact and date of such amendment, and that such copy is a true copy of the original amendment, shall be filed and recorded in the office of the secretary of state, and when so filed and recorded, and not until then, said amendment shall become and be in law an integral part of the articles of incorporation of said corporation, and all the property, real and personal, the title thereto, and all the rights and ·credits, corporate powers and franchises, and all endowment fund or funds, gifts and bequests, legacies, mortgage securities and promissory notes, and all powers, rights and privileges of every kind belonging to, vested in, claimed or possessed by said original corporation shall, by said amendment, pass to, be assigned, transferred and vested in, and held, enjoyed and exercised by the said corporation,·named, created and organized by said amendment for the promotion of all the objects of its creation and organization. And said new corporation shall be liable for and perform all the lawful obligations, contracts and undertakings of said original corporation. For recording such amendment and furnishing a certified copy or copies thereof, the secretary of state shall receive a fee of twenty cents per hundred words, to be in no case less than five dollars. (87 v. 8.)

**Sec. 3763.** [Restrictions under which medical colleges and teachers may receive bodies for dissection.] All superintendents of city hospitals, directors or superintendents of city or county infirmaries, directors or superintendents of work-houses, directors or superintendents of asylums for the insane, or other charitable institutions founded and supported in whole or in part at public expense, the directors or warden of the penitentiary, township trustees, sheriffs, or coroners, in possession of bodies not claimed or identified, or which must be buried at the expense of the county or township, shall, before burial, hold such bodies not less than thirty-six hours and shall notify the professor of anatomy in any college which by its charter is empowered to teach anatomy, or the president of any county medical society of the fact that such bodies are being so held and shall, before or after burial, by such said superintendent, director, or other officer, on the written application of the professor of anatomy, the president of any county medical society, deliver to such said professor, or president, for the purpose of medical or surgical study or dissection, the body of any person who has died in either of said institutions from any disease, not infectious, if such body has not been requested for interment by any person at his own expense;

[Body to be delivered to claimant.] If the body of any deceased person so delivered, be subsequently claimed, in writing, by any relative or other person for private interment, at his own expense, it shall be given up to such claimant;

[Interment of body after examination or dissection.] After such bodies shall have been subjected to such medical or surgical examination or dissection, the remains thereof shall be interred in some suitable place at the expense of the party or parties in whose keeping said corpse has been placed.

[Notification to relatives of deceased person.] In all cases it shall be the duty of the officer having such body under his control to notify or cause to be notified, in writing, the relatives or friends of such deceased person;

[Penalty for refusal to deliver body, or acceptance of consideration for same.] And any superintendent, coroner, or infirmary director, sheriff, or township trustee, failing or refusing to deliver such bodies when applied for, as herein provided, or who shall charge, receive, or accept money, or other valuable consideration for the same, shall be fined in any sum not exceeding one hundred dollars, and not less than twenty-five dollars, or be imprisoned in the county jail not exceeding six months; provided, however, that in no case shall the body of any such deceased person be delivered until twenty-four hours after death.

[Body of stranger or traveler.] The bodies of strangers or travelers, who die in any of the institutions herein named, shall not be delivered for the purpose of dissection, except said stranger or traveler belong to that class commonly known as tramps; and all bodies delivered as herein provided shall be used for medical, surgical and anatomical study only, and within this state,

[Unlawful to have unauthorized body in possession; penalty.] And the possession of the body of any deceased person for the above purposes, and not authorized under this section, shall be unlawful, and the detention of the body of any deceased person, claimed by relatives or friends for the interment at their expense, shall also be unlawful, and the person so detaining said body unlawfully, shall be fined in any sum not exceeding one hundred dollars, nor less than twenty-five dollars, or be imprisoned in the county jail not exceeding six months. (93 v. 84; 78 v. 33; Rev. Stat. 1880; 67 v. 25, § 1.)

Sec. 3764. [Penalty for having unlawful possession of corpse.] Any person, association, or company, having unlawful possession of the body of any deceased person shall be jointly and severally liable with any and all other persons, associations, and companies that had or have had unlawful possession of such corpse in any sum not less than five hundred dollars and not more than five thousand dollars, to be recovered at the suit of the personal representative of the deceased in any court of competent jurisdiction, for the benefit of the next of kin of deceased.

**Secs. 3765-3766.** Repealed 1880, March 26; 77 v. 85.

**Sec. 3767.** [Organic rules which may be prescribed in certain articles of incorporation.] An association incorporated for the purpose of receiving gifts, devises or trust funds to erect, establish, or maintain an academy in any department of fine arts or a gallery for the exhibition of paintings or sculpture or works of art, or a museum of natural or other curiosities, or specimens of art or nature promotive of knowledge, or a law or other library, or courses of lectures upon science, art, philosophy, natural history, or law, and to open the same to the public on reasonable terms, or an industrial training school, or a mechanics' institute for advancing the best interest(s) of mechanics, manufacturers and artisans, by the more general diffusion of useful knowledge in those classes of the community, or homes for indigent and aged widows and unmarried women and whose directors or trustees may be of either sex, may in its articles of incorporation prescribe the tenure of office of the trustees or directors, the mode of appointing or electing successors, the administration and management of the property, and trust and other funds of the corporation, and such other organic rules as may be deemed expedient or acceptable to donors which shall be and remain the permanent organic law of the corporation. (1887, February 21; 84 v. 31; 83 v. 40; Rev. Stat. 1880; 75 v. 135; §§ 1, 3.)

**Sec. 3768.** [May add to the objects of the corporation; acceptance of statutory provisions.] Such corporations may by certificate, duly acknowledged by the trustees or directors, and filed in the office of the secretary of state, add to the original objects and purposes of the corporation any of the several objects and purposes, mentioned in the preceding section which were not provided for by the articles of incorporation, and in any such corporation heretofore incorporated under the laws of the state may by certificate, reciting the organic rules adopted by such corporation as its permanent organic law, and duly acknowledged by the trustees or directors, and lodged in the office of the secretary of state, except the provisions of the preceding section. (1886, March 26; 83 v. 41; 75 v. 135, § 3.)

**(3768-1) Sec. 1.** [Authorizing certain mechanics' institutes to borrow money; liability of directors and trustees.] Any mechanics' institute, incorporated under the laws of this state prior to the year eighteen hundred and fifty-one, be and it is hereby authorized and empowered to borrow money, issue bonds or notes therefor, at no more than the legal rate of interest, and secure the same by mortgage upon its real estate. (82 v. 118.)

(3768-2) **Sec. 2.** [Directors **not** personally liable.] The directors and trustees of such corporation shall not be personally liable for debts contracted by virtue of this act. (82 v. 118.)

**Sec. 3769.** [Accounts and receipts of disbursements.] The officers of the corporation charged or intrusted with the receipts and disbursements of its funds or property shall make and keep like accurate and detailed accounts of such funds, and the receipts and disbursements thereof, as are required to be kept by the fund commissioners of the state; the trustees shall, on or before the third Monday in January of each year, file with the clerk of the court of common pleas of the county in which the corporation is located an abstract of their account, which abstract shall correspond in date. amount, person to whom paid, and from whom received, and on what account, with the voucher taken or given on account of such receipts and disbursements; they shall at the same time, annually, file in such clerk's office a report of the names of the donors, the kind, amount, or value of gifts of each, and a brief statement of the conditions and purposes of the gifts; and the filing of such abstract and report, and the supplying of any omission in either, may be enforced by order and attachment of the court of common pleas of the proper county, against the trustees, on motion of any respectable citizen. (75 v. 135, § 4.)

**Sec. 3770.** [Trustees ineligible to other office.] No trustee shall be eligible to any office or agency of the corporation to which any salary or emoluments is attached, nor shall the trustees be allowed any salary, emoluments, perquisites, except the right of free ingress to the grounds, rooms, and buildings of the corporation. (75 v. 135, § 5.)

**Sec. 3771.** [Attorney general may, by action, enforce duties of officers.] On application to the attorney general of five citizens of the proper county, in writing, verified by the oath or affirmation of one of them, setting forth specific charges against any of the fiscal or other agents or trustees of such corporation, involving a breach of trust or duty, he shall give notice thereof to the trustees or agents complained of, and inquire into the truth of such charges, and for this purpose he may receive affidavits, or enforce, by process from the court of common pleas of Franklin county, the production of papers and the attendance of witnesses before him; and if, on testimony or other evidence, he believes the charges, or any of them, to be true, he shall proceed, by action in that court, in the name of the state, against the delinquent trustee or trustees, fiscal agent or agents, and, on the hearing, the court may direct the performance of any duty, or the removal of all or any of the agents or trustees and decree such other and further relief as may be equitable. (75 v. 135, § 6.)

**Sec. 3771a.** [How number of trustees of certain colleges increased.] The board of trustees of any university or college heretofore incorporated, but not under the patronage of conferences or other ecclesiastical bodies of any religious denomination, as described in section 3736, may increase the number of such trustees to twenty-four, exclusive of the president, or a less number, and may divide said trustees into six classes, each class to serve six years, and one class to be chosen each year, for said term; but one trustee of each class may be chosen by the votes of the alumni of such university or college, if the board of trustees shall so provide by by-law, in which case it shall also be the duty of the board of trustees to provide, by such by-laws, a method of nominating and electing such appointee of the alumni. The president of such university or college shall, ex-officio, be a trustee perpetually, and shall not be included in the classes going out in rotation. If it shall be necessary, in the first enlargement of the board of trustees, under this section, to distribute new members to the several classes, whose terms shall expire by rotation, the distribution may be made in such manner as the board may direct, so that no trustee shall be elected for a longer term than six years. (87 v. 188; 86 v. 341.)

# APPENDIX.

---

## FORMS AND INSTRUCTIONS.

---

### I. NOTICE OF ELECTION.

Notice is hereby given that an election for members of the board of education in ——— school district, ——— county, Ohio, will be held on the ——— day of November, 190—, at the usual voting places in said district. At said election there will be [*state number of members to be elected and length of term.*]

————————————, *Clerk of the Board of Education.*

————————, Ohio.

————————, 190—.

NOTE:—Notices must be published in a newspaper of general circulation in the district or posted in five public places in the district at least ten days before elections. All school elections, except those for director in township sub-districts, are conducted under the general election laws.

### II. NOTICE OF ELECTION IN SUB-DISTRICTS.

Notice is hereby given to the qualified voters of sub-district No.——, of——— township, ———county, Ohio, that the next annual school meeting for the election of a director in said district will be held at the ——— school house in said sub-district on Monday, the —— day of April, 19—, beginning at —— o'clock p. m. [A. M.], and closing at —— o'clock p. m.[a. m.]

————————————, *Director.*

NOTE.—The above notice to be posted in three or more conspicuous places, at least six days prior to the election. Section 3921*a*.

### III. POLL BOOK

Of the election held in sub-district No. ——,in the township of ———, in the county of ———, and state of Ohio, on Monday, the ——— day of April, in the year A. D. 19—.

A. B., Chairman, and C. D., Clerk, judges of said election, were severally sworn, as the law directs, previous to their entering on the duties of their re- spective offices.

Forms and Instructions.

| Number and names of electors. | Number and names of electors. |
|---|---|
| No. 1 .............................. | No. 5 .............................. |
| 2 .............................. | 6 .............................. |
| 3 .............................. | 7 .............................. |
| 4 .............................. | 8 .............................. |

It is hereby certified that the number of electors who voted at this election is ———.

——————————, *Chairman.*

——————————, *Secretary.*

*Judges.*

## IV. TALLY SHEET

Of the election held in sub-district No ———, in the township of ———, in the county of ———, and state of Ohio, on Monday, the ——— day of April, in the year A. D. 19--, to elect a director for said sub-district.

| Names of Candidates. | Tallies, showing number of votes given for each candidate. | | | | | Total. |
|---|---|---|---|---|---|---|
| | 5 | 10 | 15 | 20 | 25 | |
| .................................. | ........ | ........ | ........ | ........ | ........ | ........ |
| .................................. | ........ | ........ | ........ | ........ | ........ | ........ |
| .................................. | ........ | ........ | ........ | ........ | ........ | ........ |
| .................................. | ........ | ........ | ........ | ........ | ........ | ........ |
| .................................. | ........ | ........ | ........ | ........ | ........ | ........ |
| .................................. | ........ | ........ | ........ | ........ | ........ | ........ |
| .................................. | ........ | ........ | ........ | ........ | ........ | ........ |

We hereby certify

That ——————— received ——————— votes for director.

That ——————— received ——————— votes for director.

That ——————— received ——————— votes for director.

And that ——————— was duly elected director for a term of one year.

——————————, *Chairman.*

——————————, *Secretary.*

*Judges.*

Forms and Instructions.

The poll book and tally sheet must be signed by the judges of election before they separate. No signing after such separation is valid. They must be delivered within eight days to the clerk of the board of education.

### V. MINUTES OF SUB-DISTRICT SCHOOL MEETING.

SUB-DISTRICT, No.————,

————TOWNSHIP, ———— COUNTY, OHIO.

———— ————, 19—.

At a meeting of the qualified voters of said sub-district, held on the ———— day of April, 19 —, ———————— was appointed secretary.

Whereupon said voters proceeded to elect by ballot, a director of said sub-district for the term of one year, and upon inspection of the several ballots given at said election, it was found and publicly declared, that ———————— was duly elected for the term of one year.

————————, *Chairman.*

————————, *Secretary.*

### VI. APPOINTMENT OF SCHOOL DIRECTOR TO FILL VACANCY.

This is to certify that ———————— has been appointed director of sub-district number ————, ———— township, ———— county, Ohio, to fill the vacancy caused by ———————— of ———————— said appointment to extend until the next annual election as provided for in section 3921*a*.

————————Ohio.

————————, 190—.

Attest: ————————, *President.*

————————, *Clerk.*

### VII. OATH OF SCHOOL DIRECTOR.

The following oath which may be administered by the clerk or any other member of the board of education, should be taken by each director before entering upon the discharge of his duties.

You, ————, do solemnly swear [*or affirm*] that you will support the constitution of the United States, and the constitution of the State of Ohio, and that you will faithfully and impartially discharge the duties of director, in and for said sub-district, number ————, ———— township, ———— county, Ohio, according to law and the best of your ability.

See section 3921*a*.

### VIII. DIFFERENT MODES OF ALTERING SUB-DISTRICTS.

*Resolved by the board of education of* ———— *township,* That there be transferred and united with sub-district number ————, so much of sub-district number ————, as is bounded as follows: [*describe boundary.*]

*Resolved by the board of education of* ———— *township,* That sub-district number ———— is hereby abolished, and there is hereby transferred to and united with sub-district number ————, so much of the territory of said abolished sub-district as is bounded as follows: [*describe boundary*], and so much of said abolished sub-district as is not herein united with sub-district number ————, is transferred to and united with sub-district number ————. This resolution shall take effect on the ———— day of ————, 19—.

Forms and Instructions.

*Resolved by the board of education of* ——— *township,* That so much of sub-district number ——, as is bounded as follows: [*describe boundary*], be cut off from said sub-district, and that so much of sub-district number ——- as is bounded as follows: [*describe boundary*], be cut off from said sub-district, and that the territory thus cut off from sub-districts numbers —— and ——, respectively, is hereby consolidated and formed into a new sub-district and designated sub-district number —— of ——— township.

*Resolved by the board of education of* ——— *township,* That sub-districts numbers —— and —— are hereby abolished, and that the territory included in said sub-districts at the time of their abolishment is hereby consolidated and formed into a new sub-district, and designated sub-district number —— of —— township. This resolution shall take effect on the —— day of ———, 19—.

NOTE.—When a new sub-district is formed the township board should appoint a director as provided in section 3921a.

## IX. RESOLUTIONS ON BOND ISSUE.

*Resolved,* By the board of education of ———— school district, ——— county, Ohio, That it is necessary for the proper accommodation of the schools of said district that [*state nature of improvement*], that it will require $——— to make said improvement, that the funds at the disposal of said board or that can be raised under the provisions of section 3994 of the Revised Statutes of Ohio, are not sufficient to accomplish said purpose and that a bond issue is necessary, it is therefore further

*Resolved,* That an election be held in said school district on the question of the issuing of bonds in the sum of $—— for the purpose herein specified, on the ——— day of ———— 190—, and that the clerk of the board be directed to forward a copy of these resolutions to the deputy state supervisors of elections and request said supervisors to provide election supplies and conduct said election, and that the clerk be also directed to publish the notices of said election as provided by law.

## X. NOTICE OF ELECTION FOR BOND ISSUE.

Notice is hereby given by the board of education of ————— school district, ————— county, Ohio, that there will be an election held in said district at the usual voting place [*places*], between the hours of 5:30 a. m. and 5:30 p. m., on the ——— day of ———, 190—, to consider the question of a bond issue in the sum of $——, for the purpose of [*here state purpose*] as provided in section 3991 of the Revised Statutes of Ohio.

By order of the board of education.

——————————— Clerk.

——————————— Ohio.

————190—.

### FORM OF BALLOT.

| | |
|---|---|
| For Bond Issue in the Sum of $———, Yes. | |
| For Bond Issue in the Sum of $———, No. | |

All elections on school questions should be held under the supervision of the regular election officers and the ballots be made to conform to the provisions of the general election laws.

## XI. PETITION FOR SPECIAL SCHOOL DISTRICT.

*To the Probate Judge of* ——— *County, Ohio:*

We, the undersigned petitioners, being male citizens and electors of a proposed special school district, respectfully request that a special school district be established from the territory herein described for the following reasons: [*give reasons.*] Said special school district to be bounded and described as follows: [*Give description in full*].

Respectfully submitted,

————————, Ohio.

————————, 190—.

NOTE:—The above petition must be signed by at least ten male electors and must be accompanied by a certificate from the county auditor giving the total tax valuation of the proposed district, an accurate map of the same and an undertaking with security for costs in the sum of $100.

## XII. NOTICE OF SPECIAL MEETINGS.

Notice is hereby given that there will be a meeting of the board of education of ——— school district, ——— county, Ohio, on the ——— day of ————, at —— o'clock ————, at ————, to consider any business which may be considered necessary.

————————, *Clerk.*

————————, ————————, 19—.

NOTE:—A special meeting may be called by the president, clerk or two members of the board.

## XIII. TEACHER'S CONTRACT.

An agreement entered into between ————, of ————, ——— county, Ohio, and the board of education of ——— school district in ——— county, Ohio; the said ———— hereby agrees to teach in the public schools of said district for a term of —— months, and also agrees to abide by and maintain the rules and regulations adopted by said board for the government of said schools of said school district. And in consideration of such services, the said board of education agrees to pay the said ———— the sum of ——— dollars, payable monthly at the office of the treasuer of the board of education.

Entered into this —— day of ————, 19—.

————————, *Teacher.*

————————, *President.*

————————, *Clerk.*

Any special provisions may easily be inserted.

Forms and Instructions.

## XIV.  ORDER ON THE TREASURER.

(Form prescribed by Bureau of Inspection and Supervision of Public Offices.)

RECEIVED PAYMENT,

——19——

No.———  OFFICE OF BOARD OF EDUCATION————SCHOOL DISTRICT.

$———   ——————, OHIO,—————19——

### THE TREASURER OF SAID SCHOOL DISTRICT

WILL PAY TO ——————————————————

—————————————————— DOLLARS.

out of ——————— Fund in the Treasury.

For ——————————————————

BY ORDER OF THE BOARD OF EDUCATION.

———————— PRESIDENT.  ——————— CLERK.

## XV.  ORDER ON TREASURER WHEN SCHOOL FUNDS ARE IN A DEPOSITORY.

(Form prescribed by Bureau of Inspection and Supervision of Public Offices.)

RECEIVED PAYMENT,

——19——

No.———  OFFICE OF BOARD OF EDUCATION————SCHOOL DISTRICT.

$———   ————————, OHIO,—————19——

### THE TREASURER OF SAID SCHOOL DISTRICT

WILL PAY TO ——————————————————

—————————————————— DOLLARS.

out of ——————— Fund in the Treasury.

For ——————————————————

BY ORDER OF THE BOARD OF EDUCATION.

———————— PRESIDENT.  ——————— CLERK.

Payable at ——————— Bank, ———————, Ohio.

—————————————TREASURER.

## XVI. CERTIFICATE OF ANNUAL SCHOOL LEVY.

(Form prescribed by Bureau of Inspection and Supervision of Public Offices.)

*To the Auditor of* ..............................*County*                    :

It is hereby certified by the Board of Education of ....................
School District,.........................County, that the entire amount
necessary to be levied upon the property of said school district for school purposes, during the next school year, as directed by Sec. 3958 R. S., is as follows:

For Tuition Fund ..................... ......mills. $..........
For Building Fund .................... ......mills. $..........
For Contingent Fund ................. ......mills. $..........
For Bonds, Interest and Sinking Fund ......mills. $..........
For ..................... ............. ......mills. $..........

BY ORDER OF THE BOARD OF EDUCATION.

.................................... CLERK.

.................................Ohio.  ....................19....

## XVII. CERTIFICATE OF SCHOOL FUNDS IN TREASURY.

We hereby certify that, by a count, as required by law, of all the money,
bonds and securities in the hands of ———, treasurer of ——— school district
——— county, Ohio, made this —— day of ———, 19—, in the presence of the
clerk of the board, we find ——— dollars [and bonds, etc., in value amounting
to ——— dollars] of school funds to be in the treasury on the date above
named, and we have directed the clerk to enter upon the records of the board
a copy of this report.

                                        ———————————,
                                        ———————————,
                                        ———————————,
                                        *Board* (*or committee.*)
Attest:                                 ———————————, *President.*
                                        ———————————, *Clerk.*

[See section 4043, Revised Statutes.]

## XVIII. TRANSFER OF TERRITORY.

### (Minutes of boards.)

*Resolved,* That the following described territory be and the same is hereby
transferred from ——— school district, ——— county, Ohio, to ——— school
district, ——— county, Ohio, subject to the provisions of section 3894, Revised
Statues of Ohio [*give description.*]

*Resolved,* That the clerk be instructed to notify the board of education of
——— school district of ——— county, Ohio, of the passage of this resolution,
and upon similar action being taken by said board that said clerk file a certified copy hereof with the county auditor, together with a correct map of the
territory described.

NOTE:—A majority of the full membership of the boards is necessary to
carry such a resolution and a yea and nay vote is required.

### XIX.  LEASE TO SCHOOL DISTRICT.

*Know all men by these presents:*

That ————, of the county of ——, and State of ———, for the consideration herein mentioned, does hereby lease unto the board of education of the township of ——, county and state aforesaid, its successors and assigns, the following premises, to-wit: [*Here insert description*], with all the privileges and appurtenances thereunto belonging; to have and to hold the same for and during the term of —— years from the —— day of ———, 19—. And the said board of education for itself and assigns, does covenant and agree to pay the said ———— for the said premises, the annual rent of ——— dollars. [*Insert date and place of payment.*]

In witness whereof, the said parties hereunto set their hands, this ——— day of ————, 19—.

————————————, *Lessor.*

————————————,
*President of the Board.*
————————————, *Clerk.*

Signed, sealed, and acknowledged in the presence of

————————————,

————————————,

*State of Ohio,* —— *County, ss.:*

Before me, a —— in and for said county, personally appeared ————, grantor in the above instrument, and acknowledged the same to be —— voluntary act and deed, for the uses and purposes therein mentioned.

In testimony whereof, I have hereunto subscribed my name and affixed my ——— seal, this —— day of ———, A. D. 19—.

(Title.)

If the lease be for three years or more, it must be acknowledged, attested by two witnesses, and recorded. If for a less term, it need not be executed with these formalities. See section 4112. The consideration may be money or anything else, and the form varied accordingly. The above form is for a long lease.

### XX.  OATH OF CLERK OF BOARD OF EDUCATION.

*The State of Ohio,* —— *County.* —— *Township, ss.:*

Before me, ————, personally came ————, who, being duly sworn according to law, says that he will support the constitution of the United States and the constitution of the state of Ohio; and that he will faithfully discharge his duties as clerk of the board of education of the —— school district ———— in ———— county, Ohio, during his term of office, and until his successor is chosen and qualified.

————————————,

———————————— *of said Board.*

Sworn to before me and signed in my presence, on —— day of ———, A. D. 19—.

————————————

(Title.)

## XXI. CLERK'S BOND.

The bonds required by law of all school officers must hereafter be given by a guaranty company. See section 3641c.

## XXII. FINAL RECEIPT OF CLERK.

$————.                                        ————————, Ohio, ——, 19—.

Received of ————, late clerk of —— school district, the sum of ——— dollars, the record book, account book, school laws, teachers' certificates and reports, and the other official books and papers in his hands.

————————, Clerk.

See section 4054.

## XXIII. OATH OF TREASURER OF BOARD OF EDUCATION.

*The State of Ohio,* —— *County, ss.:*

Before me, ————, personally came ————————, who being duly sworn, according to law, says that he will support the constitution of the United States, and the constitution of the state of Ohio; and that he will faithfully discharge his duties as treasurer of the board of education of the —— school district —— county, Ohio, during his continuance in said office, and until his successor is chosen and qualified.

Sworn to before me and signed in my presence, on this —— day of ————, 19——, by the said ————.

————————,

. ———— *of said Board.*

## XXIV. TREASURER'S BOND.

The bonds required by law of all school officers must hereafter be given by a guaranty company. See section 3641c.

## XXV. FINAL RECEIPT OF TREASURER.

$————.                                        ————————, Ohio, ——, 19—.

Received of ————, late treasurer of ———— school district ———— county, the sum of ———— dollars, and the following securities, bonds, and other school property, to-wit: ————————————

————————————,*Treasurer.*

## XXVI. COMPLAINT IN REGARD TO SCHOOL FUNDS.

*To the State Commissioner of Common Schools:*

Sir: I respectfully submit the following state of facts as existing in —— school district, —— county, Ohio.

(Statement of complaint containing one of the causes mentioned in section 364, R. S.)

In consideration of the above statement I respectfully request the appointment of some competent accountant to investigate the condition of the school funds of said district.

————————, *Complainant.*

*State of Ohio,* —— *County, ss.:*

I, ——————, —————, and ————, do solemnly swear (affirm) that the statements made in the foregoing complaint are true to the best of my knowledge and belief.

—————————————,

—————————————,

—————————————,

Sworn to by ————, —————, and ————, and subscribed in my presence this —— day of ——, 19—.

—————————————,

**(Title)**

I hereby certify that —————, —————, and ————, are freeholders and taxpayers, residents of —— school district.

—————————————,

*County Auditor.*

————, Ohio, ——, 19—.

# COMPULSORY EDUCATION LAW.

### XXVII.  NOTICE TO PARENT OR GUARDIAN.

*State of Ohio,* .............. *County, ss.:*

To ..................

You are hereby notified that.............., a child between the ages of ..... and ......... years, under your charge, is not attending school, that such non-attendance is in direct violation of the law and without legal excuse.

You are hereby required to cause said child to attend some recognized school within two days from the date of this notice, and you are warned that if the truancy of said child is persisted in the final consequences will be as provided by law, as indorsed hereon.

Witness my hand this.......day of............, 19..

...................,

Truant Officer.

......school district, ............ county, Ohio.

Print sections 4022-7 and 6986-7, R. S., on reverse side of form.

### XXVIII.  NOTICE TO TRUANT.

*State of Ohio,* .............. *County, ss.:*

To............, a child between the ages of ...... and ...... years.

You are hereby notified that you are and will be required to attend some recognized school within two days from the date of this notice, and you are hereby warned that if this notice is not complied with the final consequences will be as provided by law as indorsed hereon.

Witness my hand this.......day of............, 19..

................

*Truant Officer.*

...... school district, ............ county, Ohio.

Print section 4022-8 in full on reverse side of form.

### XXIX. NOTICE TO EMPLOYERS OF YOUTH.

To ............ [Here insert name of person, company or corporation]:

Your attention is respectfully called to sections 4022-2, 4022-3, 4022-5 and 4022-11, 6986-7, R. S., to compel the elementary education of children.

In compliance with the provisions of this act, you are requested to return to me on this blank the names, ages, and add residences of all minors under fourteen years of age employed by you, also all minors between fourteen and sixteen years of age, and to state whether you have a certificate from the superintendent of schools, or clerk of the board of education that authorizes you to employ such minors.

.................

*Clerk of* ......... *Board of Education.*

| Names of Minors. | Age. | Residence. | Certificate—Yes or No. |
|---|---|---|---|
| .................... | ...... | ...................... | ..................... |
| .................... | ...... | ...................... | ..................... |
| .................... | ...... | ...................... | ..................... |
| .................... | ...... | ...................... | ..................... |
| .................... | ...... | ...................... | ..................... |
| .................... | ...... | ...................... | ..................... |
| .................... | ...... | ...................... | ..................... |
| .................... | ...... | ...................... | ..................... |

In cities this notice may be signed by the superintendent of schools.

This certificate must be kept on file until the youth reaches the age of sixteen years and must be accessible to the Truant Officer and the Inspector of Factories at all times.

### XXX. AGE AND SCHOOLING CERTIFICATE.

(For minors under sixteen years of age. Employed at Labor.)

This certifies that I am the ............. of ...................... and
(Parent or guardian)  (Name of child)
that ...... was born at ........ in the county of .........., state of ........ on the .... day of .............., 18.., and is now .... years .... months old.

.........................
(Name of parent or guardian)

## Forms and Instructions.

The said ........................ having satisfactorily verified the fore-
(Name of parent or guardian)
going statement I hereby approve the above certificate of ...................;
(Name of child)
height .... feet .... inches; complexion ......; hair ....; having no sufficient
reason to doubt that .... is of the age therein certified.

I hereby certifiy that .............. can·read at sight and write legibly
(Name of child)
simple sentences in the English language.

This certificate belongs to ............ and is to be surrendered to ......
(Name of child)
whenever .... leaves the services of the person, company or corporation holding
the same; but if not claimed by said child within thirty days from such time,
it shall be returned to the superintendent of schools.

Signature ..................,

.............., 190..          *Supt. of Schools*

## XXXI—REPORT OF TRUANT OFFICER.
### (Section 4022-5).

................................, Ohio, .......... .., 19..

*To the Clerk of the Board of Education of* ............................ *County, Ohio.*
In compliance with your requirements, I hereby submit my report for ............, 19.., as shown below.

............................ *Truant Officer.*

| Name of truant or non-attendant reported. | Age. | Sex. | Warning sent. | | Notification of non-attendance sent. | | Complaint entered on refusal, failure, or neglect. | | Complaint entered of juvenile disorderly. | |
|---|---|---|---|---|---|---|---|---|---|---|
| | | | Month. | Day. | Month. | Day. | Month. | Day. | Month. | Day. |
| | | | | | | | | | | |
| | | | | | | | | | | |
| | | | | | | | | | | |
| | | | | | | | | | | |
| | | | | | | | | | | |

Forms and Instructions.

### XXXII. TEACHER'S REPORT.

(Section 4022-6.)

.............., Ohio, ............, **19**..

*To the Clerk of the Board of Education of ........, ........ County, Ohio.*

The following is a correct list of the pupils attending my school during the month ending ............, 19..

...................., *Teacher.*

| Names of pupils. | Age. | Residence. |
| --- | --- | --- |

# INDEX.

## A

## Index.

## Index.

## B

## Index.

## Index.

Index.

Index.

Index.

## Index.

## Index.

## Index.

## Index.

## Index.

## Index.

# D

## Index.

## E

## Index.

Index.

# F

## G

Index.

## H

## Index.

# I

# J

# K

# L

## Index.

## Index.

## Index.

## Index.

Index.

Index.

---

---

## Index.

## Index.

## Index.

Index.

## Index.

## Index.

## Index.

## Index.

Index.

# W

# Y

Index.

## Z